THE CONCEPT OF TIME

The Concept of Time

Roger Teichmann
Lecturer in Philosophy
University of Oxford

First published in Great Britain 1995 by
MACMILLAN PRESS LTD
Houndmills, Basingstoke, Hampshire RG21 6XS
and London
Companies and representatives
throughout the world

A catalogue record for this book is available
from the British Library.

ISBN 0–333–64550–2

First published in the United States of America 1995 by
ST. MARTIN'S PRESS, INC.,
Scholarly and Reference Division,
175 Fifth Avenue,
New York, N.Y. 10010

ISBN 0–312–12703–0

Library of Congress Cataloging-in-Publication Data
Teichmann, Roger, 1963–
The concept of time / Roger Teichmann.
p.   cm.
Includes bibliographical references and index.
ISBN 0–312–12703–0 (cloth)
1. Time.   I. Title.
BD638.T44   1995
115—dc20   95–13885
                                                              CIP

10   9   8   7   6   5   4   3   2   1
04   03   02   01   00   99   98   97   96   95

Printed and bound in Great Britain by
Antony Rowe Ltd, Chippenham, Wiltshire

Contents

Part III: Time, Change and Causation

Introduction

Augustine famously remarked that if he wasn't actually asked the question, 'What is time?', he knew well enough what time was, but that upon being asked that question, he found that he didn't know.[1] This remark of Augustine's is quoted by Wittgenstein in the *Investigations*: Wittgenstein uses it to illustrate the idea that a person can be completely competent in the everyday use of some concept or concepts, but at sea when it comes to talking *about* those concepts in the manner characteristic of philosophy. 'Something that we know when no one asks us, but no longer know when we are supposed to give an account of it, is something that we need to *remind* ourselves of', says Wittgenstein; and, 'We remind ourselves . . . of the *kind of statement* that we make about phenomena. Thus Augustine recalls to mind the different statements that are made about the duration, past, present or future, of events.'[2]

There are many different kinds of statement that we make 'about temporal phenomena'. Indeed, there are more kinds of such statements than there used to be: for modern physics has much to say about time. Physicists may well need some sort of 'reminding' of what they are actually saying, but the task of reminding them is one requiring more expertise than I possess. In this book, I have contented myself with looking at aspects of our everyday temporal talk. But this is hardly a restriction; for, as will be seen, there are plenty of philosophical puzzlements arising from temporal notions which we all grasp (temporal concepts in the everyday use of which we are all competent).

The view that philosophical puzzles are susceptible of therapy through an examination of language is a pudding whose proof is in its eating. Essays like the present one can aim not only at solving or dissolving puzzles but at bearing out the at least partial truth of Wittgenstein's well-known conception of proper philosophical method. (Of course, if this essay fails of its first aim it will not thereby have undermined that conception.) What counts as an 'examination of language' is a pretty flexible matter. Trotting out lists of English idioms cannot be all that is needed, since – for one thing – this on its own is unlikely to help a reader attain that 'overview of the language-game' which it is hoped he should attain. We may, in the course of the investigation, need to consider formal as well as natural languages, possible as well as actual ones, if only so as the better to appreciate features of our own language. And naturally a whole battery of more traditional argumentative devices is to hand to supplement linguistic analysis and description, especially for purposes of arguing *against* philosophical positions. The *reductio ad absurdum, modus tollendo tollens,* and their kin, will always be with us.

Arguing against a given philosophical position is something which I am more at pains to do in Part I than in Parts II and III; it is in Part I that the phenomenon of tense is discussed, and this phenomenon has generated one particular and notable species of puzzlement, which finds expression in the question, 'Is time itself tensed, or is tense merely a feature of language?'. (There are other problems that arise from the phenomenon of tense, such as those concerning the 'openness' of the future, with which I have not been able to deal.) As the phrase 'merely a feature of language' would suggest, this question is one that tends to be taken most seriously by philosophers who do not hold with the view of philosophical problems as susceptible of linguistic treatment; and a good many of these philosophers will say that time is not tensed, but is rather ('in itself') tenseless. Against this, I would want to argue that, if *linguistic* tense can be shown to be an irreducible and autonomous phenomenon, then we have as good grounds as we could ever have for saying that 'time is tensed'; though one would need to say a little about 'irreducibility' and 'autonomy'.

Hence, what has been dubbed 'the debate between the tensed and tenseless views of time' not only encapsulates a certain philosophical problem, or set of problems, but can be taken, at least in the form in which I present it, as a locus for two rather different approaches to philosophical method. Some proponents of the 'tenseless' view could probably only be dissuaded from that view at the cost of changing the way they do philosophy.

Part II has to do with dates and duration-terms, and with attendant questions about the times at which things happen and the times things take to happen. (This slightly irritating ambiguity in the English word 'time' is difficult to avoid if one is loath to replace 'time when' by 'moment when'.) After a discussion of the semantics of dates and duration-terms, I examine conventionalism about clocks, and then turn to the question whether the notion of a durationless instant is a coherent one, arguing that it is not.

In Part III I turn to that most metaphysical of tangles, the entanglement of Time, Change and Causation. It hardly needs saying that only certain aspects of this tangle receive attention; thus, I avoid as far as possible getting involved in questions directly to do with causation, such as, 'What is it for one event to cause another?'. My concern in this part of the book is basically with the idea that certain temporal notions are somehow constitutively connected with notions having to do with change or with causation. An example is the 'direction of time': in what sense, if any, is the earlier/later relation constitutively related to the cause/effect relation? I put considerable methodological weight on the concept of a 'criterion'; the alternative notion (in this context), of truth-conditional reduction, is argued to be inadequate.

There is, I think, a more general rationale for at least sometimes adopting a 'criterial semantics' than that it solves particular puzzles, such as those introduced in Part III. But in a way the general rationale is presented most vividly in the course of looking at particular problems. (For example, the particular problem of the ascription of mental predicates to other people is notoriously one where the need for talk of constitutive but defeasible grounds quickly makes itself felt.) There are, however, some general worries that can be voiced concerning the notion of a criterion, and I have tried to deal with one of the more notable of these worries in the Appendix.

Some readers may be annoyed at the lack of an overarching 'thesis'. I make no apologies for this lack; but hope that the many interconnections between the different topics discussed lend the book more coherence than it would have had merely in virtue of its broad subject matter and the philosophical 'method' employed. This is not to say that I don't sometimes discuss a topic above all for its own sake, rather than for its contribution to any broader argument: examples would be section 3.3, and, to some extent, section 2.3. On the other hand, while the findings of Chapter 4 might look to be relatively self-contained, they inform certain of the arguments of Chapters 6 and 7 in a significant way. And although it is true that the point of Chapter 1 is largely to get McTaggart 'out of the way', the McTaggartian conception of time comes back on the scene right at the end of Chapter 7.

Writers sometimes tell their readers that particular sections of a work may be skipped if one wants to keep on the track of the main argument. I have not done this, mainly because it seems to me that it would be misleading to do so. Though I spoke above of its being more my concern in Part I than in the other Parts to argue against a certain position, nevertheless I cannot claim in Part I to be hunting down a conclusion. This is because (as will be stressed shortly) there is no single debate centring on the question, 'Is time (really) tensed?'. If philosophers are wont to suggest that there *is* a single issue here, or that one can approach the subjects of tense and tenselessness in a 'linear', rather than a discursive, manner, those philosophers, it seems to me, are simplifying things. Still, I hope that readers will not feel lost without a compass *too* frequently.

Finally, I would like to thank various people and institutions. I wrote this book while I had tenure of a British Academy Postdoctoral Research Fellowship; I am grateful to the British Academy for their support. For comments on certain sections of the book, I would like to thank Michael Martin and Adrian Moore. Versions of Chapters 6 and 7 were read to seminars and meetings at the universities of Birmingham, Cambridge, Glasgow and Stirling; I am very grateful for the feedback I had from those institutions. Chapter 6 appeared in a slightly different form in *The Philosophical Quarterly* for April 1993.

Part I
Tense and Tenselessness

Preamble

'Temporal discourse' can be defined as discourse that makes use of temporal vocabulary. Propositions such as 'The Second World War ended in 1945', 'Socrates was born before Plato', 'The milkman will call tomorrow' all count as bits of temporal discourse; '1945', 'before' and 'tomorrow' are expressions belonging to different species of the genus of temporal expressions. But in this case, it looks as if *all* indicative discourse, at any rate in English and most other languages, counts as 'temporal discourse'. For (in English and most other languages) all indicative sentences are grammatically tensed, and surely tense betokens temporality?

Grammatical tense is typically embodied, not in a special vocabulary, but in special modifications of vocabulary – in modifications of verbs, in fact. But this need not lead us to regard tense as a prevalent, but theoretically redundant, inflexional phenomenon, akin to gender in French or Latin. A difference of tense typically goes with a difference of meaning, a difference of truth-conditions. It is for this reason that tense *can* be represented, as it is in tense logics, by means of a special vocabulary – e.g. one incorporating the sentential operators 'It was the case that', 'It will be the case that', and 'It is the case that'.

The grammatical tense of a verb does not always correspond to what we may call its 'real' tense – though clearly it must for the most part so correspond. The expression 'is coming' is, grammatically speaking, a present continuous form, and indeed the 'real' tense of a sentence like 'That gorilla is coming towards us' is that of the present. The 'real' tense of a sentence like 'The plumber is coming tomorrow' is, however, not present but future.

The connection between grammatical and 'real' tense is of course an intimate one. Roughly speaking, certain grammatical forms are picked out partly by morphology, but partly also by semantic function: the function of indicating 'real' tense. It is a necessary truth that grammatically past-tensed statements are for the most part logically past-tensed; but, since grammatical form is partly a morphological matter, it is possible for a grammatically past-tensed statement not to be logically past-tensed.

How, then, can we characterise 'real' or 'logical', as opposed to grammatical, tense? The answer, for unembedded sentences, is relatively simple. We need only appeal to the different sorts of truth-conditions had by differently-tensed sentences, thus:

(1) An utterance of 'It is the case that p' is true iff 'p' is true at the time of utterance;

(2) An utterance of 'It was the case that p' is true iff 'p' is true before the time of utterance;

(3) An utterance of 'It will be the case that p' is true iff 'p' is true after the time of utterance.

(1)–(3) are about 'utterances'; if need be, we could extend their scope to cover inscriptions, thoughts, beliefs, or whatever. The locution 'is true' might appear to be a 'timeless (tenseless?) present'. As we shall see later on (p. 39), (1)–(3) would be less misleadingly rendered as subjunctive conditionals, from which 'is true' has been altogether excised. The question remains whether (1)–(3) are to be regarded as tensed or as tenseless – but at this stage it is important to recognise that we have not (by the mere use of 'is true') committed ourselves one way or the other. *Prima facie*, (1)–(3) would seem to be construable as tenseless, as disjunctively-tensed (with 'is true' equivalent to 'was or is or will be true'); or, indeed, as present-tensed. We shall compare these three approaches in Chapter 3.

An unembedded sentence which can be paraphrased as 'It was the case that p', for some 'p', such that this paraphrase has the truth-conditions given at (2), is past-tensed: its 'real' tense is past. Similar comments apply to sentences paraphrasable as 'It is the case that p' and 'It will be the case that p'. A simple consequence of this would appear to be that every unembedded indicative sentence is present-tensed, since any unembedded indicative sentence 'p' can, seemingly, be paraphrased as 'It is the case that p'. If this is so, talk of 'the' tense of a sentence is to some extent misleading; a past-tensed or future-tensed sentence will also be a present-tensed sentence. (From here on, I shall use 'sentence' to mean 'indicative sentence', unless otherwise specified.)

This last point would not be affected if, like Prior, we decided that 'It is the case that' is redundant in our account. For in that case we will still have to say that a present-tensed sentence is one that, if true, is true at the time of utterance (whenever uttered), and clearly this applies to all sentences. If 'It is the case that' is redundant, we might indeed characterise 'pure' present-tensed sentences as ones that are (perspicuously) paraphrasable as sentences *with no initial tense operators*; but, until supplemented by some characterisation of the present tense, our account would be indistinguishable from one in which there was no present tense: the 'root' sentences, to which past- or future-tense operators were attachable, might as well be called 'tenseless' as 'present-tensed'. I shall indeed argue later on that they cannot be so characterised; but this is because they, like past- and future- tensed sentences, must be regarded as having characteristic *truth-conditions*.

Though every unembedded sentence is present-tensed, we cannot so easily jump to the view that every unembedded sentence is past- or future-tensed. 'p' cannot necessarily be paraphrased as 'It was the case that q'. 'It was the case that it would be the case that p', or 'It was going to be the case that p', is clearly not equivalent to 'p', although in a metric tense logic we can get closer to an equivalence: 'A year ago it was going to be the case a year later that p' *will in fact* be materially equivalent to 'p'. And 'It was the case that it would *now* be the case that p' *will in fact* also be materially equivalent to 'p'; and this latter might seem after all to be a paraphrase of the form 'It was the case that q'. In fact, it isn't such a paraphrase: as we shall see later on (section 2.3), 'now', when it occurs in a sentence like 'It was the case that it would now be the case that p', takes wide scope, so that we cannot simply symbolise this last sentence as: 'It was the case that: (it is going to be the case that: (it is now the case that: p))'.

As for 'n units ago it was going to be the case n units later that p', this would fail to amount to 'p' if time had a beginning, and 'p' reported that beginning (e.g. if 'p' was 'The Big Bang went bang'); for then 'p' would be true while 'n units ago it was going to be the case n units later that p' would not be true. And the mere possibility of time's having a beginning (whenever) would be enough. For a sentence to be 'really' past-tensed, its past-tensed paraphrase must be synonymous with it, not merely materially equivalent to it. Similar remarks apply, *mutatis mutandis*, to the thesis that every unembedded sentence is future-tensed.

These latter observations make appeal to the possibility of time's having an end or a beginning, and to that extent must count as provisional. For the questions whether it really *is* possible, even logically possible, that time have a beginning, or an end, are complex ones, too knotty to go into at this juncture. (We shall return to them later on: see Chapter 6.)

Thus far I have merely been giving a basic characterisation of 'real (as opposed to grammatical) tense'. Nothing very controversial has been put forward. The precise role, for instance, played by the truth-conditions for tensed statements has been left open, as have certain features of those truth-conditions themselves, such as the construal of 'is true', and of 'the time of utterance'. I will, however, say here that I think giving truth-conditions like the above does help in, and is indeed necessary for, the elucidation of the phenomenon of tense. Necessary, perhaps; sufficient, no: for there are certain constitutive connections, for example between the past tense and memory, or between the future tense and intention, which would need to be adduced in a full account of tense. We shall return to *these* connections in Part III.

It would appear to be merely common sense to say that logical tense plays an essential part in rendering much, if not all, of our discourse 'temporal'. Tense allows us to talk about time in certain ways: it allows us to talk about past, present and future. The proposition that 'Time is really tenseless' must therefore count as *prima facie* implausible. Implausible, that is, to the extent that it has a clear sense at all.

Tense, after all, whether grammatical or logical, is first and foremost a feature of language, so that the application of 'tensed' or 'tenseless' to *time* looks to be in some degree metaphorical. It is not surprising, therefore, that there are several different theses that can be associated with the slogan 'Time is tenseless', some of them metaphysical in appearance, some of them linguistic. Here are just nine of them (there may be more):

(1) The past, the present, and the future are *illusions*;
(2) There is no 'ontological' asymmetry between past and future: the future is as 'real' as the past;
(3) There are no such properties (of events, etc.) as pastness, presentness, or futurity;
(4) *Spacetime* is the proper concept to use in the scientific description of the physical world;
(5) Time does not 'flow';
(6) The only 'facts' (or 'truth-makers') there are are tenseless ones;
(7) The meaning of tensed statements can be given by tenseless ones;

(8) The truth-conditions of tensed statements can be given by tenseless ones;

(9) 'Past', 'present' and 'future' are nothing but relational expressions, relating events/periods to utterances/thoughts.

It would seem that (1)–(9) are logically independent. Nor is it likely that they all follow from some single thesis. Hence to talk of 'the' debate between the 'tensed' and 'tenseless' views of time is probably misleading, and I will endeavour not to talk in such a way. To make our task a little easier, I will in what is to come construe the assertion that time is tenseless as at least committing one to *some* kind of debunking attitude towards logical tense. 'Purely' metaphysical or scientific views, if there be such, will not receive direct attention. Given this, my plan is as follows: to examine various lines of thought associated with the slogan, 'Time is tenseless', to see what, if anything, they establish, and where, if anywhere, a debate is to be found. Our rather meandering line of enquiry will in fact end up centring on a very linguistic-sounding question; namely, the question, 'In what sense, if any, is a genuinely tenseless language possible?'. At this stage, the dialectical boot will effectively be transferred to the other metaphysical foot.

More specifically, Part I will proceed as follows.

I will start (Chapter 1) by looking at McTaggart's famous argument for the unreality of time, most closely associated with theses (1) and (3), above. This discussion will be more or less self-contained.

In Chapter 2, I will begin by briefly but critically considering the notion of 'tenseless facts', especially in connection with thesis (6), above. I will then argue that one *can* indeed get a grip on the notion of tensed/tenseless facts, *via* the notion of tensed/tenseless beliefs, but that this provides us with good grounds for insisting that there must be tensed facts – since there are many kinds of irreducibly tensed beliefs.

In the third chapter we will come on to the question of truth-conditions. Of the nine theses above, the ones particularly at stake will be (7) and, more importantly, (8). In section 3.1, I will try to clear up some confusions about what truth-conditions are, and about how we are to interpret such claims as that made by thesis (8). I will then (in sections 3.2 and 3.3) pass on to the so-called 'timeless' truths of logic and mathematics; these are both of interest in themselves, and important to the broader discussion, insofar as they might be a *model* for tenseless propositions generally. For at this stage the question will be emerging: 'What would tenseless truth-conditions for tensed statements *look* like?'

This last question will be directly addressed in the next section, section 3.4. A very natural picture of tenseless propositions will there be examined, and problems facing that picture, of a technical as well as a philosophical nature, will be spelt out. In section 3.5, *tensed* forms, as representable in a standard tense logic, will be discussed; both for comparison with the just-discussed picture of tenseless forms (in regard to 'root sentences'), and because it will turn out that what might have been thought to be a theoretical niche for tenseless sentences turns out to be no such thing.

Finally, in section 3.6, I will argue that for general philosophical reasons *there could be no* genuinely, non-parasitically tenseless sentences, in any possible language. This will clearly lead to a rejection of thesis (8), above – and to other, wider conclusions about time, tense and tenselessness.

What about those theses in our nonet not directly mentioned? Several of them, if the various arguments of Part I are to be believed, will have to receive a negative answer. But not all. Thesis (3) must, it seems to me, be correct: this has largely to do with what a 'property' is. Thesis (4), on the other hand, is one of those claims that lies beyond the scope of this book. Thesis (5), being metaphorical, raises all sorts of interesting questions. And it is to McTaggart, who thought that if only time were real, (5) *must* be false, that we now turn.

1

McTaggart's Argument

It seems appropriate to begin with possibly the most famous argument to take a debunking attitude to the phenomenon of tense: that of McTaggart. The argument is also, notoriously, an attempt to debunk our notion of time itself.

McTaggart[1] uses 'B-series' to mean the series of 'positions' in time, as they are related to one another by the relations 'earlier than' and 'later than', and relations derived from these. He uses 'A-series' to mean the series of 'positions' in time, as they are past, present or future. One could talk of events in history rather than positions in time without materially affecting McTaggart's argument, and this in fact is what I shall do. McTaggart takes the thesis that time is real to imply that the A-series is real, and proceeds to argue that the A-series is incoherent and therefore unreal; and by *modus tollens* he concludes that time is unreal. A proponent of a 'tenseless' view of time will probably deny that the thesis that time is real implies that the A-series is real. Like Mellor,[2] he may claim that the reality of the B-series is unimpugned by McTaggart's argument, and is sufficient for the reality of time. Whether or not the reality of the B-series is thus sufficient, we can assess McTaggart's argument against the reality of the A-series independently; and this is what I shall try to do.

McTaggart's argument is essentially this. The predicates 'is past', 'is present' and 'is future' are clearly incompatible predicates: no two of them can be true of one thing (event). However, if the A-series is real, we must admit that every event starts as future, becomes present, and finally becomes past. In that case, every event will have each of three incompatible properties (pastness, presentness, futurity). This is impossible; so the A-series cannot be real.

If the force of McTaggart's argument relied on his using 'is past', 'is present' and 'is future' as genuine predicates – with 'event A', 'the death of Caesar', and so on, functioning as true subject-terms – then it would, I think, founder. For, as has been argued elsewhere,[3] the logical parsing of a sentence like, 'The death of Caesar

9

is past', is not into 'the death of Caesar' (subject) and 'is past' (predicate); rather the sentence amounts to: 'It was the case that: Caesar dies' (operator plus sentence). But, as Dummett has pointed out, the argument can be rephrased so as not even to appear reliant on such a subject–predicate construal of such sentences as 'Caesar's death is past':

> Time involves change, and if there is change, then . . . some objects must have different predicates applying to them at different times; here indeed we may have to count 'is no more' and 'is not yet' as predicates. But this just means that to one and the same object incompatible predicates apply; for example, the paper was white and is yellow, so the incompatible predicates 'white' and 'yellow' apply to the paper.
>
> ('A Defence of McTaggart's Proof of the Unreality of Time', in *Truth and Other Enigmas*, Duckworth 1978, p. 352)

Nevertheless, I will continue to phrase the argument as McTaggart expressed it, since nothing does turn on it, and so that I can use 'McTaggart' as the name of my opponent.

To evaluate McTaggart's argument, it seems a good idea to begin with some account of what makes for compatibility and incompatibility in predicates. A first stab might be as follows. Predicates 'is F' and 'is G' are incompatible if they cannot both be true of one and the same thing (and compatible if they can be). McTaggart claims that 'is future' and 'is present' are incompatible. ('Is future' here means 'is wholly future'.) But are they? He himself points out that any event will start off future, and become present. Whence the idea that these predicates are incompatible?

If 'is future' and 'is present' are incompatible, this must be because they cannot be true of one and the same thing *at once*. (Indeed, this is the standard explanation of incompatibility.) If at any given time something is yet to happen, then it is not at that time happening, and if at a given time something is happening, then it is not at that time yet to happen. So our definition of incompatibility needs an extra clause. Predicates 'is F' and 'is G' are incompatible if they cannot both be true of one and the same thing at the same time. Our *first* definition (understood as unqualified) was a definition of something quite strong: examples of predicates thus 'strongly incompatible' would be 'is a man' and 'is a horse', and indeed 'substantial' or 'essential' predicates generally. If Bill is *ever* a man, then he is *never* a horse; while if he is *ever* a horse, then he is *never* a man. For Bill cannot change from being a man into being a horse (or *vice versa*) without ceasing to be Bill altogether.

No one is committed to the view that 'is future' and 'is present' are, as I have put it, 'strongly incompatible'. No one need say that if some event is ever future then it is never present, or that if it is ever present then it is never future. The predicates 'is present' and 'is future' are only incompatible in the weaker, ordinary sense. From now on, I will use 'incompatible' to mean incompatible in this ordinary sense.

Now the question arises: does the use of the A-series, or of tensed discourse, commit one to saying things, with the help of incompatible predicates such as 'is future' and 'is present', that cannot possibly be true? Well, what specific use of incompatible predicates results in propositions that cannot possibly be true? The answer to this comes straight out of our definition of 'incompatible'. Two predicates are incompatible if they cannot both be true of the same thing at the same time. The sort of necessarily-false proposition one might get using 'is future' and 'is present' will thus result from predicating them both of the same thing at the same time.

Is one who believes in the A-series committed at all to predicating 'is future' and 'is present' of the same event *at the same time*? In particular (since this is McTaggart's ground for the claim), is this commitment evident in the recognition that, if the A-series is real, any event will 'start off future, become present, then become past'?

It seems that the answer to this is 'No'. To say, of a given event, that it starts off future, becomes present and then past, is not to say of it that at some or any time it satisfies more than one of the predicates: 'is future', 'is present', 'is past'. There is of course a rather deviant sense in which one can be said to apply each of these predicates to the event 'at the same time': for one can, *in a single statement* and *on a single occasion*, say that the event satisfies, at different times, each of those three predicates. But this possibility has nothing to do with compatibility or incompatibility.

Where can McTaggart have got the idea that the A-series commits one to applying incompatible predicates to a thing so as to produce a contradiction? The answer, I think, is this. McTaggart thought that one who allowed the reality of the A-series would have to say, for example: 'Caesar's death is all of the following: past, present, and future'. This does look like a contradiction. It looks like the same sort of sentence as, 'Bill is all three of the following: over six foot tall, between five foot and six foot tall, and less

than five foot tall'. But the latter is a contradiction because it amounts
to saying that three incompatible predicates all apply at once to Bill;
the present tense of the statement leads one to read it that way.
(The fact that Bill started off under five foot, became taller than five
foot but shorter than six foot, then became more than six foot, does
not lead us to embrace the contradiction.)

Only if we take the sentence about Caesar's death as saying that
the three predicates all apply to Caesar's death at once, do we need
to call it a contradiction. But we cannot infer that the predicates
all apply to something at once from the fact that something began
as future, then (later) became present, and (later) became past. In
other words, the contradiction does not follow from acceptance of
the A-series.

These remarks allow us to see that rebutting McTaggart's argument does not, *pace* various philosophers, set one off on an infinite
regress. According to these philosophers, the debate will kick off
roughly like this:

> *McT*: You must admit that every event is past, present and fu-
> ture.
> *Anti-McT*: No. A past event, say Napoleon's death, *was* future, then
> *was* present, and *is* past. A present event *was* future, *is* present,
> and *will be* past. And a future event *was* future, *will be* present, and
> *will be* past. No event *is* past, present and future.
> *McT*: You've just introduced such complex tenses as 'will be past',
> 'was past', etc. But you must admit that every predicate for a
> complex tense applies to every event; including incompatible
> predicates, such as 'past in the past' and 'present in the future'.
> *Anti-McT*: No; it may, for some event, E, be true that: (it *is* the case
> that it was the case that E was the case), and that: (it *was* the case
> that it is the case that E will be the case). It can't be that E *is* 'past
> in the past' and *is* 'present in the future'.

The McTaggartian then points out that yet more complex tenses
have been invoked, and that every predicate for such a complex
tense will apply to every event. And so on.

As has been noted in this debate, it is the status of 'is' in a sentence like 'Every event is past, present and future' that determines
what we should say about the putative regress. But it is not necessary
for the proponent of the A-series to deny the possibility of a tenseless
'is'. Let our 'is' be tenseless. Then why can't it be admitted that
'Every event is past, present and future' is *true*? For this sentence
just means 'Every event is at some time past, is at some time present

and is at some time future'; and this is compatible with the (ordinary) incompatibility of 'past', 'present' and 'future'. What is false is: 'Every event is at some time past, is at the same time present, and is at the same time future'. But this doesn't follow from 'Every event is past, present and future', with tenseless 'is'. On the other hand, if the 'is' is construed as present-tensed, then clearly no one need admit that every event is (now) past, present and future – a proposition that *would* conflict with the incompatibility of 'past', 'present' and 'future'.

The riposte I have here spelt out to McTaggart is essentially that about which Dummett wrote:

> It is because people suppose that McTaggart can be refuted by some such objection . . . that they do not take him very seriously. . . .

and Dummett goes on to say:

> I believe that this [sc. putative] solution rests on a grave misunderstanding. If it gave a correct account of the matter, then only stupidity could explain McTaggart's failure to use a quite analogous argument to show the unreality of space and the unreality of personality. Every place can be called both 'here' and 'there', both 'near' and 'far', and every person can be called both 'I' and 'you': yet 'here' and 'there', 'near' and 'far', 'I' and 'you' are incompatible.
>
> (Ibid., p. 353)

Dummett's view is that McTaggart's argument rests on a certain assumption: namely, that 'reality must be something of which there exists in principle a complete description'. Expounding this assumption, and what McTaggart thinks follows from it with respect to time, Dummett writes:

> The description of what is really there, as it really is, must be independent of any particular point of view. Now if time were real, since what is temporal cannot be completely described without the use of token-reflexive expressions [i.e. tensed expressions], there would be no such thing as the complete description of reality. There would be one, as it were, maximal description of reality in which the statement 'The event M is happening' figured, others which contained the statement 'The event M happened', and yet others which contained 'The event M is going to happen'.
>
> (Ibid., p. 356)

Time is different from space, for example, because what is spatial *can* 'be completely described without the use of token-reflexive expressions'.

What sort of a statement is 'Reality is something of which there exists in principle a complete description'? And does McTaggart's argument rest on such a principle?

Nothing in fact prevents the devotee of the A-series from accepting the principle as it stands. He may say: 'Yes; reality *is* completely describable! That is, it *is now* completely describable, using tensed sentences, etc. Tomorrow, it will still be completely describable, though the description will have changed.' Dummett's statement of the principle he ascribes to McTaggart can only be taken as underlying McTaggart's argument if it is construed tenselessly, or as conjunctively-tensed. In 'There exists in principle a complete description . . .', the verb 'exists' cannot just mean 'exists now'; it must mean effectively, 'has existed, exists, and will exist'. Indeed, a less misleading statement of the principle would be: 'Reality is something of which there exists in principle an unchanging description'. And, of course, the principle spelt out thus is one which a proponent of a 'tensed' view of time will simply reject.

Perhaps it is right to say that McTaggart was tacitly assuming the above principle about what is real. But if so, then McTaggart's argument seems to involve a fairly blatant *petitio principii*. It is hard to say whether this would betoken less or more 'stupidity' than would a piece of fallacious reasoning involving the term 'incompatible'. A precise diagnosis of philosophical confusion is, however, frequently impossible – a tangle of temptations may have lured McTaggart to say what he did.

Several philosophers, apart from Dummett, have seen much to endorse, or at any rate to discuss, in McTaggart's argument for the unreality of the A-series. If my treatment of McTaggart has been brief, it is because I am at odds with these philosophers: I cannot help feeling that there is a relatively simple mistake involved in what McTaggart says – simple, that is, to spell out, though maybe not a simple matter to avoid in the first place. Other versions of the argument seem to me not to do any better.

We shall at a much later stage find something to endorse in McTaggart: namely, his view that the A-series, and not the B-series, contains the 'essence' of time – or rather, for McTaggart, the 'essence' of what time would be if there were such a thing.

2
Facts, Knowledge and Belief

2.1 FACTS

Some philosophers assume that if our topic is time and the nature of time, we will be talking off the subject so long as we discuss language. These philosophers do not necessarily eschew the use of such expressions as 'tensed' and 'tenseless', however. I pointed out earlier on that since tense is first and foremost a feature of language, an application of such an adjective as 'tensed' to *time* looks to be more or less metaphorical; certainly, applications of this sort will stand in need of explanation. And philosophers who professedly want to 'get away from' the merely linguistic, while using *prima facie* linguistic terminology, owe us that explanation.

The urge to 'get away from' the merely linguistic is evidenced, in the literature on time, by Hugh Mellor. In a debate with Graham Priest, he asserts that a parallel drawn by Priest

> fails, because to draw it he has to take what I call 'tense' to be a feature of verbs, despite initially defining it as 'pastness, presentness and futurity' and saying rightly that the question at issue is whether tense so defined is 'an objective feature of reality'.... This of course is a question about time, not about verbs....
>
> ('Tense's Tenseless Truth Conditions', *Analysis*, vol. 46, p. 167)

How would one go about characterising the tense (or TENSE, as Mellor decides to call it) which is 'an objective feature of reality'? Mellor's way is to talk about McTaggart's A-series:

> What I call TENSES are temporal positions in McTaggart's A-series, 'that series of positions which runs from the far past through the near past to the present, and from the present through the near future to the far future' (McTaggart 1927, p. 10).
>
> (Ibid., p. 167)

The same characterisation of TENSE is to be found in Mellor's *Real Time* (Cambridge University Press, 1981). In a way, it is perfectly innocuous: if tense is a matter of anything, it is a matter of past, present and future. (Talk of a 'series of positions' adds nothing to this.) The question is: how can one distinguish 'real' tense from grammatical tense? Grammatical, as well as 'real', tense is (vacuously) a matter of past, present and future: there are past verbs, present verbs and future verbs. To say that 'real' tenses are (or would have to be) features of events, or of stretches of time, while grammatical tenses are only features of verbs or sentences, does not help us. For a start, characterising 'real' tenses as *features* of anything, whether events or anything else, may turn out to be wrong. But in any case, what backs up the idea that events (stretches of time, etc.) can be 'really' tensed? Only the fact that in sentences like 'He is coming tomorrow' we can distinguish between the grammatical tense of the verb or sentence, and what we should like to call the 'real' tense (*of the verb or sentence*). I have already suggested how to characterise *this* distinction (pp. 3–4), in terms of the truth-conditions of utterances. The distinction between grammatical and 'real' tense is essentially that between the grammatical and logical form of sentences; to say that a sentence is 'logically' past-tensed is to say that it is paraphrasable as one of the form 'It was the case that p' (for some 'p').[1] The dichotomy between 'mere grammar', on the one hand, and 'full-blooded metaphysics', on the other, is a false one.

Even if it is a little hard to characterise metaphysical 'reality' without a little help from such a logico-linguistic notion as that of logical form, perhaps it is still of interest to ask: 'Well, for all that, *is* tense in fact real?'. (If we have *explicated* the notion of 'reality' – *via* that of logical form – we ought to be in a position to *use* it.) And having formulated this question, we can, perhaps, begin to assess the 'tenseless' view of time.

Of course, the trouble now is that, in distinguishing grammatical from 'real' tense, we have guaranteed that there *is* such a thing as 'real' tense. In the sentence 'He is coming tomorrow', we say, the verb is grammatically present-tensed, but the 'real' tense of the report is future. So the future tense of the report (or of the event, fact, etc., reported, if you prefer) must be real enough: for we have just said that the 'real tense' of the report (event, fact) is future.

If we want to deny that tense is ever 'really real', we will need some new characterisation of '(un)reality', and not the one with

which we began. The one with which we began traded on a distinction that it did seem necessary to make; will our new notion of
'reality' have as good a *raison d'être*?

This, of course, depends on how we characterise our new notion.
One way of characterising it is in terms of 'facts': the thesis that
tense is unreal then becomes the thesis that there are no 'tensed
facts'.

It should need no pointing out that the concept of 'fact' being
employed is not that to be found in such ordinary locutions as 'It's
a fact that . . .'. Clearly, an utterance such as, 'It's a fact that he will
come' (and the reassembled 'That he will come is a fact'), is perfectly capable of being true, just so long as the simple 'He will
come' is capable of being true. And we are not at the moment
taking the latter to be in any doubt. Nor does a quantificational
locution like, 'I know certain facts' (or the reassembled 'There are
facts which I know'), provide the proponent of thesis (6) of the
Preamble with a foothold: '. . . such as that he will come' is a perfectly possible 'namely'-rider for 'I know certain facts'. (Other verbs
than 'know' could equally well be used to make this point; 'certain
facts are contingent' will do.)

The metaphysician's 'fact' has a history: it is to be found particularly in classical formulations of the correspondence theory of truth,
such as Wittgenstein's in the *Tractatus*. (Wittgenstein's term is
Tatsache.) To the extent that a philosopher uses 'fact' in association
with a correspondence theory of truth, he will make himself vulner-
able to all the charges that have been levelled against such theories.
Philosophers who talk of facts as 'truth-makers' come to mind in
particular. One of the main charges levelled against correspondence theories was that they failed to provide a notion of 'fact' that
was sufficiently independent of the very notion to be explained by
reference to facts: namely, the notion of the true sentence or proposition. And this charge will certainly be pertinent in the present
case. For the philosopher who wants to assert that there are 'tenseless
facts' while denying that there are 'tensed facts' will have to be able
to reject the principle that to non-synonymous true sentences there
correspond different facts. This is because he will want to say that
the fact that makes an utterance at time t of 'It's raining' true is *the
same fact* as that which makes the allegedly tenseless 'It's raining at
time t' (uttered whenever) true. But the idea that (an utterance of)
'It's raining' and 'It's raining at time t' might be *synonymous* is fraught
with problems, as well as being *prima facie* unbelievable. The notion

of 'fact' will to that extent have to be independent of the notion of a true proposition: the 'criteria of identity' for facts won't go hand in hand with the 'criteria of identity' for propositions (i.e. synonymy). But, so it would seem by now, no such criteria of identity are forthcoming.

There is also the problem of 'making true'. The nature of this alleged relation is obscure, just as that of traditional 'correspondence' was. Indeed, that the truth of any sentence at all is explicable by reference to some *relation* between it and something else is very problematic. If we have a *bona fide* relation here, expressible as a two-place predicable, in whose two places we should be able to put singular terms, then we are landed with such putative singular terms as 'The fact that p'. An entity to which both 'p' and 'The fact that p' somehow correspond, despite their difference of syntactic category, is a very rum thing.[2]

Moreover, grounds would have to be given why 'truth-makers' such as Bill's going to arrive shouldn't do the job of making utterances like 'Bill will arrive' true. This problem is a close cousin in the material mode of one posed by Graham Priest for certain views about 'tenseless truth-conditions', with which problem we shall have to do later on (pp. 41–2).

The appeal to 'facts' is often (though not invariably) a manifestation of a certain view of philosophy, a view I have already hinted at with the word 'metaphysics'. According to such a view, the philosopher, like the scientist, wants to know the nature of things 'out there': he wants to know what the 'furniture of the world' *really* is. ('Really' here will tend to mean: 'independently of our minds or language'.) 'Facts', if they exist, will be just another bit of the world's furniture, along with tables, chairs and force-fields – if, indeed, such as these do exist.

Another traditional view of the philosopher's task is more purely epistemological. According to this view, the philosopher above all seeks after knowledge – perhaps after certainty also. There is less emphasis on what his knowledge must be knowledge *of* (e.g. the world 'out there', the world 'within', the eternal verities . . .). And if one bit of knowledge can be shown to be, *qua* knowledge, a thoroughly new bit of knowledge, then, according to such a view, this must be a matter of philosophical importance.

In the context of the debate over tense and tenselessness, the question of *knowledge* gets raised once it is seen that 'tensed' knowledge may be different from, and irreducible to, any 'tenseless' knowledge. Moreover, one might further weaken the position of the fact-fetishist by pointing out that types of knowledge provide a promising route to our so far lacking criteria of identity for facts: if a person knows something he didn't know before, isn't it quite appropriate to say that he knows certain *facts* he didn't know before? In which case, if there is essentially 'tensed' knowledge, then there are essentially 'tensed' facts. And the question whether there is essentially tensed knowledge is definite enough for one to get a proper grip on it.

2.2 TENSED BELIEF AND THE EXPLANATION OF ACTION

Most latter-day accounts of knowledge classify propositional knowledge (knowing *that* such-and-such) as some sort of true belief. Just what sort of true belief has been the main concern of epistemologists for a long time – but this concern will not be ours in what follows. Knowledge *qua* belief will be the primary focus of our discussion. But let us first, as they say, wind the clock back. . . .

Nigel Molesworth, a schoolboy and noted under-achiever, is observed from 2.45 p.m. onwards on a Friday afternoon by an empirical psychologist. From 2.45 p.m. until 3.30 p.m. he exhibits a wide variety of displacement behaviours, such as making ink blots and throwing things at Peason; but at 3.30 p.m., his demeanour alters markedly. He piles his meagre possessions together into his briefcase and, regardless of the teacher's protests, charges from the room yelling. How are we to explain this phenomenon? It is not an isolated event either: Molesworth, and indeed most of 3b, regularly act in this deplorable way.

The explanation is simple. Molesworth was driven to his exit by acquiring a new piece of knowledge. Acquiring new knowledge is a standard, perhaps the standard, route to new behaviour, even for Molesworth; for instance, on learning that a certain shop sells one's favourite chocolate, one may well go to that shop. So what important piece of knowledge did Molesworth acquire on Friday afternoon? The answer is: at the moment (or just before) he moved, Molesworth came to know that it was 3.30 p.m., the time scheduled for the end of the lesson. This did not just hit him, to be sure – he had had his eye on the clock.

Molesworth's state needn't have been one of *knowledge* for him to have acted, of course. He would have charged from the room yelling if he had *falsely* believed that it was 3.30 p.m. So the empirical psychologist can appeal simply to Molesworth's belief that it was 3.30 p.m. in his final report. Be that as it may, the knowledge which Molesworth acquired was clearly tensed knowledge. He could have expressed his knowledge thus: 'It is now 3.30 p.m.'; and we can report Molesworth's knowledge indirectly: 'He came to know that it was then 3.30 p.m.'.

A somewhat similar case was introduced by Prior, in his paper 'Thank Goodness That's Over!'. As Prior points out concerning the eponymous exclamation:

> It certainly doesn't mean the same as, e.g. 'Thank goodness the date of the conclusion of that thing is Friday, June 15, 1954', even if it be said then. (Nor, for that matter, does it mean 'Thank goodness the conclusion of that thing is contemporaneous with this utterance'. Why should anyone thank goodness for that?)
>
> ('Thank Goodness That's Over', in *Papers in Logic and Ethics*, ed. Geach and Kenny, Duckworth 1976, p. 84.)

It does seem natural to think that when one thanks goodness, one is thanking goodness *that so-and-so* – in the present case, that one is thanking goodness that the lesson is now over, for example. However, an opponent of tensed knowledge may deny that we have in 'Thank goodness that...' (or in 'He thanked goodness that...') any sort of propositional operator. Such an opponent may regard 'Thank goodness that's over!' as more like an avowal, in the Wittgensteinian's sense, or like a combination of an avowal and a proposition. Hugh Mellor writes:

> The fact is that 'Thank goodness that's over' is not really a single statement at all: it is a conjunction of 'That's over' and 'Thank goodness'. This can be seen in the fact that the conjuncts are just as naturally joined the other way round: 'That's over; thank goodness'.
>
> (*Real Time*, Cambridge University Press, 1981, p. 51)

This view encounters some slight problems, such as the problem of making sense of third-person statements, as, 'Molesworth thanked goodness the lesson was over'. If 'Thank goodness' is, as Mellor holds, a self-sufficient expression of relief, rather than a propositional operator or part of one, then 'Molesworth thanked goodness that the lesson was over' will have to amount to something like: 'Molesworth expressed his relief (by saying "Thank goodness"), and implied that his relief was caused by the ending of the lesson'. (This sort of analysis is gestured towards by Mellor.)

The details no doubt would need attending to; but one who adopts this general approach does not, I think, court obvious absurdity. The threat posed by straightforward tensed *beliefs*, such as Molesworth's 'It is now 3.30 p.m.', is more acute, especially if those beliefs seem to be required for the explanation of certain behaviours. John Perry[3] has written of beliefs that are both indexical and essential in the explanation of people's behaviour – beliefs that are 'essentially indexical'. The case on which he, and many others writing on the topic, have concentrated, is that of first-personal beliefs, and it will be useful to bear such beliefs in mind for comparison with tensed beliefs.

The first thing to be said, I think, is this. Whatever one says about the exact nature of epistemic contexts, like 'Molesworth knows that . . .', it is clear that one cannot replace the sentences occurring in such contexts by materially equivalent ones, *salva veritate*; nor can one replace embedded sentences by ones which simply give the truth-conditions of those sentences, *salva veritate*. This is the primary explanation of the impossibility of recasting 'Molesworth knew it was 3.30 p.m.' as anything along the lines of, 'Molesworth knew that his thought "It is 3.30 p.m." coincided with its being 3.30 p.m.'. Similar remarks apply to the impossibility of recasting 'Molesworth knew he was called "Molesworth" ' along the lines of, 'Molesworth knew that Molesworth was called "Molesworth" '.

The point is not one about the impossibility of substituting co-referring terms in epistemic contexts. In the last-quoted example, neither the indirect reflexive 'he', nor the 'I' which would have been part of Molesworth's expression of his knowledge, need be taken as referring at all. And in the tensed example, it is not that the indirect reflexive 'then', or the 'now' that would have occurred in Molesworth's expression of his belief, fail to refer to the *same thing* as '3.30 p.m.' – none of these expressions need be taken as referring at all. The classic arguments which elaborate why 'I', 'now', etc., are 'essential' (such as Perry's and Castaneda's)[4] are not in the same boat as those purporting to show why 'Cicero' can't be substituted for 'Tully' in 'Molesworth knew that Tully denounced Catiline'. But they are in more or less the same boats as all those arguments which show, for any 'p' and 'q', why 'p' can't be substituted for 'q' just because the sentences share a truth-value, or because one gives the truth-conditions (not the meaning) of the other.

The second point I want to make is that one cannot explain the 'essentiality' of indexicals like 'I' and 'now' by associating them with special 'modes of presentation', even when the latter phrase is allowed in connection with non-referring terms. The devotee of facts might claim that Molesworth's knowledge of the time was 'new' only in the sense that he came to have a new 'mode of presentation' of a fact with which he was, or could easily have been, acquainted (the 'tenseless' fact that his thought 'It is now 3.30 p.m.' coincided with its being 3.30 p.m.).

Frege's jargon, 'mode of presentation', has become possibly even less clear in import than when he first used it; however, I think that it can be shown that the special roles of 'I' and 'now' have nothing to do with 'modes of presentations of facts'.

The special mode of presentation of a tenseless fact which Molesworth is being claimed to express by saying 'It is now 3.30' presumably derives from the special mode of presentation of the *time* (3.30 p.m., Friday, 16 January, say), which mode of presentation he expresses by saying 'now'. Similarly, it will be argued, the fact that Molesworth is called 'Molesworth' is a fact which the judgement 'I am called "Molesworth"' presents to Molesworth in a special way, on account of 'I' expressing (for Molesworth) a certain mode of presentation of Molesworth.

Does this sort of account hold water? Consider 'I' first. I will not rehearse the arguments to the effect that 'I' cannot amount to any description, such as 'The thinker of these thoughts', 'The owner of this body', or whatever – others have presented the case thoroughly enough. One will usually be accused of simplification if one assimilates 'modes of presentation' to descriptions, in any case. But there are two, related, features of first-personal judgements that, it seems to me, make an application of Frege's notion quite inappropriate. I mean the *directness*, and the *simplicity*, of such judgements. Psychological examples are generally most persuasive here. One's knowledge that one is in pain is unmediated by any 'presentation' of oneself at all, and it is in this respect simple, in much the way that 'It's raining' is simple. (Indeed, some have been tempted to see the notable simplicity of 'I am in pain' as a sign that it is, at bottom, not a subject-predicate judgement at all.)[5]

A 'mode of presentation' of oneself is sometimes argued for by philosophers who say that, in making first-personal judgements, one is thereby manifesting one's conception of oneself as a body with spatio-temporal location and properties, etc. This way of talking presents us with a dilemma. Either the notions involved are being imputed, in a substantive way, to the conceptual armouries of everyone who can think 'I am in pain', in which case those notions are of a generality and abstraction the capacity for which is implausibly ascribed to children (and most adults!) – or, alternatively, 'having a conception of oneself as a spatio-temporal object' amounts to little more than being able to move around without bumping into things, and will hardly establish the 'mode of presentation' thesis (not, at any rate, in the form needed by our fact-fetishist).

Turning to 'now', one can make analogous remarks to many of those just made about 'I'. We may start by pointing out that no *description*, or description-like phrase, could do the work of 'now', or of the present tense. This effectively is the gist of the thesis that tensed sentences are not susceptible of tenseless translations (see pp. 37–8); and in the present context, one can add that a substitute for 'now' will either surreptitiously involve it (as, 'the time of the *present* utterance/thought'), or will be useless in explaining behaviour like Molesworth's (as, 'the time of the end of my fifty-third Latin lesson').

If 'modes of presentation' are more than just descriptions, on the other hand, one can again appeal to the notable directness and simplicity of present-tense judgements. The idea that, in order to make a present-tense judgement, one should have any sort of 'conception' of the present moment at all is even less plausible than the idea that making first-person judgements requires a 'conception' of oneself; unless, of course, 'having a conception of the present moment' is nothing *more* than being able to make present-tense judgements – or nothing more than being able to *behave*! Nor is it irrelevant here to mention the enormous *difficulty* of the question 'What is the present moment?'. The question is a thousand times knottier than 'What is Molesworth?', for example; and to ascribe to thinkers generally a conception which must, at least to some extent, embody an answer to that question would be to display an excessive confidence in people's mental powers.

So much for modes of presentation. Another argument to be considered concerns the grounds we have for saying that someone retains the same belief over time. Richard[6] has drawn attention to the following sort of example. If at 2.45 Molesworth thinks the lesson *will* end at 3.30, and at 3.30 thinks that it *is* ending, and at 4.00 thinks that it *did* end at 3.30, we will very often find it natural to say that his beliefs concerning the time of the lesson's conclusion do not change between 2.45 and 4.00, but rather remain steadfast. This is in contrast to what I said earlier, that at 3.30 Molesworth 'acquired a new belief'; and it seems that if we are to stick to the idea that Molesworth doesn't change his mind on this question, we will after all have to admit that the 'object' of Molesworth's belief is a tenseless, not a tensed, proposition. Given that his belief is a case of knowledge, we might then go on to say that what 'makes his belief true' is a tenseless, not a tensed, fact.

One might want to respond to Richard's argument as follows. The proponent of the view that Molesworth's beliefs must be tensed can consistently admit that a belief of Molesworth's regarding the time of the lesson's conclusion remains fixed: for he can say that at each time (2.45, 3.00, 4.00), Molesworth has the belief expressible as 'The lesson either will end, or is ending, or did end at 3.30'. The logical connection between 'p' and 'p or q or r' is simple enough for it to be not unbelievable that even Molesworth would have the disjunctive belief at each time at which he had one of the 'disjunct-beliefs'.

However, this sort of line seems to me to be too contrived. Our question centres on what counts, in certain contexts, as 'the same belief' (over time). And there seems nothing to prevent one from saying that where, for example, Molesworth believed that the lesson would end at 3.30, and later believed that it had ended at 3.30, these just are sufficient grounds for saying that he maintained the same belief about the time of the lesson's ending: what *counts* in such a context as a single belief has to do with shared truth-value and subject matter, or if you like with a certain way of explaining or describing a person's outward behaviour. It doesn't have to do (as it does in other contexts) with shared 'propositional content'. At any rate, one cannot assume that wherever we have the 'same belief', we *must* have shared propositional content, a content expressible (in principle) by a single sentence.

To be sure, if the ascription of a single belief were on occasion thus independent of the possible existence of a sentence expressing that belief, we should not be able to take 'A believed something . . .' as always amounting to, 'For some p, A believed that p . . .', given that such propositional quantification requires possible substitutions for 'p'. Even so, it is worth pointing out that we are happier saying something like, 'From 2.00 til 4.00, Molesworth's belief about the time of the lesson's ending remained unaltered' than saying something more overtly quantificational, like, 'From 2.00 till 4.00,

Molesworth had a certain belief about the time of the lesson's ending'. Moreover, it is significant that we have to use the noun phrase 'the lesson's ending', or similar: if we try to use a clause, we immediately run into the problem of tenses. 'From 2.00 till 4.00, Molesworth's belief about when the lesson would end remained unaltered' isn't quite right, since after 3.30 Molesworth had no belief about when the lesson *would* end (for by then he realised that it had already ended). But no other single verb-form is available. If we simply *postulate* a tenseless verb-form, we are no longer using what we find it natural to say about belief-retention, as evidence for the existence of tenseless beliefs and propositions.

There are grounds for thinking that 'event-terms' like 'the lesson's ending' are, at least typically, nominalisations of a verbal form. But if 'the lesson's ending', in the quoted sentences about belief-retention, is indeed paraphrasable with the aid of a clause, that clause will have to belong to the same language: standard English. And the sentence, 'From 2.00 till 4.00, Moleworth's belief about when the lesson ends remained unaltered' is just not standard English.

2.3   ASCRIPTIONS OF TENSED BELIEFS THROUGH *ORATIO OBLIQUA*

So far, I have been putting forward various considerations that suggest the irreducibility of 'tensed' knowledge and belief. But it is still a little vague what ascriptions of such knowledge or belief amount to. In this section, I want to examine what exactly is going on when we make attributions of tensed knowledge or belief. Apart from being of interest in itself, this examination will reveal ways in which tensed sentences and what they express must be regarded as irreducible to tenseless equivalents.

Consider the following:

(1)   Bill thought that it was raining, and it was.
(2)   Bill thought that it would be raining now, and it is.
(3)   Bill thinks that it was raining/will rain, and it was/will.
(4)   Bill thinks that it is raining, and it is.
(5)   Bill will think that it is raining, and it will be.
(6)   Bill will think that it was raining now, and it is.

Whether or not a redundancy theory of truth gives the whole truth about truth, it seems a good general principle that if Bill truly believes that p, then we can write: 'Bill thinks that p, and p'. But the possibility of the occurrence of indexicals, either in the belief-clause or in one of the two main clauses, means that this principle is far from exceptionless as it stands. Altham[7] has pointed this fact out for first-personal beliefs: the two occurrences of 'he' in 'Bill thinks he is on fire, and he is' are, as Castaneda *et al.* have shown, not occurrences of a single expression. In (1)–(6), the indexicality is provided by tense.

Castaneda[8] classified expressions like 'I', 'now', and 'here', which can occur in direct discourse and *oratio recta*, 'indicators'. The expressions which replace these indicators when we go from *oratio recta* to *oratio obliqua*, such as 'he (himself)', 'then', and 'there', Castaneda termed 'quasi-indicators'. Thus, the *oratio recta* report, 'Bill said, "It is raining"', can be replaced by the *oratio obliqua*, 'Bill said that it was then raining'. (Quasi-indicators of time and place are often left out in English: 'Bill said that it was raining' is sufficient.)

It is, I think, an accident of English (and other languages) that quasi-indicators replace indicators in indirect speech. We have the form 'Bill said he was on fire' because the form 'Bill said I am on fire' is reserved for another use, a use in which, as logicians say, 'I' takes wide scope. But the proposition expressed by 'Bill said I am on fire' is rather anomalous; for instance, one cannot (as one can with *oratio obliqua* sentences generally) 'infer back' to any *oratio recta* form. The same goes for other indicators than 'I'. Hence, it would be quite possible to use 'Bill said I am on fire' to be the indirect report of Bill's saying 'I am on fire'. And indeed Sanskrit works along just these lines.

In fact, English sometimes works rather along these lines, too: the first clause of (5), above, is the indirect version of, 'Bill will think, "It is raining"'. The indexical element (the present tense) is preserved in the shift from direct to indirect speech. (Likewise, in (6), some report of the form 'Bill will think, "It was raining...."' corresponds to 'Bill will think that it was raining now': the tense is preserved.) We might use 'quasi-indicator of time' to mean 'then', or just to mean the Sanskrit-like occurrence of an indicator (whether an expression or just a tense-formation) within an indirect context; whichever way we use it, we can say that both (1) and (5) involve quasi-indicators (though an occurrence of 'then' must be deemed implicit only).

A general statement of the truth-conditions of sentences containing some indicator involves a generalisation from an *oratio recta* version of sentences like (1), (3), (4), and (5). Consider 'I' once more.

'Bill says that he is on fire, and he is' can be rewritten first as, 'Bill says that he is on fire, and Bill is on fire' – the pronoun of laziness 'he' is replaced by the name it stands proxy for. We can then go into *oratio recta*: 'Bill says "I am on fire", and Bill is on fire'. To say this last is of course to say that Bill's utterance is true; and so we can now write:

Bill speaks truly if he says 'I am on fire' iff Bill is on fire.

A generalisation from the above biconditional gives us the truth-conditions for 'I am on fire':

For all x, x speaks truly if x says 'I am on fire' iff x is on fire.

Now consider indicators of time – tense operators, in fact. We can rewrite (1) as:

(1a)   It was the case that (Bill thinks that (it is now the case that (it is raining))), and it was then the case that (it is raining).

Let us hereafter put 'P' for the past tense operator, 'N' for the present tense one, and 'F' for the future tense one. (1a) amounts to:

(1a)   P (Bill thinks that (N (it is raining))), and P then (it is raining).

Depending on what we eventually say about 'root sentences', 'N' may turn out to be redundant. I include it mainly to emphasise the analogy between 'now' and 'I' (which, if 'now' were redundant, would amount to an analogy between first-personal and 'root' sentences), and also to put in practice the Sanskrit-style use of 'now' within indirect contexts. That style of use will enable us to transform (1a) into *oratio recta* in a quite automatic manner.

But what is 'then' doing in (1a)? This will become apparent in a moment. First, though, let us alter our example slightly. (1) might have involved an adverb of date, thus: 'On 1 January, Bill thought that it was raining, and it was raining then'. This last 'then' is a pronoun of laziness, just as the second 'he' was in, 'Bill says that he is on fire, and he is'. Hence, our dated sentence can be rewritten: 'On 1 January, Bill thought that it was raining, and it was raining on 1 January'. (To avoid complication, let us assume that 'It rained on 1 January' can be taken to mean 'It rained for the whole of 1 January'.) With 'at t' for 'on 1 January', (1a) can be altered accordingly:

(1a') P at t (Bill thinks that (N (it is raining))), and P at t (it is raining).

Going into direct speech, now, we can write:

(1b) P at t (Bill thinks 'N (it is raining)'), and P at t (it is raining).

A few steps of generalisation will give us the sort of truth-conditions for 'N (it is raining)', with which we are familiar (p. 4):

For all t, for all x, P/N/F at t (x thinks truly if x thinks 'N (it is raining)') iff P/N/F at t (it is raining).

('P/N/F at t (p)' is short for 'P at t (p) OR N at t (p) OR F at t (p)'; we have 'generalised' from plain 'P at t'.)

What is going on here?

The rule for determining whether 'Bill says he is on fire' (or its Sanskrit-style equivalent, or its *oratio recta* version) reports a true statement was this: replace the quasi-indicator (or Sanskritly-embedded indicator, or indicator in *oratio recta*) by the name governing the intentional verb 'says', and the resulting sentence of the form 'A is on fire' is true iff A's reported utterance is. The analogous rule for (1b)'s first clause, 'P at t (Bill thinks that (N (it is raining)))', *alias* 'On 1 January, Bill thought that it was raining', is this: replace the quasi-indicator (i.e. Sanskritly-embedded indicator) by the indicator governing the intentional context 'Bill thinks that', and the resulting sentence of the form 'δ (it is raining)' – i.e. the sentence for which the indicator has widest scope – is true iff Bill's reported thought was true. In other words, replace 'N' by 'P at t' to get 'P at t (it is raining)'.

(1) lacked a date, of course. But the thought reported by the undated 'P (Bill thinks that (N (it is raining)))' isn't true iff the simple 'P (it is raining)' is true – Bill's thought wasn't *that* immune from error. That was why we had to insert 'then' into (1a). How are we to construe that 'then' when there seems to be no preceding adverb of date for it to go proxy for?

The obvious solution is to take (1a), and hence (1), as amounting to:

(1a) For some t, P at t (Bill thinks that (N (it is raining))), and P at t (it is raining).

With a sentence like the first clause of (1), then, the rule for determining whether the thought reported is true is a shade more complex.

The quantifier governing the indicator governing the intentional context also governs the result of replacing the quasi-indicator by the indicator.

The above account will help us explain what is going on in both (1) and (5). (For (5), just replace 'P' by 'F' in the preceding paragraphs.) It can also be applied to (4), at any rate on one reading of (4).

That (4) should be susceptible of more than one reading may well be doubted. But, as I have been suggesting, the use of a present-tense indicator in an indirect context sometimes means one thing, sometimes another – given that the present tense can itself be taken as an indicator. An embedded present-tense indicator may take wide scope, relating it, if you like, to the time of utterance of the whole; this is what happens with 'now' in (2) and (6). Alternatively, such an indicator may take narrow scope, relating it, if you like, to the time of utterance of the reported utterance (thought, or whatever); this is what happens with the present tense in (5). The latter use is what I have been calling the 'Sanskrit-style' use. Which use is being made of the present tense in (4)?

From sentences like (2) and (6) one might draw the conclusion that the *function* of 'now' when it occurs in indirect contexts is to take wide scope (whereas, perhaps, that of the embedded present tense – where it occurs – is to take narrow). Could we then conclude that (4) is like (5)? – and further, that it can be approached in the same way as we approached both (5) and (1)?

This would be a little hasty, if only because it does not seem to alter the sense of (1) much if we insert 'now' to get: 'Bill thinks that it is raining now, etc.'. If we had begun with this version, and noticed how 'now' behaves in (2) and (6), we might have decided to approach (4) in whatever way we approach (2) and (6)!

At this point, we should consider *oratio recta* once more. (1) and (5) are indirect reports of thoughts that Bill might express thus: 'It is raining'. The thoughts reported by (2) and (6), on the other hand, respectively weren't and won't be so expressible; they were/will be *true* iff 'It is raining' is true when the *report* is made (the conditions on this truth-value link will be discussed in a moment). The question to ask of (4), then, is this: Could Bill express his thought as 'It is raining', or could he only express it by some sentence that is true iff 'It is raining' is true at the time of the report?

It is quite possible that Bill's thought, as reported by (4), is one he could, and would, express as 'It is raining'. In which case, (4) would be assimilable to (5) and to (1), as I have already hinted. Going formal, we could rewrite (4) as (4a):

(4a)   N (A thinks that (N (it is raining))), and N (it is raining).

Adopting the rule we used for (1a'), we can say: replace the quasi-indicator (Sanskritly-embedded indicator), 'N', by the indicator governing the intentional context – 'N' again – and the resulting sentence, 'N (it is raining)', is true iff the reported thought is. (Dates, as well as quantifiers with date-variables, are here superfluous.)

We need now to consider what sort of thought Bill might be having, other than one expressible as 'It is raining', which is true iff it is raining (at the time of the report). This leads us also to (2) and (6). The question we are addressing is analogous to: In 'Bill thinks I am on fire', in which 'I' (like 'now'), takes wide scope, how might Bill express the thought which he has? These questions about 'I' and 'now' are discussed at some length by Castaneda, and what I have to say will bear some affinity to what Castaneda says.

Take (2) first. Bill might have had his thought about today's weather yesterday, and it might have been expressible as, 'Tomorrow it will rain'. This would be enough for (2)'s first clause to be true. 'Tomorrow' amounts to 'in a day from now'; and any thought of Bill's using the future tense and a specified interval-length ('three years from now', etc.) would do. For (6), Bill's thought would have to employ the past tense in conjunction with any such interval-specification (e.g. 'yesterday'). For (4), it would have to employ the present tense; but the specification of an *interval*-length would be out of place – except of course that of the 'null interval', which Bill would have 'specified' if he had added the redundant 'today' to 'It is raining'.

What if we replace interval-specifications by dates? In the case of (2), Bill might have said, 'It will rain on 22 March'. Given that 22 March is the date of the report constituted by (2), this would be enough for (2)'s first clause to be true. Similar comments apply to (6). But with (4), we find that, although 'on 22 March' would add something to Bill's thought, his unqualified present-tense thought is enough for the truth of (4)'s first clause – and in that sense, once more, the added extra (the date) is just superfluous. (This was why dates weren't needed for (4a), above.)

It is, of course, the tensedness of the thoughts so far attributed to Bill which is making for some disparity between (4), on the one hand, and (2) and (6), on the other. What if untensed thoughts were involved? Might Bill's thought (in any of (2), (4), (6)) identify the present moment by its date alone, or by its temporal relation to some event, without the temporal relation between the present moment and the thought itself coming into it at all? Might Bill's thought, in Castaneda's terminology, have appealed only to 'non-perspectival properties' of the present moment?

Bill awakes from a drugged sleep, his sense of time adrift and without the means of finding out what date it is. He remembers, however, that before he had been drugged, his sister's birthday party was coming up in a week or so, being arranged for 8.00 p.m. onwards on 5 June. The time of his awakening happens to be 8.30 p.m., 5 June. His belief about the time of his sister's birthday party may perhaps be expressed tenselessly – or at any rate as disjunctively-tensed: 'My sister's birthday (tenselessly) takes place from 8.00 p.m. onwards on 5 June'. Let us imagine that all this is happening now: that it is now 8.30 on 5 June. Can we say of Bill that he thinks that his sister's birthday party is taking place *now*? (The same question can be asked if 'the tenth evening after Bill had his last haircut', or some such, is substituted above for the time and date.)

The answer, surely, is 'No'. If Bill thought that his sister's party was going on now, he would think that he was missing it, whereas he may well suspect that it is still a pleasure in store for him. In this respect, 'now' is perhaps different from 'today', or 'this evening': it seems appropriate – at least in many imaginable contexts – to say of the awakened Bill that he thinks (knows) that his sister's party is today, or that it is this evening. Does this indicate that 'now' will not take wide scope if inserted in the indirect context of a present-tense sentence like (4); that it must take narrow scope, indicating the present-tensedness of the thought reported?

No – what is shown by our example is rather that for 'Bill thinks his sister's party is going on now' to be true, Bill's thought must be (present) tensed, rather than untensed or disjunctively-tensed; it is still possible for the 'now' to be taking wide scope, for it to be relating the time of Bill's sister's party to the present moment. For consider the case where Bill's awakening was on 1 June, and his sister's party is going on now, at 8.30 on 5 June. Will we be able to say: 'On 1 June, Bill thought (knew) that his sister's party would (was going to) be taking place now'? Again, we *can* say: 'On 1 June, Bill thought (knew) that his sister's party would take place this evening'. But this is different. If on 1 June Bill had thought (known) that his sister's party would be going on *now*, he would have had to have had some future-tensed thought like: 'My sister's party will be happening in four days' or 'My sister's party will be happening at 8.30 on 5 June' – which, given his disoriented condition, he would not have had. (For all Bill knew, his sister's party was over.) If he *had* had such a thought, the 'now' in 'Bill thought that his sister's party would be going on now' would clearly relate to the present time, not to the time of Bill's thought. 'Now' does always take wide scope in English, but it is only appropriate in an indirect context where the reported thought or utterance was/is/will be itself tensed (and not just disjunctively tensed). A thought using just dates or the like will never be enough.

I think that similar remarks to the above apply to 'here' – a thought-experiment involving a spatially-disoriented Bill will test intuitions. The case of 'I' is a little different. 'Bill thinks that I killed his frog' is perhaps verified if Bill thinks, 'The man who came to read the gas meter killed my frog', and I am indeed the man who came to read the gas meter; and it is certainly verified if Bill thinks, 'Roger killed my frog', given that I am Roger, even if Bill doesn't know that the person he is looking at right now is Roger. (The analogue of a name, in the case of time, is a date; but as we have seen, a dated but untensed thought of Bill's would never be reportable as the thought that so-and-so *now*.) We might account for this difference along these lines: in the case of time and space, the paradigm way for a thinker to think about other times and places is as they are related to whenever/wherever he is, whereas the paradigm way for a thinker to think about other people is not an indexical way at all, but perhaps by the sort of 'direct reference' effected by names. There are, of course, 'metaphysical', or better, probably, 'physical' reasons for all this. We are – though it does not add much to say this – creatures that last through time and move about in space, and having our spatio-temporal bearings (relations to other objects) is essential for us.

If what I have said here is right, a modification of Castaneda's account is needed. Castaneda lumps the indicators 'I', 'here', and 'now' together when discussing their (wide-scope) occurrence in indirect contexts, and says that the original (*oratio recta*-style) form of the thought reported may have made use of (a) a single indicator, or (b) a name, or (c) an indexical description (e.g. 'my friend', or 'five years ago today'), or (d) a Leibnizian description, i.e. a description containing no indicators. It seems though that for a wide-scope occurrence of 'now' or 'here' in an indirect context to be appropriate, it is *not* enough that the form of the reported thought use just a name (date or place-name), nor that it use just a Leibnizian description of the time or place of the reporting utterance. An indicator, or indexical description, is needed. In the case of time, the original thought must be *tensed*.

Let us return to (1)–(6) above (p. 25), and to the question whether the proponent of tensed belief and knowledge can provide a proper construal of such sentences. It seems that he can. The resulting account of Bill's knowing that p is considerably more complicated than the first stab: Bill knows that p iff Bill (justifiably . . .) thinks that p, and p. But that was only to be expected. And it is clear that not only does a right construal of (1)–(6) not require tenseless sentences to enter in at any point, but, *au contraire*, tensed sentences are notably essential throughout. The original thoughts reported in (1), (3) and (5) are clearly tensed; but so must the thoughts reported in (2), (4) and (6) be.

3

Truth-Conditions

3.1 INITIAL REMARKS

We have looked at various possible ways of assessing the thesis that 'Time is tenseless'. So far, that thesis has been lent little if any support by what we have found. There remains to be considered what is arguably the most promising way of setting up a case for the 'tenseless' view: I mean, by proposing that tensed sentences are susceptible of tenseless truth-conditions.

We have already encountered the view that there are no 'tensed facts'. The notion of a 'fact' will often be in a philosopher's mind when he is talking of truth-conditions. Indeed, 'there are no tensed facts' is sometimes used as little more than a 'material mode' slogan for the thesis that tenseless truth-conditions can be given for tensed sentences, but not *vice versa*. But the conflation of facts and truth-conditions may lead to confusion; the thesis to do with truth-conditions is ill-encapsulated by 'there are no tensed facts'. For a sentence's truth-*conditions* are the conditions, actual *or possible*, under which the sentence is true, whereas 'fact' is generally used to mean a constituent of the actual world only. (A false proposition has truth-conditions, but has no fact corresponding to it.)

I have already mentioned the views of Hugh Mellor, a well-known advocate of the thesis that 'time is tenseless'. Though he thinks *time* to be tenseless, Mellor admits the indispensability of linguistic tense. That is the point of his attempt, alluded to on p. 15, to keep the questions of linguistic tense and REAL tense apart. An aspect of the indispensability of linguistic tense, for Mellor, is its untranslatablity into tenseless forms; but in arguing for this unexceptionable view, Mellor gets into a confusion about truth-conditions of just the sort I have noted above. He writes:

> Let X = Cambridge and T = 1980, and let R be any token of 'Cambridge is here' and S be any token of 'It is now 1980'. ('R' and 'S' must of course not themselves be token-reflexive names or descriptions.) Then R is true if and only if it occurs in Cambridge,

and S is true if and only if it occurs in 1980. If a sentence giving another's truth-conditions means what it does, R should mean the same as 'R occurs in Cambridge' and S should mean the same as 'S occurs in 1980'. But these sentences have different truth conditions. . . . At all other places and times those tensed sentences would have been false, whereas their alleged translations are true everywhere and always.

(*Real Time*, Cambridge University Press, 1981, p. 74)

This passage is a little confusing. Let us concentrate on the tensed example. Mellor says that S is true if and only if S occurs ('tenselessly') in 1980, and from this infers that *if* truth-conditions give meanings, then S ought to mean what 'S occurs in 1980' means; from this inference *we* can infer that Mellor took his initial statement (that S is true if and only if S occurs in 1980) to be a statement of S's truth-conditions. 'S occurs in 1980' *gives* the truth-conditions of S. But then Mellor writes that S and 'S occurs in 1980' 'have different truth conditions'. How can a sentence *giving* another sentence's truth-conditions have different truth-conditions from that sentence?

To dissolve the confusion, we should start by looking at the assertion, 'these sentences have different truth conditions', and the reasons given for that assertion. As Mellor says, the sentence 'It is now 1980' would, at all times other than 1980, have been false; which is to say, any utterances of 'It is now 1980' at times other than 1980 would have been false. This is an observation about the truth-conditions of 'It is now 1980'. But S, *ex hypothesi*, is a particular actual utterance of 'It is now 1980' – to enforce this, I stipulate that S be the first announcement of 'It is now 1980' that was (actually) made in 1980. In saying that any utterances of 'It is now 1980' at times other than 1980 would have been false, one is not saying that any utterances of S at times other than 1980 would have been false. (An utterance of 'It is now 1980' in 1975 would not have been S.)

We can of course talk about S's truth-conditions; but we must make clear which of two very different things we are doing. We may be talking about S alone, or we may be talking about the conditions under which similar utterances (i.e. utterances of 'It is now 1980') would have been true. This is why we must be careful in interpreting 'S is true if and only if S occurs in 1980', which as it stands is about S alone. If Mellor intends this as a general statement of truth-conditions, then 'is true' (and 'occurs') must either be untensed, or alternatively amount to 'was, or is, or will be true' (or 'did, or does, or will occur'). So long as we hang on to the fact that S was the first utterance of 'It is now 1980' made in 1980, we can see that the left- and right-hand sides of this biconditional must indeed share their truth-value at all times. S wasn't true in 1975 – it hadn't yet been uttered – but it was going to be true (in 1980, when it was going to be uttered); so our biconditional was as true in 1975 as in 1980. (Alternatively, if we take seriously the idea that 'S' is a *name* of an utterance, and also adhere to a causal theory of names, then we may want to deny that propositions expressible by means of 'S' existed in 1975, including the biconditional 'S is true iff S occurs in 1980'. But this will not amount to an *exception* to the truth of the biconditional – it will not be a case where the two sides of the biconditional differ in truth-value.)

It may well be thought, however, that a sentence's truth-*conditions* ought to be the conditions, actual or merely possible, under which it could be true. A question like, 'Could S itself have been true if uttered in 1975?' would have to be answered *via* the tricky question 'Could S have been uttered in 1975?'. These difficulties are surely a red herring; it would be more natural, indeed, to talk about S's truth-conditions by talking about the conditions under which similar utterances would be true. If we do this, of course, we will need a new formulation: 'Any utterance of "It is now 1980" is true iff that utterance occurs in 1980'. This is as correct as 'S is true iff S occurs in 1980' was.

What is incorrect is the hybrid, 'Any utterance of "It is now 1980" is true iff S occurs in 1980', i.e. 'For any utterance of "It is now 1980", that utterance is true iff S occurs in 1980'. When Mellor observes that S and 'S occurs in 1980' differ in their truth-conditions, he is effectively drawing our attention to the incorrectness of the hybrid statement. But the hybrid is not a statement of S's truth-conditions, on anyone's account. As I have said, the best candidate for a statement of those truth-conditions is, 'Any utterance similar to S is true iff that utterance occurs in 1980'. What is clear is the fact that 'It is now 1980' (the sentence) and 'S occurs in 1980', where 'S' picks out some utterance of 'It is now 1980', must differ in their truth-conditions.

I have dwelt on this matter because one attempt to argue for the 'tenseless view' takes the following form: 'Though tenseless truth-conditions are unavailable for tensed sentences, tenseless truth-conditions are available for all *actual tensed utterances'*. It seems probable that 'truth-conditions for actual utterances' are thought to amount to something like 'facts'.

L. Nathan Oaklander writes:

> there is no inconsistency in claiming that tensed and tenseless sentence-*types* have tokens with different truth conditions, while also claiming that tensed and tenseless sentence *tokens* themselves have the same truth conditions.
>
> ('A Defence of the New Tenseless Theory of Time', *The Philosophical Quarterly*, January 1991, p. 30)

Oaklander argues that S does indeed have the same truth-conditions as 'S occurs in 1980', because S is a *token* sentence (an utterance by my present stipulation). As I have allowed, 'S is true iff S occurs in 1980' is perfectly correct – leaving aside the question as to how we are to understand 'is true' and 'occurs' (since either a tenseless or disjunctive-tensed interpretation is possible). But it cannot be taken as a statement of S's truth-conditions. An utterance can only have truth-conditions *qua* utterance of a certain type. And the type of sentence to which S belongs – namely, the sentence(-type) 'It is now 1980' – has truth-conditions different from those of the sentence (-type) 'S occurs in 1980'.

We have already encountered (p. 4) schemata which give (the forms of) truth-conditions for statements in the past, present, or future tense. A naive view of such truth-conditions would be that they effectively gave the *meaning* of the tensed sentences – for example, so that a sentence like 'It is raining now' just *means* 'It is raining simultaneously with this utterance/thought'.[1] And it might further be supposed that the latter sort of paraphrase was tenseless. This would amount to the thesis numbered (7) in the Preamble (p. 6).

There are various things wrong with such a view, I think, but it will be instructive to look at just one. In the above-proposed paraphrase of 'It is raining now', we have the demonstrative phrase 'this utterance/thought'. Now either we are to rest content with such a demonstrative, exempting it from further (meaning-) analysis, or we are to attempt to give its meaning by means of some such analysis. Let us consider the second option first. What sort of analysis of statements containing 'this utterance' is available to us? A definite description seems to be needed to replace 'this utterance': something starting, 'the utterance which . . .'. And the definite description we seem to be driven to is 'the utterance which I am now producing'. (Other features of one's utterances, such as what room they are uttered in, are features that will vary from occasion to occasion, as well as being features of which one may be ignorant, without however being ignorant, of any utterance, that it is 'this utterance'.)

The definite description, 'the utterance which I am now producing', contains two indexical elements, 'I' and 'now'; but we can forget 'I' for the moment, since the reappearance of 'now' is enough to scupper our enterprise. Our final analysis of 'It is now raining' is just a longer statement also containing 'now'; and the same is going to go for statements like 'It was raining' and 'It will be raining': their 'analyses' ('It is raining earlier/later than this utterance') will also be longer statements containing 'now'. Hence we will not have shown that tensed statements are susceptible of tenseless paraphrases.

What if we were to stop our analysis at 'this utterance'? We could allow that truth-conditional accounts of statements containing such demonstratives, though they might be the only way of 'giving the semantics' of such expressions, nevertheless did not capture the *meaning* of those expressions. But why should we not say all this of indexicals like 'now' and 'hitherto'? If indexical demonstratives are unanalysable, why shouldn't indexical tenses-operators be?

Let us then turn to the thesis that tenseless truth-conditions are available for tensed sentences, where such truth-conditions fall short of providing *definitions*. In fact, there are really two theses to consider here, not one. One is the thesis that tenseless truth-conditions *must* be given for tensed sentences – so that attempts to give tensed truth-conditions for such sentences must, for some reason, fail. The other is the modest thesis that tenseless truth-conditions *can* be given for tensed sentences – whether or not tensed such truth-conditions are also possible. I shall consider each of these theses in turn.

Consider again the truth-conditions given on p. 4 for the past-tense form 'It was the case that p':

(2)   An utterance of 'It was the case that p' is true iff 'p' is true before the time of utterance.

What is necessary for us to be able to say that (2) gives *tenseless* truth-conditions for 'It was the case that p', and cannot be properly interpreted as giving tensed truth-conditions? One thing that seems to be necessary is that we should be able to say that 'is true', as it occurs (twice) in (2), must itself be a tenseless verb, not a tensed one.

Before proceeding further, we need to note that since (2) applies to possible as well as merely actual utterances, it looks as if it amounts in fact to a subjunctive conditional – roughly:

(2′)   Were anyone to utter 'It was the case that p', he would speak truly if and only if 'p' were true before the time of utterance.

The 'were' on the right-hand side of this biconditional cannot be replaced by 'was'. If it were so replaced, the subjunctive conditional on the left-hand side would be a self-contained sentence; and this is not possible, given the anaphoric status of 'the time of utterance', a phrase falling within the scope of 'anyone'. ('The time of utterance' means 'the time of his utterance'.) Since, in effect, the subjunctive mood has wider scope than 'anyone', the mood of the biconditional's left-hand side must be shared by its right-hand side. (2′) is a subjunctive biconditional.

It seems impossible to classify either 'would speak truly' or 'were true' as of any *tense* at all. Does this immediately establish the 'tenseless' view?

Obviously not. The semantics of subjunctive conditionals is a very thorny topic, but it is relatively clear that (2′) is *prima facie* construable in a 'tensed' fashion. (2′) might amount to: 'Were anyone now to utter . . .'; or it might amount to: 'Were anyone in the past to have uttered . . . he would have . . . AND were anyone now to utter . . . he would . . . AND were anyone in the future to utter . . . he would . . .'. In short, (2) may be taken as straightforwardly present-tensed (with a qualification we shall come to in a moment), or as a conjunction of tensed sentences. The question is thus better put as one about the tensedness, or otherwise, of (2′) than as one about the tensedness, or otherwise, of 'is true', as it occurs in the slightly misleading (2).

Consider first the possibility that (2′) – or (2), construed as its equivalent – is present-tensed; that it amounts to, 'Were anyone now to utter . . .'. In this case, admittedly, it is somewhat unclear what we are talking about in talking about (2′). We might either be talking about a particular present-tensed utterance (inscription), or about a schema for present-tense utterances of a certain form. (2′) is already schematic, of course, in that it includes the free variable 'p' – but we could eliminate this schematicity by binding 'p' with a quantifier. (Since 'p' is mentioned, not used, in (2′), our quantifier would seem to have to bind variables for names of indicative sentences: 'For any "p", were someone to utter . . .'.)

What, then, of taking (2') as a schema for present-tensed sentences of a given form? This course might seem unsatisfactory, insofar as a mere schema *says* nothing; so that one might wonder how (2') could 'give the truth-conditions' of past-tensed sentences. But such an objection is rather feeble as it stands. To the question, '*How* could (2') give the truth-conditions for past-tensed sentences?', it seems adequate to reply, 'By providing a schema for present-tensed statements which, whenever uttered, would give the then truth-conditions for past-tensed sentences'. Note that this answer appears to distinguish what a present-tensed utterance of the form of (2') would give ('the then truth-conditions') from what (2') itself gives ('the truth-conditions'). It would be naive to infer from this that we are committed to a past-tensed sentence's having two 'kinds of' truth-conditions: truth-conditions at a time, and timeless truth-conditions. The sentence, '(2') gives the truth-conditions . . .' should be construed as being about the truth-conditions that any or all present-tensed utterances of the form of (2') give, or would give. We could, indeed, construe '(2') gives the truth-conditions . . .' as meaning roughly: 'One can learn from (2') what (present-tensed) utterances count as giving the truth-conditions for past-tensed sentences'.

Whether utterances of the form of (2'), with determinate 'p', made at different times, give '*different* truth-conditions' for 'It was the case that p', is a further question; but since it is characteristic of the 'tensed' view to regard a given tensed sentence as expressing the *same* proposition whenever uttered, this question would probably get a negative answer from one interpreting (2') as present-tensed.

Taking (2') as schematic in the way adumbrated above relies on being able to count present-tensed utterances of the form of (2') as themselves 'giving truth-conditions', whenever uttered. So we might think it simpler just to take (2') itself as a present-tensed utterance. But what is '(2') itself'? The inscription occurring a few paragraphs back in this book? But which book is 'this book'? – If we are looking for a 'token utterance', we will also be looking (vainly, it would seem) for a 'token book'. And if the original (2) were at issue, we should have the undecidable choice between the inscription on p. 4 and that on p. 38. All in all, if (2') is to be regarded as present-tensed in form, then what I have here done ('in this book-type' . . .) does perforce seem to have been to give a schema, rather than a single salient instance, of a sentence. It is rather as with Descartes's *cogito*: Descartes has seemingly to be taken as providing for his readers the schema for certain first-personal thoughts – his own first-personal thoughts being of no use to them.

Of course, a philosopher *could* content herself, in the context of the present debate, with giving voice or pen to particular, distinguishable, present-tensed utterances of the form of (2′), aspiring to no 'generality' beyond this. But I think this would show an overfastidious attitude to schematic forms.

Some readers will have been wondering what to make of 'the time of utterance' in formulae such as (2) and (2′). This is a topic to which we shall return later, so I will not here pursue it. Suffice it to say that, so flexible a notion will 'the time of utterance' turn out to be, it would appear to make no trouble at all for the construal of (2′) as schematising certain present-tensed utterances.

We have not exhausted the possibilities open to one who would interpret (2′) as a tensed, rather than a tenseless, formula. For where a proponent of the 'tenseless' view sees atemporal truth, his opponent can always discern omnitemporal truth instead. For simplicity, I will revert to (2), and will take the question to be whether, in (2), 'is true' could be said to amount to, 'was, or is, or will be true'. This is not quite right; to be perfectly precise, the formula we are interested in is itself a tripartite *conjunction* of biconditionals. Using subjunctive conditionals, the conjuncts would be: (a) 'If anyone were to have uttered . . . then he would have spoken truly iff . . .'; (b) 'If anyone were now to utter . . . then he would speak truly iff . . .'; and (c) 'If anyone were in the future to utter . . . then he would speak truly iff . . .'. But no confusion should follow from framing the question as one about 'was, or is or will be true'.

A concomitant of such an approach would appear to be that tensed truth-conditions may be given for tenseless sentences – assuming the existence of such sentences. Thus, truth-conditions could be framed for a putatively tenseless 'It rains':

'It rains' was true iff it rained, is raining or will rain
AND
'It rains' is true iff it rained, is raining or will rain
AND
'It rains' will be true iff it rained, is raining or will rain.

Graham Priest has made much the same point,[2] and correctly drew the lesson that at this more or less formal level there is going to be a straight symmetry between the 'tensed' and 'tenseless' positions; and that it would take more philosophical considerations to show that the truth-predicate must, can, or cannot be tenseless.

These remarks are relevant to an objection which it is tempting to raise in connection with the approach just outlined: namely, that 'was, is or will be true' is not *genuinely* tensed: that *really* it is tenseless. But what on earth could be meant by 'not genuinely tensed'? It can't be that we are *forbidden* from constructing such complex tenses; it is a condition of adequacy on any theory of tensed language that it can give an account of just such complex tenses. A tense is expressed in tense logic by a one-place tense operator, such as 'PFp' ('It was the case that it will be the case that p'); the complex tense we are here considering would be expressed in tense logic as the one-place operator 'Pp or Np or Fp', or in Polish spirit, 'P-or-N-or-F(p)'.

It might be said that certain operations with tenses bring us to untensed results. But what could support such a claim? That tenseless verbs (if such there be) can be systematically substituted for disjunctively-tensed ones is in the present context beside the point: such a possibility would only show that a tenseless interpretation of the likes of (2) is, for all that has been said, possible, not that it is mandatory. And so far we have been only considering the view that a tenseless interpretation of the likes of (2) is thus mandatory.

It is somewhat hard to assess the claim that disjunctively-tensed verbs are 'really' tenseless until we have a better idea of what tenseless verbs are, or might be. It is time to examine this question, and with it the question whether genuinely tenseless language is possible at all. Is a tenseless construal of (2) and of formulae like it even possible? The 'philosophical considerations' to which Priest alludes will soon have to be brought to bear.

3.2   THE ETERNAL VERITIES

Not only are tenseless propositions *possible*, it might be said; they are *actual*. To know what tenseless propositions are like, it is only necessary to consider the eternal truths (and the eternal falsehoods) of logic and mathematics. If we can abstract, from logic and mathematics, a notion of tenselessness applicable to propositions in general, then we can intelligibly posit a tenseless interpretation of sentences like (2). From which it would follow that tenseless truth-conditions can be given for tensed sentences. If logical and mathematical propositions turn out not to be genuinely tenseless, on the other hand, this will have been a blind alley; while if such propositions cannot be taken as models for putatively tenseless propositions of other kinds (e.g. contingent ones), then the provision of tenseless truth-conditions for tensed sentences generally will not have been made intelligible.

The thesis that necessary truths, such as those of logic or mathematics, are 'timelessly true' can be interpreted in one of (at least) two ways:

(a) Necessary truths are true for all time, throughout all time;
(b) Necessary truths are really 'timeless': they are, so to speak, 'outside time'.

(a) and (b) differ in various respects. It would seem that a proponent of (b) must deny that it *makes sense* to prefix tense operators or other temporal adverbs to such sentences as '2 + 2 = 4'. 'Yesterday two plus two made four' will amount to nonsense if (b) is correct. A proponent of (a), on the other hand, seems to be saying that '2 + 2 = 4' (for instance) is true at every time, past, present or future; which seems to mean that attaching a temporal adverb to '2 + 2 = 4' always yields a true – and hence meaningful – sentence (except for adverbs like 'At no time', of course!).

The position I have labelled (b) was discussed by Prior, in the following passage:

If . . . it is maintained that either dated propositions or any other propositions (e.g. Moore's example of '2 + 2 = 4') are non-temporal in the sense that it 'makes no sense' to prefix tense-operators to them, we do encounter one serious problem, namely, does it make sense to prefix such operators to compounds, e.g. conjunctions and disjunctions, of which one part is temporal and the other not? Wittgenstein says that 'the logical product', i.e. conjunction, 'of a tautology and a proposition says the same as the proposition. Therefore that product is the same as the proposition.'[3] Equating non-temporal propositions with Wittgenstein's 'tautologies', if they are true, and with his 'contradictions', if they are false, this would suggest that if we use a, b, etc., for non-temporal propositions and p, q, etc., for temporals, Kap [i.e., a & p] is the same proposition as p when a is true, and the same as a when it is false; and Aap [i.e., a ∨ p] is the same as p when a is false, and as a when that is true. . . . But if this means that it makes sense to prefix, say, 'It will be the case that' to Kap if a is true and does not if it is false, and that the converse holds with Aap, this is a very awkward formation-rule indeed.

(*Past, Present, and Future*, Oxford University Press, 1967, pp. 102–3)

Of course, it is arguable whether a conjunction of a necessary and a contingent proposition can be called 'the same proposition' as one of the two conjuncts, in the sense required to wreak havoc with (b). The Wittgensteinian principle seems to have to do with strict logical equivalence, and there may be a finer-grained notion of 'propositional identity' where (b) is at issue. A proponent of (b) may deny that prefixing tense operators to any conjunctions involving necessary propositions makes sense, regardless of the fact that some such conjunctions are logically equivalent to propositions to which it does make sense to prefix tense operators: to replace a conjunctive sentence by a non-conjunctive but equivalent sentence is not here to put 'the same for the same'.

But there is a problem with (b), and one which is more pertinent to our present theme. It is this: given that our hope is eventually to give tenseless truth-conditions for tensed sentences, it will hardly be possible to use sentences that report facts 'outside time' as models for sentences which report facts 'within time'. For not only will the modification of the former kind of sentence by tense operators make no sense; as has been noted, the modification of those sentences by any temporal adverbs at all will have this result. But when it comes to giving truth-conditions for sentences like 'It was raining', we must be able to qualify the tenseless sentence corresponding to the tensed one with a temporal adverb. Take the tenseless truth-conditions for 'It was raining':

Any utterance, U, of 'It was raining' is true iff it is raining at some time prior to the occurrence of U.

The tenseless 'It is raining' which appears on the right-hand side of the biconditional has to be qualified by 'at some time, etc . . .'. Sentences of the form 'It is raining at time t' must thus be available to us. But, according to (b), '2 + 2 = 4 at time t' can make no sense. Rainings, even if tenseless, must nevertheless be in time; mathematical truths, according to (b), are outside time.

I shall take it, then, that it is to (a) that we are to look for an account of necessary truths that we might use as a model for tenseless truths generally. From now on, I shall use 'Albert' as a dummy name for the proponent of the view that necessary truths are tenseless, that (a) is correct, that tenseless discourse in general can be understood by reference to the case of necessary truths, and that tenseless truth-conditions can be given for tensed sentences.

Albert has two distinct options with regard to '2 + 2 = 4':

(i) '2 + 2 = 4' is, in some sense, equivalent to a sentence of the form, 'It always was, is, and will be the case that p'; or

(ii) there is no such equivalence, but prefixing any tense operator (including, of course, 'It always was, is, and will be the case that') to '2 + 2 = 4' yields a true sentence.

It may be objected here that it has not been shown that Albert need allow that it makes any sense at all to prefix tense operators to '2 + 2 = 4', despite what I have just said. (Both of the options just outlined for Albert would seem to commit him to allowing that '2 + 2 = 4' be prefixable by tense operators: the second option does so explicitly, the first implicitly, at any rate if sentences of the form 'It was, is, and will be the case that p' – and sentences equivalent to these – are themselves prefixable by tense operators.) What *has* been shown (three paragraphs back) is this: Albert, along with anyone else who thinks tenseless truth-conditions can be given for tensed sentences, must allow that tenseless sentences are qualifiable by certain temporal adverbs, such as 'at time t'. For Albert, the same will hold of '2 + 2 = 4', since he thinks that tenseless sentences generally are to be understood by appeal to the likes of '2 + 2 = 4'. But it does not follow from this Albert need accept that '2 + 2 = 4' is qualifiable by *tense operators*.

However, we must ask why 'It was the case on 1 January that two plus two made four' should lack a sense when 'On 1 January, two plus two is four' does not. If 1 January is in the past, and a true sentence has been truly qualified by 'on 1 January', shouldn't we then say that the truth in question *did* hold on 1 January? And isn't this to say that the sentence reporting the truth ('2 + 2 = 4') can – and indeed must, if we are also to use 'on 1 January' – be qualifiable by the past tense operator, 'It was the case that'?

This is not to say that '2 + 2 = 4' must itself be a tensed sentence, or equivalent to one; Albert's *second* option, option (ii), is a live one, for all that's been said. In section 3.5 (p. 61 ff.), we shall see that the thesis that the 'simple' sentences in front of which we put tense operators are tenseless sentences is a problematic one; but I will not pre-empt that discussion here.

If Albert chooses option (i), and allows that '2 + 2 = 4' is in some sense equivalent to a conjunctively-tensed proposition, nevertheless he need not say that it is to be understood simply in terms of the latter. Albert may claim that '2 + 2 = 4' is not parasitic on the conjunctively-tensed proposition, or on any other tensed proposition (e.g. in any of the senses of 'parasitic' to be given in section 3.6, pp. 73–4). One thing that Albert cannot very easily say is that '2 + 2 = 4' is *itself* the value of 'p' in 'It always was, is and will be the case that p'. For if '2 + 2 = 4' is equivalent to a conjunctively-tensed proposition, then prefixing the conjunctive tense operator to '2 + 2 = 4' will yield something equivalent to: 'It always was, is and will be that: (it always was, is and will be that: p)'. For fear of an infinite and vicious regress, we must take the embedded 'p' to be something distinct from '2 + 2 = 4'. It is rather awkward that there seems to be no sentence which will do duty here: we have postulated an expression of a similar species of elusiveness to that which in the *Tractatus* attends Wittgenstein's 'names of simples'.

'It always was, is and will be the case that 2 + 2 = 4' will not itself be equivalent to '2 + 2 = 4'; it will rather be a translation of the 'higher-order' sentence, 'It is timelessly true that 2 + 2 = 4'. This point applies also to opponents of the view that '2 + 2 = 4' is tenseless. It follows that Albert cannot claim, in support of his view, that his opponents are committed to an implausible construal of the apparently simple '2 + 2 = 4' as a tripartite conjunction ('It always was, is, and will be the case that 2 + 2 = 4'). They are not so committed; for they may say that the tripartite conjunction is a translation of 'It is timelessly true that 2 + 2 = 4', insisting that '2 + 2 = 4' is present-tensed.

But, Albert will object, isn't it also unbelievable that '2 + 2 = 4' should be *present-tensed*? If someone says 'It is raining', then though it may be superfluous, it surely nevertheless makes *sense* to ask: 'When is it raining?' – to which the answer will of course be, 'Now'. But if someone says '2 + 2 = 4', and another asks: 'When does two and two make four?', the correct answer will not be 'Now', but rather will be 'Always' (or perhaps, 'Now and always').

This is not, however, a very compelling argument. A tourist who remarks, on seeing King's College Chapel for the first time, 'That chapel is enormous', will not answer 'Now' if asked the question: 'When is that chapel enormous?'. If he feels any answer to be appropriate, he will probably feel 'Always', or 'Now and always', to be the appropriate answer. But it doesn't follow from this that his remark was not present-tensed. A present-tensed report of a changeless state, or of a general fact, as opposed to a report of an event or process, is very often inappropriately qualified by the adverb 'now'. And this connects with something important about the notion of 'the present'. It might be thought that the truth-conditions for present-tensed utterances made reference to momentary instants: that 'the time of utterance' meant some durationless point in time. In fact, a moment's reflection will convince one that this can hardly be so, without a good dose of adhoccery; utterances take time. But neither does 'the time of utterance' mean just the time taken to make the utterance in question. An utterance of 'That chapel is enormous' is true iff the chapel pointed to is (was, will be) enormous at the time of utterance. What is the time of utterance here? Not just the time taken to say 'That chapel is enormous'. Imagine that King's College Chapel underwent huge contractions – to the size of a matchbox – and resumptions of its actual size, every eight seconds; someone who said 'That chapel is enormous' while the chapel was in its 'big' phase would at least be misleading, given what generally counts as 'the present time' for buildings.

The fact is that 'the time of utterance' is a context-dependent matter, and a vague matter to boot; and this is an important point to recognise when discussing the truth-conditions of tensed sentences, as represented by (1)–(3) at p. 4. Could we say, in the case of 'That chapel is enormous', that the time of utterance is the actual lifetime of King's College Chapel? No; for the chapel may have been added to extensively in the last century, rendering it enormous, so that for most of its lifetime it would have been false to say that it was enormous. 'That chapel is enormous' seems to amount to *something* like, 'That chapel is enormous these days' – so long as we ignore the conversational implicature in this last version. ('That chapel is enormous' doesn't conversationally imply that the chapel hasn't always been enormous.) And the sense of an adverb like 'these days' is obviously vague. It is worth considering another type of example: 'People leave home earlier than in previous centuries'. In this case, the time spoken of ('the time of utterance') seems to be an entire century: the salient century is probably AD

1900–2000. Nevertheless, the tense is surely present; for a contrast is being implicitly made between 'People leave home by such-and-such an age (this century)' and 'People used not to leave home by such-and-such an age (in past centuries)', which latter is clearly past-tensed.

Thus the view that '2 + 2 = 4' is present-tensed cannot be dismissed on the grounds that one would not answer 'Now' to the question, 'When does two and two make four?'. One would not answer 'now' to the question 'When is King's College Chapel enormous?', but 'King's College Chapel is enormous' is clearly not tenseless (if only because it wasn't always a true proposition; perhaps it wasn't always a proposition at all). It is not a reliable test of whether a proposition is present-tensed to ask, 'Can it appropriately be qualified by "now"?'. But nor will we be able to determine whether any sentence is present-tensed by sticking to a single interpretation of 'time of utterance' (e.g. 'time taken to utter the sentence'). A surer general indication of present-tensedness is the possibility of a contrasting past- or future-tensed proposition. 'People leave home by the age of eighteen – *but they didn't used to*'; 'Pigs can't fly – *but in fifty years they'll be able to*'; 'two plus two makes four – *but that wasn't always the case*'. To be sure, the last proposition is necessarily false. But it makes sense. The second conjunct does not *contradict* the first, except in the sense in which 'p & ¬p' contradicts 'q'.

Returning to Albert's position, there remains the general worry that if '2 + 2 = 4' is to be our model for the possible tenseless sentence, 'It is raining', we will have somehow to deal with the fact that the mathematical truth, and not the contingent one, is eternally true. (There are times when it isn't raining.) It seems hard to conceive of how the 'eternal' proposition '2 + 2 = 4' could serve as a model for a putatively tenseless, but hardly 'eternal', 'It is raining'. If '2 + 2 = 4' is somehow equivalent to a conjunctively-tensed proposition, it will differ markedly from 'It is raining', which corresponds more to a disjunctively-tensed one. Two further possibilities remain: that '2 + 2 = 4' be taken as equivalent to no such proposition, but merely as truly qualifiable by any tense operators, and that it be (like 'It is raining') equivalent to a disjunctively-tensed proposition.

But now what is there to choose between Albert's position and his opponents'? Albert wants to say that timeless propositions such as '2 + 2 = 4' may make clear to us how there can, indeed, be such untensed propositions as 'It is raining', in order (eventually) that he might make appeal to the existence of these latter when arguing for the framing of tenseless truth-conditions for tensed sentences generally. But if '2 + 2 = 4' is taken, either as equivalent to no tensed proposition, or as more akin to a disjunctive than to a conjunctive tensed proposition, then its timelessness boils down to nothing more than the truth of 'For all t, 2 + 2 = 4 at t'. Albert's opponent expresses the timelessness of '2 + 2 = 4' in his own way: 'It always was, is, and will be the case that 2 + 2 = 4'. Why would the tenseless formulation be considered more natural, more 'intuitive', or in general more appropriate, than the tensed formulation? As was said above (p. 45), it is hard to see why 'It was the case that 2 + 2 = 4' should not follow from '2 + 2 = 4 at t', whenever 't' means a past time; and the connection between 'It always was, is and will be that 2 + 2 = 4' and 'For all t, 2 + 2 = 4 at t' is just as intimate.

All in all, it looks as if the 'timelessness' of necessary truths such as '2 + 2 = 4' will not provide us with a conception of tenselessness which we might apply to contingent sentences, in the hope of constructing tenseless truth-conditions for tensed sentences generally. In reaching this conclusion, I have tried not to rely on a particular answer to the question whether necessary truths are themselves properly spoken of as 'tenseless'; though the view of such truths as present-tensed seems to me to be preferable. In the next section, I want to make a slight detour from our main concerns, by outlining a certain position on the 'timelessness' of necessary truths, whose effect should be to steal at least some of the thunder from those who too closely connect that timelessness with tenselessness.

3.3 'TRUE AT ALL TIMES' AND 'TRUE OF ALL TIMES'

In what follows, I will have in mind especially the truths of logic and of mathematics when I write of 'necessary truths'. Such putative 'metaphysical' necessities as that every event has a cause I won't deal with. Statements of identity, on the other hand, or at any rate some species of these, will get a mention.

A characteristic and well-known feature of many logical and mathematical truths is their *generality*. Now, it may be that this generality is, in many cases, best expressed in the formulation of these truths themselves. (Thus it has been argued that we ought to view a form like 'p → p' as short for '(∀p) (p → p)', eschewing

schematic letters in favour of bound variables.) Generality typically gets expressed by means of universal quantification. This
means that if the generality which we are trying to express is to
be expressed by means of higher-order universal quantification –
quantification employing variables for expressions other than names
– then our resulting formulations will enjoy the following sort of
*omni*temporality: the possible substituends for our bound variables
must include expressions of any tense, in a language which involves tense at all. (In a tense logic with tense operators like 'It was
the case that', these operators will yield (tensed) sentences from
sentences, (tensed) predicables from predicables, (tensed) adverbs
from adverbs. . . .)

For example, the truth of '($\forall$p) (p $\rightarrow$ p)' will clearly rest as much
on the truth of instances like 'If it was raining, then it was raining'
as on that of ones like 'If it is raining, it is raining'. And we may
look upon '($\forall$p) (p $\rightarrow$ p)' as itself present-tense, without forgoing
the right to say that it is true of all times, i.e. true irrespective of the
tenses of any of its possible substituends.

In the previous section, our concern was with sentences' 'being
true at all times'. The notion we now have under discussion is that
of sentences' 'being true *of* all times'. The proponent of a 'tenseless'
view of time will naturally want to stress the possibility of sentences that are true at all times, and will cite necessary truths for
this purpose. But might not a good part of the celebrated timelessness of necessary truths reside in their being true *of* all times? There
is an analogy here with the celebrated necessity of necessary truths:
the necessity of those truths is not just a matter of their being true
in all possible worlds, but of their being true *of* all possible worlds.

There are, though, truths of logic and maths that seem to be both
'timeless' and perfectly general, while not being of the kind of generality that is capturable by higher-order quantification. 'If it's raining, then it's raining' and 'If there are two cows, and there are two
further cows, then there are at least four cows', are examples of the
sorts of truths I mean. These might be said to be true at all times
– but it makes little sense to say they are true *of* all times.

Let me now make good my claim that at least many logical and
mathematical truths are true of all times in the sense above adumbrated, being expressible by means of higher-order universal quantification. I have already mentioned one important type of logical
truth: the type which encapsulates the forms of truth-functional
tautologies. As I said, there is reason to think these truths tantamount

to ones of the forms, '(∀p) (. . . p . . .)', '(∀p) (∀q) (. . . p . . . q . . .)', and so on. I will not go into the arguments for regarding forms like 'p → p' as short for universal generalisations, except to say that if the alternative is to regard such forms as schematic sentences, then it would seem hardly possible to call them 'timeless truths': a schematic sentence is not a sentence, after all, and so cannot express a truth, let alone a timeless truth.

What about statements of first-order identity, such as 'Cicero is Cicero', and 'Cicero is Tully'? One might well suppose that these statements, however necessary, cannot express timeless truths. For the proposition that Cicero is Cicero, whether tensed or untensed, itself only came into existence with Cicero. This is a consequence, at any rate, of one theory of names, the causal theory. But consider such propositions as that there was a time when Cicero hadn't yet been born – the latter expressible as: 'It was the case that: it is not the case that: Cicero is born' (or 'P¬(Cicero is born)', for short). This proposition exists *now* – indeed, it is true. And its truth doesn't depend on there having ever been a proposition expressible as 'Cicero hasn't yet been born'. 'Cicero *always was* Cicero' might therefore also be (now) true. The predicable '__ was always Cicero' (or: 'It always was the case that: __ = Cicero'), it could be argued, is now (necessarily) true of Cicero. To settle this, however, something needs to be said about what 'Cicero is Cicero' means.

Invoking Leibniz's Law, we can perhaps equate or at least associate 'Cicero = Cicero' with: '(∀F) (Fc iff Fc)', with 'c' for 'Cicero'. This piece of higher-order quantification is verifiable by sentences of any tense; a possible substituend for 'F__' will be 'It was the case that: it is not the case that: __ is born'. The present-tense '(∀F) (Fc iff Fc)' is true, and more over, 'true of all times'. What about 'It was (always) the case that: (∀F) (Fc iff Fc)'? Is this true? To put it another way, is '(∀F) (Fc iff Fc)' true *at* all times?

The answer, I think, is 'No'. In a nutshell, this is because, as we have noted, there wasn't always such a proposition as 'Cicero = Cicero'. Before Cicero existed, there were no propositions of the form 'F(Cicero)'. And *a fortiori* no proposition, '(∀F) (Fc iff Fc)' (still with 'c' for 'Cicero'). The past-tensed quantified sentence, 'It always was the case that: (∀F) (Fc iff Fc)', must consequently be false.

'Cicero is Cicero', then, would appear to be a necessary truth that is true of all times, though not true at all times – at any rate, if we can equate if with the quantified '(∀F) (Fc iff Fc)'. The same goes for 'Cicero = Tully', of course, if the latter is a necessary truth. The timelessness of first-order identity-statements thus *has to* be distinguished from tenselessness.

What about statements like 'Water is water', or indeed 'Water is H_2O'? These kinds of sentence are not first-order statements at all, I think; even if we decide that 'water' ('tiger', etc.), being natural kind terms, are 'rigid', we do not need to conclude that they are *designators*. (This is a topic to which we shall return – see section 4.2.) The logical categories of expression with which we have to deal in such cases are such categories as those of the predicable and sentence. Sentences containing 'tiger' are perspicuously paraphrasable as ones containing the predicable '__ is a tiger'; ones containing 'water' are perspicuously paraphrasable as ones containing the predicable '__ is a body of water' – or perhaps as ones containing the feature-placing sentence 'There's water'.

Statements like 'Water is water' and 'Water is H_2O', therefore, amount to statements of 'higher-order identity', and so can be grouped along with such statements as: 'To be a vixen is to be a female fox', and 'The proposition that Hilda is a vixen is the same as the proposition that Hilda is a female fox'. How could higher-order quantification come in here?

Prior[4] gives the following account of 'propositional identity', an account which essentially invokes a higher-order version of Leibniz's Law:

The proposition that p is the same as the proposition that q iff for all δ, δp iff δq.

The quantifier 'For all δ' binds variables for expressions that yield sentences from sentences. And such expressions will clearly have to include tense operators, if there are such.

The Prioresque account of what may be called 'property-identity' would be roughly this:

The property of being F is the same as the property of being G iff for all α, αF iff αG

where the quantifier 'For all α' binds variables for expressions that yield predicables from predicables (i.e. variables for what have been called second-level predicables). Again, such expressions will have to include tensed ones, since tense operators yield second-level predicables from second-level predicables: an example might be 'It will be the case that nothing . . .'.

If we take the right-hand sides of our two biconditionals as giving the forms of the perspicuous expressions of statements of higher-order identity, then we may say that a timeless truth like 'To be a bachelor is to be an unmarried man' is true of all times. It is also true at all times. However, with 'Water is water/H_2O' (or: 'To be of water is to be of water/H_2O'), the matter is different, if a causal theory of natural kind terms *à la* Kripke is correct; for in that case, if only because there wasn't always water around, there wasn't always such a proposition as 'Water is water/H_2O'. 'Water is water' and 'Water is H_2O', though they may be true of all times, won't be true at all times.

Let us turn now to mathematical truths. The idea that mathematical truths are 'timeless' has tended, with the more Platonistically minded, to go with the idea of numbers' inhabiting a 'timeless realm', a 'realm outside time' (as also outside space, of course). There are plenty of arguments, which need no rehearsing here, against mathematical Platonism of this sort; but since mathematical examples still tend to take centre-stage in discussions of 'timeless truths', it will be useful to see whether, and how, the attribution of 'truth of all times' can be made in their case.

In a logicist programme, the sentence 'There are exactly two cows' gets rendered in the following sort of way:

$$(\exists x)\ (\exists y)\ (Cx\ \&\ Cy,\ \&\ x \neq y,\ \&\ (\forall z)\ (Cz \rightarrow z = x \lor z = y))$$

(where 'C' means 'is a cow'). Such 'concrete' number-statements are the statements from which are derived the more abstract and general statements of mathematics.

How are mathematical statements 'derived' from 'concrete' number-statements? In various ways. But, at least according to one kind of logicist approach, these various ways will have in common that we ascend from the first-order quantification of number-statements to higher-order quantification. (The ascension is not surprising: one would expect the truths of mathematics not to involve the 'ontological commitment' that comes with first-order quantification.)

The first step up from 'concrete' number statements is to statements like 'Two plus two is four'. We cease to restrict ourselves to cows, or whatever, and generalise: what we do can be likened to introducing universal quantification with predicable-variables. 'Two plus two is four' will amount to something like 'For all F, for all G, if there are two Fs and two Gs, then there are at least four things that are F or G'. Let us abbreviate the sentence above which translates 'There are two cows' as '$(\exists 2x)(Cx)$', and abbreviate sentences of the same form similarly, and sentences of analogous forms analogously (i.e. for numbers other than 2). Let us also abbreviate

$$(\exists x) \, (\exists y) \, (Cx \, \& \, Cy, \, \& \, x \neq y)$$

(which will mean 'There are at least two cows') as '$(\exists*2x)(Cx)$', abbreviate sentences of the same form similarly, and abbreviate sentences of analogous forms analogously. Then we can render 'Two plus two is four' as:

$$(\forall F) \, (\forall G) \, (\text{If } (\exists 2x) \, (Fx) \, \& \, (\exists 2y) \, (Gy), \text{ then } (\exists*4z) \, (Fz \vee Gz)).$$

Once more the argument goes: since we are dealing with universal quantification, the possible substituends for 'F' and 'G' will have to include predicables of all tenses – 'is a cow', 'will moo', 'has eaten some grass', and so on.

From simple arithmetic the rest of mathematics follows. Thus statements of the form 'For some number n . . .' involve us with quantifiers the substituends for whose variables are themselves quantifiers (for 'There are two __s', etc., are quantifiers). The details of this derivation of maths from arithmetic have been worked out elsewhere.[5] But omnitemporality was introduced with the first step of generalisation, when we abstracted from the case of cows.

I do not want to suggest that the logicist approach to mathematics is entirely uncontroversial. And one could, I think, endorse a form of the argument presented here without espousing logicism as a programme for *deriving* mathematics from logic, or for *justifying* mathematics by reference to logic. The logicist way of looking at things merely highlights what is in any case a plausible thesis: that at least part of the timelessness of mathematical truths is a matter of their being true of all times, just as they are true of all things (cows, solar systems, or what have you).

3.4   ROOT SENTENCES IN A TENSELESS LANGUAGE

I have suggested that we do not get, from reflection on the propositions of logic and maths, a notion of tenselessness which we can use in framing tenseless truth-conditions for tensed sentences generally. In this section, I want to consider certain problems connected with the idea of tenseless propositions, having to do with 'root' sentences; and I will go on afterwards to discuss, by contrast, the status of 'root' sentences in tensed languages.

Consider the following remarks by Hugh Mellor:

> The dates of events do not change with time, so adding another date to a 'dated' statement never makes a false statement true or a true one false. Indeed, the pointlessness of adding dates is so obvious that it sounds very odd to do it at all: to say, for example, 'On February 2, Jane arrives (tenselessly) on February 1'. If this says anything, it says the same as 'Jane arrives (tenselessly) on February 1'. Either both statements are true or both are false.
> (*Real Time*, Cambridge University Press, 1981, p. 23)

A certain sort of tenseless language is presumed in this passage, and if we suppose a tenseless language to be possible, it is natural to think that it would be of the sort Mellor has in mind – at any rate, if we are considering a tenseless language capable of making temporal statements, statements about time. The basic structure of the language would be this: tenseless 'root' sentences, for example 'Jane arrives', would be modifiable by dates, for example 'on 2 February', to produce sentences whose truth-value (true or false) would be unchanging and 'eternal'. 'Jane arrives on 2 February 1980', if ever true, would always have been true and would always be true.

An adverbial expression of date, such as 'on 2 February', would be an expression that formed sentences out of sentences. This suggests that the attaching of dates (as I shall call such adverbial expressions) would be an *iterable* process; and Mellor does appear to allow this when he says that adding a date to an already dated sentence would produce a sentence with the same truth-value as the first. But now difficulties begin to present themselves.

Let us assume that, as we would say in normal English, Jane did in fact arrive on 2 February 1980. In our tenseless language, we will express this fact thus: 'On 2 February Jane arrives'. According to Mellor, we can also say: 'On 1 February, on 2 February, Jane arrives'. The simple 'On 1 February, Jane arrives' must however be false. In which case, 'On 2 February, on 1 February, Jane arrives' will be false also (since adding a date to a sentence doesn't alter its truth-value). It appears that we must distinguish 'On 2 February, on 1 February, Jane arrives' (false) from 'On 1 February, on 2 February, Jane arrives' (true). And this distinction will be a scope-distinction: the date with narrowest scope, and governing just the 'root' sentence, will be what one would intuitively call the actual date of Jane's arrival, while any dates with wider scope will be, in the sense Mellor expounds above, redundant.

But now we must ask: what are the truth-conditions for a singly-dated sentence, such as 'On 2 February, Jane arrives'? One might suppose that the last-quoted sentence is true iff 'Jane arrives' is true on 2 February. (I am allowing that the whole of this argument be presumed tenseless, including 'is true'.) But a tenseless sentence is meant to be such that, if it is ever true, it is always true. Won't 'Jane arrives' be as true on 1 February as on 2 February?

If 'Jane arrives' is a true tenseless sentence, then any sentence of the form, 'At t, "Jane arrives" is true', would seem to be true. We must either distinguish 'Jane arrives' from ' "Jane arrives" is true', or deny that 'Jane arrives' is, after all, a tenseless sentence. Or we might instead decide that a true tenseless sentence is *not* in fact true at all times.

Distinguishing 'p' from ' "p" is true', in the way that would be needed, is a hard course to take; especially since the point at issue isn't just one to do with the truth-*predicate*. If 'Jane arrives' is a true tenseless sentence, then any sentence of the form, 'At t, it is true that Jane arrives' will be true, so long as tenseless sentences have unchanging truth-values. Can 'p' thus differ from 'It is true that p' – to the extent of producing a difference in truth-value in an apparently extensional context?

(It has been suggested to me that this problem can be avoided by construing 'Jane arrives on 1 February' as, 'Jane's arrival occurs on 1 February'. But whatever other merits, or faults, this proposal has, it will clearly not avoid the argument just given. The threatened chain of reasoning is: (a) 'Jane's arrival occurs' will be tenselessly true; so (b) ' "Jane's arrival occurs" is true on 2 February' will be true; so (c) 'Jane's arrival occurs on 2 February' will be true.)

What of the view that a true tenseless sentence is not, after all, true at all times? To avoid the problems to do with dating which I have alluded to, the idea would seem to have to be that a tenseless sentence is true simultaneously with the state or event which it reports, and not at other times. But it will be insufficiently informative simply to say that 'Jane arrives' is true just when Jane is actually arriving; 'Jane is actually arriving' is clearly in the same boat as

'Jane arrives'. We will have to say something like this: any utterance/inscription of 'Jane arrives' is (would be) true which is made simultaneously with one of Jane's arrivals. Unfortunately, in saying this, we lay down for 'Jane arrives' the truth-conditions of a present-tensed sentence. Indeed, it was by reference to truth-conditions of this form that we delineated the class of present-tensed sentences way back on p. 4.

Let us then examine the possibility that 'root' sentences do not in fact have truth-values at all; that 'Jane arrives' on its own doesn't express a 'complete proposition', needing a date (or a date-variable with initial quantifier) to achieve truth-conditions. The case would be similar, but only up to a point, to the case of indexical sentences. 'You are on fire' may be said to lack a truth-value until a context has been specified. But truth-*conditions* can be given for 'You are on fire', of roughly the form: 'For all x, y: if x remarks to y, "You are on fire", x's remark is true iff y is on fire'. In any appropriate context, an utterance of 'You are on fire' will achieve a truth-value. Truth-conditions cannot be given for a putatively tenseless 'Jane arrives'; for there is *no* context, on our present hypothesis, in which an utterance of that sentence on its own expresses a thought with a truth-value. A *linguistic* context, i.e. some more words, need to be added to 'Jane arrives' before it can say anything. It is not an atomic sentence at all – for it is not really a sentence at all, logically speaking. Only expressions with truth-conditions can be counted indicative sentences.

Something like this story has sometimes been told for 'feature-placing' sentences, like 'It's raining'. These, it has been claimed, require a locative adverb, such as 'in London', or 'over there', before they express a proposition with truth-conditions. The same sorts of problems face this account of feature-placing sentences as (we shall see) face the analogous account of 'root' sentences in a tenseless language. We shall see that a preferable account of locatives is available, in which 'here' has a special status, similar to that of 'now'.

The basic problem I want to draw attention to is this: if, in a sentence like 'On 2 February, Jane arrives', the embedded element ('Jane arrives') is not itself a sentence, it is very hard to assign a category to it at all – and of course, correspondingly hard to assign a category to the date.

Of course it is not that every sentence must be dated. For, unless there is a ban on quantification, it looks as if we will have to be able to say things like. 'For some t, Jane arrives at t'. But the latter will only be possible if we can take dates, or date-adverbs, as genuine syntactic units, and likewise the expressions which they modify. (If a date were like 'in the', which belongs to no syntactic category, quantifying with date-variables would be impossible.) But the categories of 'Jane arrives' and 'on 2 February' look to be suspiciously *sui generis*. And this is despite all the evidence that they would, in fact, be sentence and adverbial expression, respectively. This at any rate appears to be the case so long as we assume the tenseless language to bear a minimal likeness to actual languages with respect to certain inference-patterns.

Consider, for example, the following:

(a)   'On 2 February, Jane arrives and Jane's mother rejoices'.

Prima facie, this sentence appears (subject to a minor qualification) to be equivalent to the conjunction:

(b)   'On 2 February, Jane arrives; and on 2 February, Jane's mother rejoices'.

The 'minor qualification' is just this: if the tenseless language inherits some of the nuances of English, (a) might carry an implication of temporal succession not carried by (b). However, this detail need not bother us. The inference from (a) to (b) is closer to equivalence than that from, 'On some day, Jane arrives and Jane's mother rejoices', to, 'On some day Jane arrives, and on some day Jane's mother rejoices'. And this is all I need for my argument.

The equivalence, or close logical relation, between (a) and (b) is very hard to account for unless one admits that the embedded 'Jane arrives' and 'Jane's mother rejoices' are proper sentences. (b) is admitted by all sides to be a conjunction of two (dated) sentences; how convert it to (a), except by seeing 'Jane arrives and Jane's mother rejoices' as a similar conjunction, with the initial date being a 'distributable' adverb? 'Jane arrives and Jane's mother rejoices' is not even a proper sentence, on our present hypothesis, since it lacks a qualifying date or date-variable. But unless it *is* one specific kind of sentence – the conjunctive sentence – the equivalence between (a) and (b) is pretty mysterious. (What is the 'and' doing in (a), if not conjoining two sentences to yield a further sentence?)

We might try construing 'On 2 February, Jane arrives' as of the form, 'For some t, such that t = 2 February, Jane arrives at t', where the 'Jane arrives' of the first sentence corresponds to the 'Jane arrives at t′ of the second.[6] (We could of course use adverb-variables rather than the seeming name-variable 't', with a higher-order analogue of '=' that connects adverbs.) The relation between (a) and (b) would then be pretty much the same as the relation between (c) and (d):

(c) 'For some x, such that x = A, x is sitting and x is laughing'
(d) 'For some x, such that x = A, x is sitting; and for some x, such that x = A, x is laughing'.

Wouldn't this do as an explanation of the logical connection between (a) and (b), an explanation which avoided ascribing truth-conditions to 'Jane arrives' as it occurs in 'Jane arrives on 2 February'? For spelt out fully, this 'Jane arrives' would really amount to, 'Jane arrives at t′, i.e. 'Jane arrives at that time' (where 't' and 'that time' are variables that want binding).

(c) and (d) can both be reduced by logical steps to 'A is sitting and A is laughing'. Hence their equivalence. If (a) and (b) are to count as analogous to (c) and (d), an analogous reduction will be possible. 'For some t, such that t = 2 February, Jane arrives at t′ boils down to, 'Jane arrives on 2 February'. The 'Jane arrives' of this latter cannot, as before, be construed as elliptical for 'Jane arrives at t′. We are back with 'Jane arrives on 2 February' and the question, 'Of what category is "Jane arrives", if not that of the sentence?'. (The clause which occurs in (c) and (d), 'such that x = A', is crucial in achieving a putative analogy with (a) and (b). Without it, (c) would indeed entail (d), but not *vice versa*. 'such that x = A' corresponds to 'such that t = 2 February', which clause is clearly essential to the quantificational renditions of (a) and (b).)

Similar remarks to the above can be made in connection with the view that feature-placing sentences (or indeed sentences generally) are incomplete without modification by locatives or bound locative-variables. 'p in London, and q in London' will be equivalent to, or at the very least inferable from, '(p and q) in London'. But this equivalence will be hard to explain unless it is admitted that 'p' and 'q' are genuine sentences, having their own truth-conditions and susceptible to such logical procedures as that of conjunction.

My argument has presupposed some degree of similarity between the tenseless language with dates and actual (tensed) languages. Someone might object that in a dated tenseless language, inferences of the sort exemplified by my inference from (a) to (b) may not exist, or count as valid. The language may just be too alien for us to be able to include such a condition in our description of it.

Perhaps a sentence representable as 'Jane arrives on 2 February' is atomic, rather in the way in which the English 'It's raining' is atomic.

The main problem with this sort of view of the matter is that it becomes unclear what is being said when it is claimed that there might exist a genuinely tenseless language with dates. *Some* similarity with actual languages must be presupposed, if we are to make sense of such terms as 'date', 'sentence', and indeed 'tenseless'. I will return to this question later (p. 72 ff.), when I examine the thesis that there might be tenseless languages (including dated ones) in the light of what it would take for creatures to have such a language. (The 'atomic' conception of dated tenseless sentences will there come under scrutiny.) It should also be pointed out that in the specific context of the thesis that tenseless truth-conditions can be given for tensed sentences, it is absolutely requisite that tenseless sentences be logically pretty similar to the tensed sentences in whose truth-conditions they are meant to be playing a role – otherwise they could hardly play that role.

Quine[7] has suggested that dates be regarded as forming singular terms out of singular terms, leaving the tenseless verb unmodified. 'On 2 February, Jane arrives' would then come out as: 'Jane-on-2-February arrives'. Again, if we assume that what count as good inferences involving the actual expressions 'Jane', 'arrives', '2 February', etc., should have at least close-ish counterparts in the imagined tenseless language, as we will have to if we are giving tenseless truth-conditions for tensed sentences, then we will run into problems. What is the 'dated singular term' in (a)? If it is the monstrous 'Jane-and-Jane's-mother', then what is the verb? 'Arrives-and-rejoices' will have to be distinguished from 'rejoices-and-arrives', since 'Jane-and-Jane's-mother rejoices-and-arrives' would appear to mean 'Jane rejoices and Jane's mother arrives'; etc., etc. It seems that Quine will just have to convert (a) into (b) before he starts analysing. Further problems will then need to be met, as: what is the dated singular term in 'It's sunny on 8 October', given that 'It's sunny' cannot be analysed as a subject–predicate sentence (to change the example)? Someone with Quine's taste for radical recasting will probably be content with: 'The-sunniness-on-8-October exists', or perhaps: 'The-sunniness-on-8-October is self-identical'. But the rest of us may not be. And all this is quite apart from questions about what would be needed for any creature's linguistic behaviour to *count* as being translatable by means of such bizarre forms.

3.5 ROOT SENTENCES IN A TENSED LANGUAGE

Turning once again to tensed languages, we have the question: what is the status of the 'root' sentence in any language with sentential tense operators? On the assumption that such a language gives the perspicuous form of tensed languages generally, then our question will clearly bear on tensed discourse as such. (In the same way, it was because a tenseless language of the sort sketched above might well be thought to give the perspicuous form of possible tenseless languages generally, that problems with such a language are problems for the 'tenseless view' of time.) It might, for instance, turn out that 'root sentences' in tensed languages are themselves to be regarded as tenseless.

I will use 'root expression' to mean the expression (*prima facie* a sentence) which is left, after all tense operators, and all operators with wider scope than the tense operator with narrowest scope, have been dropped. Thus, the root expression in, 'It is not the case that: it was the case that: it is possible that: Jane arrives' is 'It is possible that Jane arrives'. On the whole, we will be looking at simpler examples, such as 'It was the case that Jane arrives'.

There are three possible answers to the question as to the status of root expressions which I will consider:

(1)   that they are tenseless sentences;
(2)   that they are present-tensed sentences;
(3)   that they are expressions without truth-conditions until modified by tense operators (or bound tense operator variables).

One might think that option (3) could be dismissed for similar reasons to those adduced just now in dismissing the view that the 'root expressions' in Mellorese are not genuine sentences. But this is not so. A proponent of (3) will not need to explain an equivalence analogous to that between (a) and (b). 'It was the case that: p and q' is not equivalent to 'It was the case that p, and it was the case that q', and of course the same goes for other tense operators. With *metric* tense operators, we do get an equivalence, to be sure: just replace 'It was the case that' by 'It was the case n units ago that' in the example just quoted. But metrically tensed discourse is a more sophisticated development from ordinary tensed discourse, and it is to the latter that the proponent of option (3) can legitimately appeal.

The feature of ordinary tense operators mentioned in the last paragraph is a symptom of a more general fact. Tense operators constitute a more powerful equipment than, for instance, dates. That the prefixing of additional tense operators should be a repeatable process is essential to tensed discourse. Complex tenses are not the spurious items that 'complex dates' appear to be. And from the possibility of complex tenses Prior has argued to the conclusion that root expressions must be present-tensed:

> For suppose we do take the view that tensed utterances can be formed by attaching some sort of modifier to timeless propositional contents, e.g. that 'I shall see John' amounts to something like '(Me seeing John) future', where the element in brackets is supposed to be a non-temporally characterized 'content'. Then if attaching 'future' to such a content forms a future-tense sentence, '(Me seeing John) future' will not itself be the sort of thing 'future' or 'past' can be attached to, since it is not a content but a tensed sentence. The building up of complexes like Findlay's '(x past) future' requires that tensing be an operation of which the subjects are themselves tensed sentences, and when we have got inside all other tensing to the 'kernel' of the complex, *its* tense will have to be present.
>
> (*Past, Present and Future*, Oxford University Press, 1967, p. 15)

This argument might be objected to in the following way.

Take operators of the form, 'A thinks that'. It seems evident that 'It's raining' falls into a category of sentence into which neither 'John thinks that it's raining' nor 'Bill thinks that John thinks that it's raining' fall. Let us call this category 'non-epistemic', and the complementary category 'epistemic'. If Prior's reasoning in the above passage were cogent, then we could argue thus: 'If attaching "John believes that" to a putatively non-epistemic sentence, "It's raining", forms an epistemic sentence, then "John believes that it's raining" will not itself be the sort of thing "Bill thinks that" can be attached to, since it is not a non-epistemic sentence but an epistemic one. But since we *can* attach "Bill thinks that" to sentences like "John thinks that it's raining", the "kernel" sentence, "It's raining", must be epistemic after all.'

Reading slightly between Prior's lines, however, we can arrive at an interpretation of his argument according to which it does have considerable force, though not the force to establish Prior's desired conclusion. If by 'propositional content' Prior meant something that cannot be expressed by a genuine sentence, something without truth-conditions, then the possibility of complex tenses *is* in conflict with the idea that root expressions are, or convey, mere contents. (That Prior *did* mean this is suggested by his using the form '(Me seeing John) future', rather than 'It will be that (I see John)'.) For we have to be able to assign a category to tense operators, and if we can 'pile up' tense operators in the way we clearly can, then it seems that their category will have to be that of the sentential operator: operators that yield sentences from sentences. In which case, root expressions will themselves have to be genuine sentences. Similarly, the 'kernel' inside a complex of belief-operators must itself be a sentence.

It is no use objecting to this that expressions of one category may attach to expressions of more than one category: that, for instance, the predicable '__is mortal' can be attached both to a name, e.g. 'Karen', and to a quantifier-expression, e.g. 'Nobody'. The different 'attachments' in such cases can be distinguished, in particular by appeal to the different *scope* had by, say, '__is mortal', in the two sentences: 'Karen is mortal' and 'Nobody is mortal'. (A categorial grammar will typically *define* categories in terms of their capacity to 'wrap round' other expressions to yield sentences, where a 'wrapping' expression has wider scope.)[8] But both 'It was the case that (it will be the case that (it's raining))' and plain 'It was the case that it's raining' are both of the form 'It was the case that p'; in both sentences, the past-tense operator is doing the same thing, namely wrapping round something. And what it wraps around would appear to have to be a sentence.

However, we do not now have an argument to the conclusion that the root expressions in tensed discourse are (present-)tensed sentences, any more than we have an argument to the conclusion that the root expressions in belief contexts are 'epistemic sentences'. What we have is an argument against the thesis that root expressions convey mere 'contents' and are not genuine sentences, lacking their own truth-conditions. Option (3) must go; but option (1) remains.

But now we must ask: how is (1) any better off than (3)? If (3) can be dismissed on the grounds that 'root expressions' must be genuine sentences, and genuine sentences have truth-conditions, the proponent of (1) must be able to attribute truth-conditions to tenseless sentences. Of course, it will not be enough just to parrot the T-schema: 'It's raining' is true iff it's raining. One does not establish moral realism by blandly laying down that 'Murder is wicked' is true iff murder is wicked. We might ask: 'To what tensed sentence is the tenseless "It's raining" equivalent? – or to what tensed sentence does it correspond?'. The answer to this question would give us a grip, for example, on when somebody might correctly say 'It's raining' (intended tenselessly) – and the truth-conditions of a sentence are, at least typically, a matter of when someone might correctly utter that sentence.

Perhaps the tenseless 'It's raining' embedded inside 'It will be that it's raining' is equivalent to the disjunctive: 'It was, is, or will be raining'? This equivalence between tenseless and disjunctively-tensed was what we assumed when considering what sort of sentences would have to be used in the framing of tenseless truth-conditions for tensed sentences (see, e.g., p. 48). Unfortunately disjunctively-tensed sentences will not help us here. 'It will be that: (it was, is, or will be raining)' would be true if 'It will be that it was raining', *alias* 'It will have been raining', were true, even if 'It will rain' weren't. For 'It will be that (p or q or r)' is true if 'It will be that p' is true. (*Which* disjunct is involved doesn't matter.) But if the tenseless 'It's raining' isn't equivalent to the disjunctively-tensed sentence, it is hard to see what tensed sentence it could be equivalent to. Certainly not the conjunctively-tensed one!

The truth-conditions of a tenseless root sentence seem to be elusive. And one's doubts are sustained by reflection on the fact that it is certainly difficult to imagine *when* someone might correctly utter 'It's raining', given that this was not just the usual present-tense statement, nor equivalent to a disjunctively-tensed statement.

At this point, it may be wondered whether the emphasis which I have laid upon *truth-conditions* is justifiable. Let us retrace our steps a little. When attacking the idea of a language of tenseless sentences constructed from root expressions ('Jane arrives') and dates ('on 2 February'), I presented a dilemma: either one must deny that 'It is true that p' need be equivalent to 'p', where 'p' is a sentence, or one must say that root expressions like 'Jane arrives' are not really sentences at all. This latter course was an option only because it seemed necessary to *avoid* the question as to what 'It is true that Jane arrives' should mean: if 'Jane arrives' is not on its own an expression with truth-conditions, 'It is true that Jane arrives' won't be one either, and the question of an equivalence (i.e. shared truth-conditions) won't arise. I was thus using 'sentence' interchangeably with 'expression with truth-conditions'. And I suggested what sort of expression 'Jane arrives' *might* be (if not a sentence in this sense) – namely, an 'incomplete' expression, needing a date or bound date-variable to 'complete' it, where completion would yield something which did have truth-conditions. It seemed clear, though, that in order to account for such an equivalence as that between 'On 1 February: p and q' and 'On 1 February p, and on 1 February q', we could not regard 'p' and 'q' as 'incomplete' in the sense just outlined. 'p' and 'q' would have to be, as they appear to be, proper sentences.

But was this last move justified? The sense of 'sentence' according to which it is true to say that the equivalence just mentioned drives us to view 'p' and 'q' as sentences, does not seem to be the sense earlier given to 'sentence': namely, 'expression with truth-conditions'. Rather, the argument from equivalence showed that 'p' and 'q' must be sentences, only in the sense that they must be susceptible to certain sorts of logical procedures, such as conjunction. If expressions susceptible to such logical procedures are not all of them expressions with truth-conditions, then my argument will have been fallacious. And similar remarks apply to the arguments I gave against options (1) and (3), concerning the status of root expressions in tensed discourse. The argument from complex tenses showed only that root expressions must be the sorts of expressions that are susceptible to the prefixing of sentential operators, not that they must be expressions with truth-conditions. So if the expressions mentioned in (3) were meant to be the sorts of 'incomplete' expressions earlier considered in connection with tenseless discourse, it does not necessarily matter that such expressions would lack truth-conditions. And the elusiveness of the truth-conditions of tenseless root expressions will likewise not necessarily matter for the proponent of (1).

There are of course expressions that are susceptible to such logical operations as conjunction, disjunction, etc., but which lack truth-conditions. Predicables are an obvious example; one might also add sentence- and predicable-*variables*. But none of these kinds of expression can be meant by the proponent of (3). Perhaps there is a position according to which tense operators are applicable primarily to predicables, not to sentences – i.e. according to which they are adverbial expressions without being sentential operators. But such a position (not without its own faults) is not our concern. We are concerned with the usual battery of tense operators, 'It will be the case that', etc., and with the 'sentence-like' expressions to which they get attached. The question is whether these 'sentence-like' expressions might lack truth-conditions.

If calling our root expressions 'sentence-like' does not commit us to endowing them with truth-conditions, to what does it commit us? Perhaps we should be looking to some 'bare logical notion' of a sentence. Well, even the 'bare logical notion' of a sentence is such that if something is a sentence, then it can occur on its own; it does not need any additional expressions tacked on in order to constitute a well-formed formula. And now we must ask what it is for an expression of a language to be able to occur on its own, since in the end we have to be able to apply our 'bare logical notion' to actual or possible tensed *languages*. If an expression of a language can occur all on its own, then using it on its own would constitute a complete speech-act. It might, of course, be other than an indicative sentence – it might be an imperative, or an optative, for instance. But the 'root expressions' with which we are concerned could hardly be said to be imperatives, optatives, or whatever. What, then, would the complete speech-act 'Jane arrives' accomplish? How would it have committed the utterer? It seems hard to avoid the conclusion that if 'Jane arrives' can say something on its own, then someone who said it would thereby have committed himself in the way one does with a (contingent) *indicative*: by saying something that might be true, might be false.

All in all, then, we seem driven to the conclusion that Prior was right: the 'kernel', after all tense operators have been dropped (along with all operators having wider scope than the tense operator of narrowest scope), must be a present-tensed sentence. It cannot be a non-sentential 'content'; nor a tenseless sentence; nor a 'sentence' *sans* truth-conditions. And this, indeed, is a conclusion very much in keeping with common sense. When one says that it will rain, one is thereby committed to the following: that it will be the case, at some time, that any utterance of 'It is (now) raining' made at that time would be an utterance of the actual truth. But the future truth of a (hypothetical) present-tensed utterance amounts to the future truth of a present-tensed proposition. In 'It will be the case that p', our proposition gets expressed by 'p'. 'p' itself, therefore, is a present-tensed sentence.

A McTaggartian 'material mode' of speech also conforms to the Priorian view. 'President Bush will die' can be rephrased as, 'President Bush's death will be (or become) present'. (The continuation,

'... and it will then be (or become) past' just amounts to adding '... and then he will have died' to our original.)

If our basic sentences, our root expressions in a language with tense operators, are present-tensed, then a present-tense operator ('It is now the case that') is redundant. This is in any case suggested by the fact that prefixing such an operator to a sentence already containing a number of tense operators never alters the sense – for which reason, as was noted on p. 4, every sentence may be regarded as present-tensed. 'p' and 'It is now the case that p' are equivalent; and there is no reason to suppose it otherwise with our root sentences.

The word 'now' is by no means redundant, however, for, as we have seen (section 2.3), this word, and sometimes the present tense itself for that matter, may function within a certain context (e.g. epistemic) as an expression having 'wide scope'. In this respect, as philosophers have noted, 'now' is like 'actually'. But the non-redundancy of these words does not entail the need for an operator corresponding to each or either in a formal language. We have already seen how 'now' in epistemic contexts can be dealt with, though I did not give exact translations of the sentences in question. Other tactics can be employed to show the redundancy of a formal 'now' operator, analogous to tactics employable in showing the redundancy of a formal 'actually' operator.[9]

The basic status of the present tense is also interesting from a more purely philosophical standpoint. The first judgements we learn to make are present-tensed ones; past- or future-tensed judgements come later, and in a certain sense presuppose present-tensed ones. These are matters which we shall soon go into in greater depth. For the moment, it is enough to note the *prima facie* plausibility of the view that the sentences, or sentence-like expressions, which get cast as root expressions in (the formalisation of) a natural language such as English will be, or will correspond to, the sentences that form a basis for the more complex sentences of the language. It should be added that being 'basic to a language' is rather a relative matter; it is the basic status of present-tensed judgements relative to non-present-tensed judgements that concerns us here.

The notion of the present is a notoriously knotty one. Questions like 'How long is the present?' have baffled philosophers for centuries. But I will leave discussion of matters such as these for later, in particular for Part II. It is time now to return once more to the question: 'Is a genuinely tenseless language possible?'.

3.6   ARE GENUINELY TENSELESS LANGUAGES POSSIBLE?

Let us recall once again the truth-conditions for the past-tense form, 'It was the case that p', variously rendered as (2) and (2'):

(2)   An utterance of 'It was the case that p' is true iff 'p' is true before the time of utterance;

(2')   Were anyone to utter 'It was the case that p', he would speak truly iff 'p' were true before the time of utterance.

(What follows will not be affected if we prefer 'had been true' to 'were true' in (2').) The question we are tackling is: 'Can such truth-conditional schemata be employed to show that (genuinely) tenseless truth-conditions can be given for tensed sentences?'.

It was because (2) amounts to something like (2') that we said (p. 39) that it would be misleading to formulate the issues here as simply being about whether or not 'is true' could, or had to be, tenseless; and in answering the question whether tenseless truth-conditions *had to* be given for 'It was the case that p', we concentrated more on the possible tensed status of the whole sentence (2'). The same approach is appropriate when it comes to our present concern. But this might suggest that a *disquotational* equivalent of (2') could as well serve as our object of study. If we put 'It is raining' for 'p', we would seem, after disquotation, to have:

(2'a)   Were anyone to utter 'It was the case that it is raining', he would speak truly iff it were raining before the time of utterance.

If the question is now, 'Is (2'a) construable as tenseless?', our task will be made the more difficult by the complexity and subjunctive mood of (2'a). Our interest is naturally focused in particular on the right-hand side of the biconditional; but we cannot abstract the right-hand side, since it is not a complete sentence at all. This is not just owing to the implicit anaphora involved in 'the time of utterance', but more significantly, to the status of 'it were raining' as subordinate clause. A disquotational equivalent of (2), with 'It is raining' for 'p', would not have a parallel feature:

(2a)   An utterance of 'It was the case that it is raining' is true iff it is raining before the time of utterance.

With (2a), our attention would of course be drawn to the form 'It is raining' just after 'iff': we should want to ask, 'Since this form cannot be present-tensed, are we entitled to take it as tenseless?'.

We cannot sensibly ask the same question of 'it were raining' – or rather, if we can ask such a question, it is because we can take 'it were raining' as equivalent to ' "It is raining" were true', and shift the question to the quoted sentence 'It is raining'. The putative tenselessness of a simple indicative sentence will thus suffice for our consideration. If (2'), with 'It is raining' for 'p', can be construed so that 'It is raining' counts as tenseless, we would at least have established the possibility of giving truth-conditions for tensed sentences framed *in terms of* tenseless ones. Whether we could then go on to say that we had effectively given truth-conditions that were themselves tenseless would have to be decided by reference to such matters as disquotation and the semantics of subjunctive conditionals.

That bridge can be crossed if we come to it; but we may not even come to it, if it turns out that simple indicative sentences cannot be construed as tenseless. In the section before last, I outlined some more or less technical problems that would be faced by one attempting to delineate a tenseless language with dates. In what follows, I want to look at some more general problems, connected with the question: 'Could any creature learn and master a language of genuinely tenseless sentences?'. A crucial effect of tackling this question will be to make clearer the sense in which a sentence, or language, might count as 'genuinely' tenseless, as opposed, say, to 'harmlessly' tenseless. For if it transpires that only 'harmlessly' tenseless truth-conditions can be given for tensed sentences, that conclusion will, as we shall see, point to the ultimate primacy (not just autonomy) of tensed language.

It would be embarrassing if the philosophical thesis just outlined were susceptible of easy empirical falsification. So the *prima facie* counterexamples to that thesis – namely, those natural languages called 'tenseless' by linguists – had better only be *prima facie* ones. By 'tenseless language' a linguist will typically mean something like, 'language without grammatical tenses'. The distinction between grammatical tense and what we are primarily concerned with, i.e. 'logical tense', is one that has already been drawn; but a lack of grammatical tense might well be thought to *indicate* a corresponding lack of logical tense. So let us examine this matter a little more closely.

Modern standard Chinese (or Mandarin) is often cited as the classical tenseless language. It lacks the paraphernalia of such tense-forms as past imperfect, perfect, pluperfect, present continuous, future continuous, future perfect, and so on, all of which, in a language such as English, are embodied in certain *verb-forms*; and in general, Chinese verbs are not inflected for tense. But of course it has ways of translating English sentences, including tensed ones. Moreover, it is in fact the case that these translations are adequate on the whole: certainly, Chinese will be able to translate a past-tense sentence as past, a future-tense sentence as future, etc.

Past-tense constructions often involve the particle 'le'. This particle can indicate, roughly speaking, a change of state; as in, 'Xiahoair ji sui le?', which can be rendered, 'Child/how many/years/become?' ('become' = 'le'), alias, 'How old is the child?' – what would usually be classified as a present-tense question in English (i.e. a question demanding a present-tense answer in English). But it can also indicate 'accomplished fact', as in, 'Ta jintian zhongwu zuo huoche le' – 'He/today/noon/sit/fire vehicle/did' ('did' = 'le'), alias, 'He took the train at noon today' – where it occurs as a final sentence particle; and as in, 'Wo xue le wu nian Zhongwen' – 'I/study/did/five/years/Chinese', alias, 'I studied Chinese for five years' – where it comes after the verb. A double occurrence of 'le', on the other hand, generally indicates a present continuation of the action or occurrence; as in, 'Wo xue le wu nian Zhongwen le', which means, 'I have been studying Chinese for five years'.

A duration-expression or date may on its own suffice to show that a sentence is past-tensed. An example is, 'Wo san tian mei chi dongxi' ('I didn't eat a thing for three days'; 'san tian' = 'three days'). How then would one say, 'I haven't eaten a thing for three days'? By using a final 'le' is the answer – the rules governing that word are notoriously difficult to encapsulate!

The future tense in Chinese can often be expressed with the auxiliary verb 'yao'. 'Wo yao qu tushuguan' can mean, 'I'll be going to the library'. (It can also mean, 'I want to go to the library', or even 'I must go to the library'; here, one must admit that the sentence is ambiguous, and needs disambiguating by context.) 'Yao' plus 'le' can produce a straight future tense. Thus, 'Yao xia yu le' means 'It is going to rain'.

Temporal adverbs and clauses, such as 'congqian' ('formerly'), 'na tian' ('that day'), and 'xiao de shihou' ('when one is young'), can all contribute to the tense of a Chinese sentence, just as they can in English – cf. 'He is coming tomorrow'.

More can be said on this topic, for example concerning negative forms; but I will leave it at that.

What of Chinese indicative sentences that lack such features as can be taken to indicate tense (certain occurrences of 'le', 'yao', temporal adverbs, etc.)? Such sentences may occur in a context – an argument, for instance – which itself supplies temporal indicators that apply throughout that context, in which case the sentences in question may have the tense(s) indicated by those temporal indicators. We may talk of the 'implicit occurrence' in these sentences of temporal indicators. But what of such sentences when they lack temporal indicators, explicit or implicit?

These, I think it is fair to say, are typically present-tensed. Certainly, translating them into English will typically involve a present-tensed sentence of English. Thus: 'Ta Yingguo cai zuo de feichang hao', which means, 'She cooks wonderful English food', can be rendered word by word: 'She/hero country/dish/make/extremely/good' ('de' simply links 'Yingguo cai' with its 'feichang hao'). Another example shows the verb 'to be' at work: 'Bu zhi zhurou er shi niurou', meaning, 'It's not pork but beef' ('Not/be/pig meat/but/be/cattle meat'). 'She cooks wonderful English food' is of course one of the sorts of sentence which some regard as tenseless, others (such as myself) as present-tensed: the debate here obviously cannot be influenced by the existence of the Chinese sentence, since exactly the same reasons will be needed to show that the Chinese sentence is 'really' tenseless/present-tensed as will be needed to show that the English one is.

That the present tense is the basic, or if you like 'default', tense, is one of my contentions, and from that point of view it is not surprising that the simple Chinese sentences of the type just referred to are generally (what I would call) present-tensed. One who took a putative tenseless form as basic in the same way could make parallel remarks, at least when it came to 'She cooks wonderful English food' and its like; to make those remarks in connection with 'It's not pork but beef' and *its* like would require saying something such as that only the context supplied the (present) tense for this otherwise tenseless sentence. But at the *prima facie* level, it could be said, 'She cooks wonderful English food' looks just as tenseless as 'It's not pork but beef' looks present-tensed: the Chinese language supplies no extra weight to either side in the philosophical debate about tenselessness.

Having taken a look at an actual candidate for the title of 'tenseless language', let us return to the question: 'Could there be a genuinely tenseless language?'.

The language in which our truth-conditions for 'It was the case that p' are formulated need not be the language to which 'It was the case that p' belongs. So if we are considering an English sentence of the form, 'It was the case that p', we do not have to take it that the sentence's truth-conditions must be in English. Hence it would not be enough to point out that English lacks tenseless sentences (if it does). Nor would it be enough to argue that no actual language has tenseless sentences (not even Chinese). For it would be of sufficient philosophical interest if tenseless truth-conditions for 'It was the case that p' in some *possible* language were conceivable; and likewise, it would be of philosophical interest if such tenseless truth-conditions in a merely possible language turned out to be inconceivable.

If, however, English (or whatever natural language we are considering) does lack tenseless sentences, the sentence quoted on the right-hand side of our biconditional (2) or (2') cannot be English – else we should not have made the first step of framing truth-conditions *in terms of* a tenseless sentence. In which case, the sentence quoted on the right-hand side will not be the sentence embedded in the English 'It was the case that' on the left-hand side. This in any case fits in with what was argued in the last section: that the root sentences in tensed language must be present-tensed, not tenseless. It seems that in their present schematic form, (2) and (2') are rather misleading; for – if either English lacks tenseless forms, or the arguments of the last section are cogent – we will have to admit an equivocation over the sense of 'p', as it occurs both on the left- and right-hand sides of the biconditional in question. It is the right-hand 'p' we are to consider, and of which we must ask: 'Could it be genuinely tenseless?'.

Let us begin by looking at tensed sentences, and the way they function. The criteria which govern the use of the past and future tenses crucially involve the present tense. Thus the sense of 'It will rain' derives above all from the 'truth-value link' between that sentence and the present-tense sentence that counts as (later) reporting its fulfilment: namely, 'It is raining'. And the sense of 'It rained' derives above all from the role which reports of direct memory have in warranting its assertion in central cases – reports that can only be made once the 'truth-value link' between those reports and present-tense observational statements ('It's raining') is grasped. (These matters will be examined in greater depth in Chapter 7.) These conceptual dependences of the past and future tenses

upon the present determine what is involved in someone's understanding variously-tensed sentences; and they link up with the
typical order in which people learn to use tensed idioms.

What could be involved in someone's understanding 'tenseless'
sentences? For the moment I mean simple, unmodified tenseless
sentences; I shall come to the case of dated tenseless sentences later.

If there is a tenseless proposition 'It is raining', then it seems that
this proposition can best be taken as equivalent in truth-conditions
to one expressible with a disjunctive combination of past, present
and future tensed statements: 'It was, or is, or will be raining'. So
if the tenseless proposition 'It is raining' is simply introduced as
short for this disjunctive proposition, it is easy to see how one might
grasp its meaning; but it is also clear that such a proposition would
not *really* be 'tenseless', any more than is its fully-spelt-out version,
'It was, or is, or will be raining'. Could one somehow grasp what
a tenseless, atemporal 'It is raining' means *without* its being introduced to one as shorthand for a tensed, omnitemporal proposition?

It might be thought that the omnitemporal proposition had
indeed to be used in the teaching of the atemporal one, but that
the atemporal proposition need not be taken as 'short for' the
omnitemporal one. If one teaches the meaning of 'Tuesday' by saying that Tuesday is the next day after Monday, where the child
already knows about Monday, the child needn't take 'Tuesday' as
short for 'the next day after Monday'. And if one teaches the meaning of 'saucer' by saying that a saucer is a little plate you put teacups on, the child needn't take 'saucer' as short for 'a little plate
you put teacups on'.

In teaching the meanings of 'Tuesday' or 'saucer', however, one
does not *have* to make reference to Monday or to teacups. One might
indeed have started the child off on Tuesday, and have told her that
Monday is the day just before Tuesday; or one might have taught
her all the days of the week in one fell swoop. And a child can be
taught what a saucer is ostensively (together with its teacup, perhaps). 'Monday' and 'saucer' belong to a different family of words
from that to which, for example, 'bachelor' or 'solar system' belong.
The meaning of 'bachelor' cannot be taught or grasped) until that
of 'married', or a synonym, has been taught (or grasped); the
meaning of 'solar system' cannot be taught until those of 'sun' and
'planet', or synonyms, have been. Now it would perhaps be going
rather too far to say that 'solar system' was just *short for* 'system of
planets orbiting round a sun'; but it seems clear that the introduction

of 'solar system' into a language will not represent any sort of 'conceptual advance'. A person who has learnt the sense of 'solar system' won't be able to do anything he couldn't already do with 'system of planets orbiting round a sun'; and nor will a community of such people.

This sort of consideration quite often crops up in philosophy. A Russellian view of everyday proper names need not be expressed as the view that an everyday name is just *short for* some definite description; it may be the view (also false) that any everyday name is to some definite description as 'solar system' is to 'system of planets orbiting round a sun'. In the philosophy of science, it can be maintained that certain terms of physics (e.g. 'mass') have to be related to other, more basic terms (e.g. 'acceleration'), even though that relation is not to be explicated in terms of *abbreviation*. And so on and so forth. What I want to say about putatively tenseless propositions is that, insofar as these propositions could be viewed as expressing temporal truths and falsehoods at all, their sense must be parasitic upon that of tensed propositions, in the way in which the sense of 'solar system' is parasitic upon the senses of 'sun' and 'planet'. They can, consequently, constitute no conceptual advance on the basic tensed propositions from which we begin. It is not an option to teach a child a tenseless 'It is raining' first, and then tell it what the tensed 'It is raining' means in terms of the tenseless sentence – the order has to be the other way around.

Someone who grasps the meaning of a sentence like 'It is raining' will typically have the capacity to recognise when the sentence is true, and when it is false. This sort of recognition obviously has its basis in perception. There may indeed be some people who grasp the sentence's meaning though lacking in this recognitional capacity; but they will have to know to defer to those who have the capacity, and – more importantly – there must *be* people who have the capacity if the sentence is to continue to be usable, i.e. continue to have a meaning. The meaning of 'It is raining' rests upon certain human capacities of recognition.

To grasp the meaning of the tenseless 'It is raining' *in the way in which we grasp the present-tense 'It is raining'*, a person would have to be able to distinguish the truth of that sentence from its false-hood. But how could someone ever distinguish the case where it (tenselessly) rains from that where it does not? The truth at a place of the 'tenseless' sentence 'It is raining' consists in its having once rained there, *or* its going at some time to rain there, *or* its raining there at the moment. A person could of course see that it was at that moment raining, and might on that account say 'It's raining'. But how could she ever manifest an ability to recognise that it is *not* (tenselessly) raining? It would be impossible ever to *recognise* the falsehood of the tenseless 'It is raining', for it would be impossible to know that it had never rained there, or that it never would rain there, in part because of the unrestricted form of this proposition ('never'), and in part because of the impossibility of knowing of the future.

Knowledge of the observational sort we are talking about in the case of the present-tensed 'It's raining' must be causally based. A human being's perception of the rain is causally dependent on the rain: this is why it counts as 'perception'. There cannot be such a thing as a capacity in general to know about future rain, for the reason that there cannot in general be backwards causation. That is, cases of backwards causation could, at most, be quirks; and the capacities on which language-learning (by any creature) depend cannot rely on quirks. (This connection between the direction of causation and the direction of time will be argued for later, in Chapter 7.)

So long as we conceive of a (possible) person's grasp of the tenseless 'It is raining' along the same lines as a person's grasp of the tensed 'It is raining', we seem to have to invoke backwards causation. And, as indicated above, this is not the only problem. One who understood the tenseless 'It is raining' would have to be able to recognise the truth of what amounts to an unrestricted generalisation ('over times', as they say). But this comes into conflict with the idea that someone's grasp of any sentence must be, in principle, manifestable to others. For to be able to manifest one's knowledge of what an *unrestricted generalisation* (or equivalent) means, it must be enough for one to be able to show that one knows what counts as good evidence for the generalisation, what logical connections the generalisation has with other sentences, and so on.[10] One will not be able to *recognise* the truth of such a sentence, in the sense in which one can recognise the truth of 'It's raining', and so will not be able to manifest such recognition.

Well – perhaps the conditions under which one could grasp (teach, explain, etc.) the tenseless 'It is raining' won't be the same kind of conditions as those under which one could grasp (teach, explain) the tensed 'It is raining'. Perhaps there will not be a recognitional capacity associated with the tenseless sentence. Perhaps indeed this will have to go for any tenseless sentence – since, we are assuming, any tenseless sentence will be truth-conditionally equivalent to a disjunctively-tensed one. Does any of this matter? Mightn't a grasp of a tenseless sentence be associated with different capacities from those associated with observation-based present-tensed sentences? Mightn't such a grasp in fact be associated with the sort of limited manifestation of competence that goes with a person's grasp of an unrestricted generalisation?

Unrestricted generalisations are connected with particular (i.e. non-general) statements; a generalisation gets its sense above all from particular propositions (notably the particular propositions that can falsify it). And tensed statements (including disjunctively-tensed ones) are connected with present-tensed statements; both memory and prediction have their roots, as I have suggested, in the present-tensed statements that confirmed or will confirm them. To the extent, then, that a tenseless sentence is assimilated to a disjunctively-tensed one, there will appear to be present-tensed sentences lurking behind it: for one who understands a disjunctively-tensed sentence must also understand some present-tensed ones and their connections with it. It may be thought that this does not in itself affect the possibility of tenseless forms. For mightn't one simply allow that tenseless sentences had to be connected to present-tensed ones in certain definite ways? (Maybe the existence of tenseless forms entails that of some tensed ones.)

The problem is: where such connections between a sentence and present-tensed sentences exist, embodied in the use of the sentence by competent speakers, it would seem that by this very token the sentence in question must be taken as disjunctively-tensed.

The issue can be seen as one of radical interpretation. What counts, in a society, as a practice of making omnitemporal, i.e. disjunctively-tensed, statements? What linguistic and other behaviour will provide the needed evidence – *constitutive* evidence – for such a piece of radical interpretation? Surely, at least in part, what is needed is that certain utterances are connected with ones interpretable as tensed utterances in the same way as the way in which our omnitemporal utterances are connected with our tensed utterances? (In the same way, a sentence will be interpretable as a generalisation if it is connected with sentences interpretable as 'particular' sentences in the way in which *our* generalisations are connected with *our* 'particular' sentences.)

Try to imagine what *use* a disjunctively-tensed sentence could have; how it could fit in with anyone's life. It should be clear that such a sentence will be quite high up in the linguistic edifice – below it will be less general sentences, sentences with more practical application – e.g. present-tensed sentences. The omnitemporal sentence will have little straightforward 'use': its life will derive from that of more basic sentences. These facts are what the radical interpreter must discern in the behaviour of his subjects. But such behaviour, linguistic and non-linguistic, will – if there is enough of it – provide sufficient warrant for the translation by means of omnitemporal sentences.

And now the question is this: If a tenseless sentence is meant to be truth-conditionally equivalent to an omnitemporal one, what behaviour of speakers could ever warrant translation of their utterances by means of a tenseless sentence *instead of* by a disjunctively-tensed one? Again, the tenseless sentence would seem on its own to have little straightforward 'use': surely we would be looking for connections with more basic kinds of sentence. (We would not get very far trying to connect a given utterance with the conditions prevailing when it was made.) What sort of sentences could these be, but just those sentences whose connections with omnitemporal sentences justified the interpreter in calling the latter 'omnitemporal'?

It appears, in fact, to be quite unclear what practices, in a given society, could possibly warrant us in interpreting utterances as the utterances of genuinely tenseless indicative sentences. If we drop the idea that (undated) tenseless sentences will be truth-conditionally equivalent to disjunctively-tensed ones, on the other hand, it becomes dubious whether the thesis that there might be tenseless forms has any definite content, or whether the content it did have could be of any use to one arguing that tensed sentences may be given tenseless truth-conditions. How are we meant to understand 'tenseless', after all? It is not enough to say: 'You know what it is for an indicative sentence to have a tense – so you must know what it is for one to lack a tense'. More pertinently, if a putatively tenseless sentence is *not* taken as equivalent to a disjunctively-tensed one, what grounds have we for regarding it as capable of expressing a temporal truth (or falsehood)? An ordinary imperative is not equivalent to any tensed statement, but an ordinary imperative cannot express a temporal truth. If tenseless propositions could say anything to us about time and temporal phenomena, they would need to bear a closer relation to tensed propositions than do ordinary imperatives.

But what about dated tenseless sentences? Mightn't a creature be taught in the first instance expressions of the form 'p at t', 'p earlier than t', etc., where 'p' is untensed? One can't give tenseless truth-conditions for tensed statements of the sort considered above with dated sentences; but instead one might try the sorts of truth-conditions exemplified by (2"):

> (2")   For all t, were someone to utter 'It was raining' at t, he would speak truly at t iff 'It is raining earlier than t*' were true, where 't*'St.

(The connective 'S' is capable of connecting a singular term for a date with a synonymous date. In (2"), 'S' connects the schematic "'t*'" – belonging to a tenseless language – with the bound date-variable, 't'. This additional complication is a necessary consequence of our keeping the right-hand side metalinguistic and foregoing disquotation: we cannot have a bound date-variable occurring quoted on the right-hand side, lest we 'quantify in'. For simplicity, I have not made use of atomic date-*adverbs*, but have made do with dates and the preposition 'at'.)[11]

In (2"), it would be claimed, we only have untensed sentences as modified by (schematic) dates. If there is no problem in learning the use of dates, then there should be no more problem in learning the use of schematic dates, or of what can replace these, date-variables, than there is in learning schematic or quantified forms generally.

Take the sentence in a putatively tenseless language which we may represent as, 'It is raining at t'. Is this to be a logically structured or unstructured sentence? If structured, then we have the further question: how could the sentence be parsed? If as sentence plus adverb of date, then there will be a propositional form more basic than what we are representing as 'p at t' – namely, the simple 'p'. (A sentence must be capable of standing on its own if it is to be a sentence.) The problems facing such a 'root' sentence have already been discussed, in section 3.4. If 'p at t' is not to be parsed as sentence plus adverb of date, how could it be parsed? It is not enough to say that we can conceive of there being *some* other parsing. If our thesis that a language containing dated sentences as basic is possible is to have any substance at all, something must be said about the logical capacities of such possible sentences.

It seems that the form we have been giving as 'p at t' must be taken as somehow unstructured, like the English 'It is raining'. It might now look as if the sentences of the language are logically isolated in a way that undermines the language itself; for if each dated sentence is unstructured, any new report of rain, say, will require a totally new sentence. 'It's raining at t3' will not (apparently) be a sentence constructable from smaller linguistic units already mastered – our way of representing the sentence in fact masks this. But continuing linguistic practice cannot thus consist in constantly inventing new expressions.

However, this argument is rather too swift. Someone who learns to tell the time masters a system of sentences that are surely logically unstructured – 'It's 5 o'clock', 'It's seven-thirty', and so on. (How would one parse 'It's 5 o'clock' into *logical* – not merely grammatical – constituents?) But a part of the person's mastery consists in knowing such quasi-necessary truths as 'Seven-thirty comes between seven o'clock and eight o'clock'. There is a stock of grammatical units ('five', 'o'clock', 'it is', etc.) which are usable in constructing new sentences, though they do not correspond to logical units, nor together yield logically complex results; the systematicity, and hence capacity for new sentences, resides simply in any competent speaker's mastery of the rules expressible as quasi-necessary sentences. (See section 4.3.)

Could a creature master a system of unstructured dated sentences as we master times o'clock? The unstructuredness of 'It's 5 o'clock' connects in part with the relatively unitary nature of the criteria governing utterances of that sentence. These criteria have to do with clocks and clock-observation. What criteria would govern a sentence like the imagined tenseless 'It's raining at t'? It seems impossible to mention fewer than two sets of distinct criteria: those on the basis of which raining is reported, and those on the basis of which the time is reported. The criteria governing 'It's raining at t1' will obviously differ from those governing 'It's windy at t1' and from those governing 'It's raining at t2'; and it is hard to take these differences as relatively 'brute'. But surely whatever criteria of use correspond to the 'It's raining' part of 'It's raining at t1' will just be those criteria that actually govern our use of the English 'It's raining'. In which case, how can we do otherwise than to *translate* the 'It's raining' of the putative language as meaning what the actual 'It's raining' means? But the actual 'It's raining' is a complete sentence; so the putative 'It's raining' will be a complete sentence also. From which it follows that the imagined 'It's raining at t' (and its kin) cannot, after all, be regarded as logically unstructured.

The view that a language might contain unstructured dated sentences founders, of course, on its need to posit sentences sufficiently like actual dated sentences to be called 'dated sentences', but sufficiently unlike actual dated sentences to be called 'unstructured'. These two requirements are in tension; a similar tension beset the view, dismissed above, that there might be logically structured dated sentences not parsable as sentence plus date.

Conclusion to Part I

It is time to take stock. In the Preamble I mentioned the slogan 'Time is tenseless'; and I said that we had to establish what that slogan might mean before proceeding to the question whether it can be taken as true. Where have we come?

We began by considering McTaggart's argument, construed as throwing doubt upon the very coherence of tensed predicates (whether they be ones like 'is past', or ones like 'was yellow'). Fault was found with the argument, a fault best brought out by asking in particular what counts as 'incompatibility' in predicates.

We then proceeded to look at the idea that there are only 'tenseless facts', where the expression 'fact' carries some degree of metaphysical import – i.e. where it amounts to more than the 'fact' in 'It is a fact that it will rain'. The metaphysician's 'facts', if taken as the worldly relata figuring in some kind of correspondence theory of truth, face all the problems of such theories, and all the problems which Platonism about abstract entities has to deal with. Such problems, it seems to me, are insuperable. Added to these problems is the difficulty of further arguing, in a non-question-begging way, against the possibility of 'tensed facts'. A place was found for the notion of tensed and tenseless facts, in connection with (putatively) tensed and (putatively) tenseless belief and knowledge; but it turned out that there was at least as much ground for admitting the possibility of tensed knowledge as there was for admitting the possibility of tenseless knowledge.

The discussion then turned to the truth-conditions of tensed statements, and in particular to the questions whether tenseless truth-conditions had to, or (merely) could, be given for such statements. The exact form that such truth-conditions would have to take was pondered; and the *prima facie* possibility of giving tensed truth-conditions for tenseless locutions scouted. It seemed that to derive any conclusions of philosophical weight, some attention would have to be paid to the question: 'What would count as genuinely tenseless truth-conditions?' – and further, to the question: 'Are genuinely tenseless sentences even possible?'.

The second question seems to demand an affirmative answer when we consider the 'timeless truths' of logic and mathematics. But a discussion of these truths (if truths they be, properly speaking) suggested, firstly, that they could not be taken as *models* for the putatively tenseless sentences that would occur in any tenseless truth-conditions for contingent tensed statements; and, secondly, that in any case a view of necessary propositions as present-tensed had at least as much going for it as a view of them as tenseless.

The next focus of discussion was the notion of the 'root sentence'. Difficulties were discerned with the conception of a (possible) tenseless language as consisting of 'root sentences' qualifiable by adverbs of date – e.g. 'Jane arrives at t'. The view of 'root sentences' as genuine sentences faced a dilemma: either 'p' must be distinguished from ' "p" is true', or any date-adverb whatever could truly qualify a true root sentence. Both horns of this dilemma being unacceptable, the prospects for regarding 'root sentences' as not genuine sentences was examined, but this view, too, was found inadequate.

The 'root sentence' in a tensed language was then considered, and reasons adduced for taking it to be, not tenseless, but present-tensed. The possibility of tenseless sentences, even if only embedded within tensed locutions, seemed to be getting more and more elusive.

Finally, the alleged possibility of tenseless sentences was attacked by invoking quite general considerations to do with meaning and language mastery. If no possible creature could develop a temporal language in which tenseless sentences were basic – i.e. were not conceptually parasitic upon tensed ones – then this threw grave doubt upon whether one could ever say that *genuinely* tenseless truth-conditions for tensed sentences could, in principle, be given. It would seem, after all, that *genuinely* tenseless truth-conditions could not consist of sentences graspable only *via* tensed locutions. At any rate, if tensed sentences must, as argued, be conceptually prior to tenseless ones (an allowed 'modest' species thereof), the observation that tenseless truth-conditions are in principle available for tensed sentences will, though true, be unable to motivate any grander claims about the 'tenselessness of time'.

Part II
How Long Things Last and When They Happen

4
Dates and Units

4.1 THE A-SERIES AND THE B-SERIES

In Part I, the phenomenon of tense was examined, in the context of a particular philosophical debate: the debate over whether time is 'tenseless' or 'tensed', and if either, in what sense 'tenseless' or 'tensed'. In this part, I shall examine two other aspects of temporal discourse, embodied in duration-terms and dates, respectively. In the next chapter, we shall encounter a well-known debate, concerning the notion of durationless instants, but this chapter will have a less dialectical form, and will have to do in the main with the semantics of dates and units.

'1 January 1992' is an example of a date; 'a year' is an example of a unit of temporal measurement. (It should be noted that I will frequently use both 'date' and 'unit' as terms for *expressions*, simply to avoid the ungainliness of 'date-term' and 'unit-term'.) For our purposes, it will be convenient to classify complex expressions like 'two years and fifteen days' as temporal units as well as simple ones like 'a year'; in general, answers to questions beginning 'How long . . . ?' may be regarded as employing temporal units. And answers to questions beginning 'When . . . ?' will employ dates. We need, in the case of dates, to distinguish two sorts of use, corresponding to two sorts of question, or two possible interpretations of the same question: 'When is the Queen's birthday?' may be a question about the Queen's forthcoming birthday, or it may be a question 'about' all and any of the Queen's birthdays (i.e. her first, second . . . twentieth . . . fifty-third . . .). On the whole, I will use 'date' to cover both sorts of case.

We cannot say, with the help alone of dates and units, what can be said using the expressions 'earlier' and 'later' – nor what can be said using the expressions 'before' and 'after'. Such a reductive translation would only be possible if the dates of a system carried with them the information as to which came before which, so that 'p on 12 May 1991, and q on 19 May 1991' entailed 'p before q'. Even then, a reduction of the simple 'p before q' would require that date-*variables* also carry such information with them, so that 'For some t1, for some t2, p at t1 and q at t2' would entail (and be entailed by) 'p before q'. As we shall see later on (pp. 103–5), the thesis that the dates of a system can be said to carry with them the information as to which come before which is at least a problematical one. And the only way in which date-variables could do so would be by means of some convention (e.g. subscripted numerals) that in effect provided abbreviations of '. . . where t1 was before t2' and the like – a convention that would render a proper *reduction* of 'p before q' impossible.

Nevertheless, the expressions 'earlier', 'later', 'before' and 'after' are in a certain sense redundant, since with *tense operators* we can say whatever can be said using 'earlier', 'later', etc. 'Earlier than' and 'later than' are themselves replaceable by the sentential connectives 'before' and 'after'. For 'p before q', where both 'p' and 'q' are tensed, various possibilities present themselves, the simplest being those in which 'p' and 'q' share the past tense, or share the future tense. 'P' means 'It was the case that'; 'Pp before Pq' can then be rendered: 'P (Pp & ¬p, and q)'. If 'p' and 'q' are 'tenseless' – and the 'harmless' sense in which they might be has been spelt out in Part I – then disjunctive tenses come to our aid: 'p before q' will amount to, 'It either is or has been or will be the case that (Pp & ¬p, and q)'.[1]

Alternatively, we can introduce temporal units and variables for these; and render 'Pp before Pq' as, 'For some n, for some m, such that n is greater than m, Pnp and Pmq', where an expression of the form 'Pnp' amounts to, 'It was the case n units ago that p', a certain unit-system being given. Again, the 'tenseless' 'p before q' comes out as: 'For some n, for some m, such that n is smaller than m, it either is or will be or has been the case that (Pnp and Pmq)'.

A metric tense logic (one involving temporal units) is obviously needed if we are to give formal translations of things like, 'p was earlier than q by a greater amount than was q earlier than r'. The possibilities for complexity are indeed manifold; for a fuller examination of these possibilities, the reader should turn to the work of Prior and other tense logicians.

There remain dates, themselves irreplaceable by such means, as will be argued in the next section. This leaves us with three types of temporal expression which together seem to give us the tools for saying whatever can be said of a temporal nature: tense operators, units and dates (plus bound variables for such). It would not be too inaccurate to say that in Part I we discussed aspects of McTaggart's A-series. And there is a sense in which Part II will have to do with McTaggart's B-series. The B-series is usually taken to consist of the events of history (or more precisely, the 'positions' they occupy), as they are ordered by the 'earlier than' relation – or, if you prefer, by its converse, the 'later than' relation. The 'positions' of the events of history are what dates record; and the topological and metrical relations between the items in McTaggart's B-series are expressible with the help of tenses and temporal units, with or without benefit of 'earlier than'.

I am not claiming any 'conceptual priority' of dates and units over 'before' and 'after', in the sense, for example, in which tensed forms were claimed in Part I to have conceptual priority over tenseless ones (which to that extent could not count as 'genuinely' tenseless). I am simply pointing out that sentences containing 'before' and 'after' could be replaced by ones containing temporal units, or bound variables for temporal units, in the way that was sketched above – and that this 'replacement' would at any rate not be a step in the direction of conceptually *posterior* forms: the employment of temporal units is not parasitic upon that of 'before' and 'after'. I thus speak merely of 'replacement', rather than of reductive translation.

4.2   THE SEMANTICS OF DATES AND TEMPORAL UNITS

Units of measurement in general typically get into the language in one of two ways. Either their sense is fixed in terms of previously understood units – as, a centimetre gets defined as one hundredth of a metre – or their sense is fixed by appeal to some empirical object or phenomenon. From this it follows that the *basis* of a system of measurement will in general have been established in this 'empirical' way, since the units in terms of which other units get defined cannot always themselves have been defined in terms of further units: at some point, units will get defined in terms of units that have been introduced *via* the empirical route. Now, an important species of 'definition by appeal to some object or phenomenon' is the kind of definition termed 'reference-fixing' by Saul Kripke.[2] And many units of measurement get introduced by means of 'reference-fixing'.

A foot was initially taken to be the length of a man's foot, a metre to be the length of the metre rod in Paris, and so on. (We need not for the moment be distracted by the difference between fixing a unit by appeal to a particular object or occurrence and fixing a unit by appeal to a type of object or occurrence.) One might consequently think that metrical statements generally could, at least in principle, be paraphrased, so as to replace unit-terms by talk of whatever it was that had 'fixed the reference': 'He was two metres high' might be paraphrased as 'He was twice as high as the metre rod'. But one will reject this as a *general* thesis as soon as one reflects, for instance, that whether men's feet are or were ever on average one foot in length is simply irrelevant to the truth-conditions, let alone the meaning, of measurements in feet. Kripke's discussion of the metre makes just these points.

It might be said that the irrelevance to measurements in feet of the length of men's feet is simply owing to standardisation. At some point, the rough-and-ready unit of a foot was made precise, presumably by appeal to some new standard. But the same arguments as were applied to men's feet apply equally well to any such new standard. The length of that standard is irrelevant, both to the meaning *and* to the truth-conditions of measurements in feet: all that is necessary for such measurements is that *the same length* be meant by 'one foot' whenever that term is used.

What about temporal units?

One can divide temporal units into three categories, exemplified by 'second', 'year', and 'day'. What has just been said about 'foot' applies also to units like 'second' and 'year': these are, in Kripke's terminology, rigid expressions. 'Day', on the other hand, seems to be non-rigid. But there exists a further distinction among temporal units which has to do with how closely associated with its 'reference-fixer' a given unit is. This distinction, as we shall see, is neither the same as, nor co-extensive with, that which holds between rigid and non-rigid expressions, in Kripke's sense. And according to *this* distinction, 'day', along with 'year' it seems to me, belongs on a different side of the fence from 'second'. I shall dub units like 'second' *pure*, and units like 'year' and 'day' *impure*.

Before proceeding, I should say that a distinction like that between pure and impure expressions, or between rigid and non-rigid expressions, is not to be taken as a hard and fast one. In some contexts, an expression may seem to function as a rigid one, while in others it functions as a non-rigid one. And when it comes to purity and impurity, there is often some indeterminacy about whether some change in the world, or in linguistic practice, would go with a 'change in meaning': what counts as meaning-change is not wholly definite. This does not render the distinction a futile one; the distinction between day and night is far from futile, despite the impossibility of 'drawing a line' between the two. Perhaps there is a 'sliding scale' from purity to impurity; I present the argument in terms of a dichotomy mainly to avoid unnecessary complexities.

Let us begin with purity and impurity. In the case of pure units, our system of units is used above all for the accurate measurement of time: the relation between such units and the processes that 'fix their reference' is in general nothing over and above the relation expressed by 'fixes the reference of'. In the case of impure units, the utility of our system is founded upon some contingent fact (about ourselves, most likely), having to do with a certain natural cycle. The most obvious example of the second sort of case is the system of *days*. Since our biological clocks are synchronised with the rising and setting of the sun, the day is too important in our lives for us to cease to be guided by it, even were the lengths of days (as measured by atomic clocks, say) to change from being twenty-four hours long to being twenty-seven hours long. Hence the truth-conditions of statements involving 'day' are dependent upon facts to do with the revolution of the earth upon its axis, relative to the sun. Were the time taken for the earth to revolve on its axis to change, the length of time signified by the term 'day' would also change, *though the sense of 'day' would remain the same.*

The case of 'year' is, I think, rather more complex. It may be that the earth's revolution around the sun is to the year as the earth's revolution on its axis is to the day; or it may be that we would not, at this stage in the history of the concept, break from the equation (or rough equation): 1 year = 365 days. In the latter case, 'year' would still count as impure, since alterations in the length of time taken for the earth to spin on its axis would affect the lengths of (what we called) years. The 'reference' of 'year' would be altered without 'year' changing its meaning.

For purposes of *measuring* time accurately, e.g. for scientific purposes, we would turn to the atomic clock in preference to the rising and setting of the sun. And it is with respect to temporal units such as those occurring in the measurements made by atomic and other clocks that we can say that the 'reference-fixer', whatever it was or is, is irrelevant to the truth-conditions of measurements involving those units. 'Second' and 'minute' are examples of such pure units. If the natural process used to determine the length of a second were to change, we would then say, correctly, that the process no longer took one second. The constancy of meaning of 'second' goes with a constancy of 'reference', if you like (though 'signifying the same duration' is not a matter of *referring* to the same thing). The reasons for all this have to do with the nature of measuring, and will receive further attention in the next chapter.

'Year', as I said above, seems to me to be like 'day' in regard to how closely its use is connected with a particular natural cycle (either the earth's revolution round the sun, or its revolution on its axis). But both 'year' and 'second' are *rigid* expressions, as is manifest in how they both behave in such modal contexts as: 'Were process P to change in duration, it would no longer take such-and-such length of time'. How can this be true of 'year', if the connection between 'year' and a certain natural cycle is as intimate as I have said it is?

Let us assume that the word 'year' stands to the earth's revolution around the sun as the word 'day' stands to its revolution on its axis. Were the time taken for the earth to go round the sun to diminish, then the earth would take less time than a year to go round the sun; and this despite the fact that the word 'year' would both maintain its sense (arguably) *and* still signify the (now shorter) time taken for the earth to go round the sun. 'The earth would take less than a year to go round' is not equivalent to, 'The earth would take less time than would be signified by "one year" to go round'; it is equivalent rather to, 'The earth would take less time than *is* signified by "one year" to go round'. To put it in terms of possible worlds, the sentence 'The earth takes a year to go round the sun' is true *in* (or 'at') every possible world, but is not true *of* every possible world, since 'year' signifies the same duration in (statements about) every possible world, whereas 'the time taken for the earth to go round the sun' does not. Perhaps a clearer case is this: in talking of what happened millions of years ago, we are not committed to anything about millions of revolutions, by the earth around the sun. These sorts of fact lend support to the claim that 'year' is, or often is, a rigid expression. That 'second' is rigid is even clearer. ('Process P takes one second' is neither true *of* nor *in* every possible world.)

'Day', on the other hand, is surely non-rigid. It does not appear to be true that, were the time taken for the earth to revolve on its

axis to diminish (or were the time taken for the sun to come back
to a given position in the sky to diminish – or whatever), then the
earth would in that case take less than a day to revolve on its axis
(or whatever). It seems to be something of a necessary truth that the
earth takes a day to revolve on its axis, or that the sun takes a day
to reappear in the same (or next closest) position in the sky. ('A
million days ago, so and so' does seem to imply something about
a million risings and settings of the sun.)

What about dates? 'Specific dates', such as '1 January 1992', are
rigid expressions; 'general dates', such as 'January', are not. Further
distinctions can be made. A system of dates depends upon some
particular system of temporal units. For example, the system of
dates BC and AD uses the unit of the year. It follows immediately
that there will be three kinds of systems of dates: systems based on
rigid, pure units like that of the second, systems based on rigid,
impure units like that of the year, and systems based on non-rigid,
impure units like that of the day. (There aren't any pure, non-rigid
units.) But a difference more directly analogous to that which exists between 'year' and 'day' on the one hand, and 'second' on the
other, also exists between dates themselves. With all actual dates,
however, though not with all actual and possible dates, this difference *is* co-extensive with the difference between rigid and non-rigid
expressions. This contrasts with actual temporal units.

Let us take 'specific' dates first. Even if a system of dates is
introduced in the first place by appeal to a particular historical
occurrence, neither the meaning nor the truth-conditions of statements employing dates from that system is typically determined by
facts about that occurrence. There are Biblical scholars who maintain that Christ's birth took place a few years BC. These scholars do
not contradict themselves; the system of dates framed with the suf-
fix 'BC' and the prefix 'AD' stays in place regardless of when, or
whether, Christ was born, simply because the system is so constituted that we end up meaning the *same time* whenever we use, for
example 'AD 2000'. It seems that dates BC and AD, and indeed
'specific' dates generally, are typically rigid, in this sense.

Are dates BC and AD like 'day' and 'year' or like 'second'? Are
they 'impure' or 'pure'? In fact, the distinction between pure and
impure units has not got a *precise* analogue for specific dates. Were
the time taken for the earth to revolve on its axis to diminish, 'day'
would come to signify a shorter period than it does now; but we
cannot say, 'Were the date of Christ's birth to change, then "AD 10"

would come to signify a different time'. The date of Christ's birth cannot change. However, we *can* say, 'Were it to turn out that Christ was born earlier than we had thought, then etc.'. After all, in the case of the hypothetical concerning 'day', we must mean, 'Were we to *notice* that the earth took less long to revolve on its axis, then . . .'; the issue is to this extent an epistemological one. And were Christ's birth to turn out to be twenty years earlier than originally thought, nevertheless 'AD 10' would signify the same time as it does now and has for centuries. Dates BC and AD are pure, *in this sense.*

Were a certain historical event to be sufficiently important to us, we could have a system of dates whose function was simply to date events in relation to that historical event. In the case of its being discovered that the 'absolute' date of the historical event had been miscalculated, all datings of events other than the historical event itself (and events whose dates could only be calculated by reference to the historical event) would require alteration in such a system. And it is no doubt this *sort* of fact which accounts for there being no such system of dates. (Perhaps scientists will one day know enough to use the Big Bang as the crux in a system of dates, a system which might 'compete' with pure systems such as the BC–AD system, in the sense that a revision of the 'absolute' date of the Big Bang – how long ago it had taken place – would require alteration of all other datings in the system.)

The dates in a system of the sort just sketched would be impure, but could nevertheless be rigid (cf. 'year'). It would be impure because of the fact that a change in (knowledge of) the time of the 'reference-fixing event' would go with a change in the 'references' of the dates of the system, i.e. a systematic change in the truth-values of propositions containing those dates. It could be rigid because it could be true to say, using such a system, things like: 'Had the Big Bang occurred a year earlier, then it would have occurred in minus one BB'.

The question remains, concerning dates BC and AD, whether the *unit* on which the system is based is itself pure or impure. Are future and possible measurements in years independent of the duration of any natural process? I indicated above that I thought *not.* If I am wrong in this, then 'year' is a pure temporal unit, like 'second', and the system of dates BC and AD will inherit some of this 'purity'; but if I am right, then the dates of that system may come at irregular intervals. In the latter case, whereas Christ's birth would serve *merely* to 'fix the reference' of the dates of the system, the period of the earth's revolution around the sun, or of its revolution upon its axis, would remain at all times relevant to the truth-conditions of dated statements.

Turning now to 'general' dates, such as 'January', it seems again that the underlying temporal *unit* may be 'pure' or 'impure'. Take the names of the months. Let us assume that 'January', 'February', etc., were in the first place introduced by reference to the cycle of seasons (though the history of the names of the months is in fact not like that) – January and February, for instance, being taken to be months that occur during winter in the Northern Hemisphere. Could we then say that the meaning and truth-conditions of statements involving month-names were bound up with the occurrence of those seasons? In fact, I suspect not. If a dislocation or alteration in the regularity of the cycle of seasons were to come about, would we not persist in our calculation of the months in terms of numbers of *days*? For the unit of the day is of more importance to us than that of the season (especially in post-agricultural societies). But it is as the underlying *unit* that the day enters in here; the claims of the *unit* turn out to be stronger, as it were, than those of the event-types (the four seasons) which we are imagining merely helped 'fix the reference' of the names of the months.

Of course, as imagined above, the lengths of days (measured by atomic clocks, say) might change over time. In which case, the lengths of the months would also. However, if the length of the year did not alter in sync., then complications would arise: stipulative changes to the number of days in some or all of the months would probably be needed.

There are general dates which do seem to be more closely connected to certain event-types. 'Midsummer's Day' is an example: it seems inconceivable that Midsummer's Day should ever come round in the middle of winter. This must largely be owing to the fact that 'Midsummer's Day' is not part of such a *system* of dates and dating as, for example, the names of the months. There is some sort of system, to be sure: Midsummer's Day 1989, Midsummer's Day 1990, Midsummer's Day 1991, and so on. But the reliance is much more upon seasonal facts than upon the year, considered as a unit of measurement (even an 'impure' one). This raises certain mind-boggling questions, as: 'Might it be that in the seasonally dislocated post-nuclear world of AD 2070, Midsummer's Day will come round twice in the year?' . . . The answer is, probably: 'Say what you like'.

Returning to the question of rigidity, it seems that general dates must be classed as non-rigid. The rigidity of 'year' was exemplified by the statement: 'Were the time taken for the earth to go round the sun to diminish, then the earth would take less time than a year to go round the sun'. Just as 'year' (it was here being supposed) has its 'reference' fixed by the revolution of the earth round the sun, a general date, D, would have its 'reference' fixed by some event-type, E. Let's say that E is some season, like summer. D might be 'Midsummer's Day'. Could we ever truly say, 'Were the cycle of seasons to alter, then D would take place at a different time from the time when it does in fact take place'?

Surely not. If sense can be attached at all to the expression 'different time' as it occurs in this last sentence, then that sense will have to be more or less stipulative. Some cycle originally synchronised with that in which E occurs could be taken as 'fixed', so that the later lack of E's synchronisation with some event in that cycle might be taken as constituting E's no longer coming round at the same time. But relative to another cycle, that in which E occurs might remain fixed, if both cycles alter in the same way. One could pick on a cycle which did not undergo change; but to appeal to such a cycle would just be a way of saying that E now come round at shorter or longer intervals than of yore. And though this would be perfectly true, it doesn't seem that it would on its own justify talk of a 'different time'. Would we really say that Midsummer's Day came round at a different time from the time it used to just because the summers became longer?

In conclusion, then, general dates appear to be non-rigid expressions, unlike specific ones. There is indeed some case for regarding general dates as, logically speaking, fragments of specific ones, or of phrases involving quantification 'over' specific ones; in which case, their non-rigidity would be unsurprising. ('Every summer it rains' would, on such a view, amount roughly to: 'For all n, it did or will rain in summer, AD n' – allowing n to be a negative number.) I have not space to go into this last question here.

But it is time to take a rather closer look at the two notions of which I have been making free use: those of purity and rigidity.

4.3 PURITY

The following remarks are meant to apply to both dates and units; for ease of exposition I will talk only of units. To convert the argument into one about pure and impure dates, just substitute 'historical event' for '(type of) process'.

The mark of a temporal unit's being pure, remember, is that there is no cyclic process such that an alteration in how long that process takes affects the 'reference' of the unit: were the process to take longer, this would not affect the durations (in terms of those units) ascribed by us to *other* processes. What is at stake here is how the unit would be used by us in a hypothetical situation, compatibly with its remaining constant in meaning; and it is part of the term's being pure that were we *not* to use, for example 'second', in the manner 'required' of us – i.e. independently of the duration of any process – then we should be using 'second' in a new way, with a new meaning. But how is this? How can it be a part of the present meaning of 'second' that some hypothetical continuation of its use would count as a shift in meaning? After all, that truth-values have to be systematically reassigned – as they would were we to link 'second' to some changing cyclic process – is not in itself sufficient for meaning-change: the existence of *impure* units shows this. If we linked 'second' to some process, wouldn't that just show that 'second' had been an impure unit all along? (Its link to the process in question only becoming an issue when the process's duration alters.)

Of course, the case of 'second' is not the most convincing one possible. For it is arguable that any process put forward as determining the 'reference' of 'second' would be put forward stipulatively. 'Year', on the other hand, is different. It would obviously not be a mere stipulation to link the duration of a year to that of the earth's revolution around the sun; but if 'year' is pure – or at any rate pure 'relative to' the earth's revolution around the sun – an alteration in the time taken for the earth to go round the sun would only affect the 'reference' of 'year' on the condition that 'year' had undergone meaning-change. For it might be that 'year' is *impure* relative to the time taken for the earth to spin on its axis, so that were we to continue to take a year as consisting of 365 days, 'year' would *not* have undergone meaning-change.

But why not just say that 'year' was, after all, impure relative to the earth's revolution around the sun, in the case of our altering our usage because of a change in the length of that cycle? It seems lame to assert that we all now intend the word's use to be independent of that process; it is probable that most of us have no such conscious intention. An appeal at this point to our unconscious intention, or to our sheer disposition to use it in a certain way in the case of the earth's taking a different time to go round the sun, immediately lands us with the rule-following considerations. Sheer dispositions aren't normative; meanings are.[3]

The question what, in general, counts as meaning-change is a very knotty one. It is not enough that there should occur a change in truth-value assignments, or a change in what counts as a definition or synonym. We also clearly make use of the notion of a concept's being 'extended' to new cases, or 'retracted' from old ones. 'Game' is regularly extended to new cases; 'fish' has been retracted from a few (whales, dolphins . . .) – neither has undergone *meaning-change*, at least in the sense in which 'toilet' has.

Assume that 'year' is indeed pure, relative to the earth's revolution around the sun. What does this amount to? If the earth came to take a lot longer to go round the sun, and we *did* alter our use of 'year' accordingly, what then? The question, it seems to me, is: how would we assess what we had done? Would we take ourselves to have merely continued with 'year' as before – or would we think that a departure had been made from previous usage?

'We' of course means: the people then speaking English. And it may be that none of those people now exists, if we take these possible natural and linguistic changes to take place two hundred years hence. It is arguable, in fact, that the future hypothetical at issue is not properly assessible for truth. So what is being said?

The future hypothetical is meant as a guide. The crux of the matter is what, in certain cases, counts as a *criterion* of meaning-change. In certain cases, that (enough) people take it that there has been a shift in meaning is itself a criterial ground for there having been a shift in meaning. This view of the matter is similar to Wittgenstein's view of what a person means by his words: the *criterion* is often what the person later says he meant. In a discussion of meaning an ambiguous word in one of the two possible ways, Wittgenstein writes:

> If asked, I shall perhaps explain this meaning, without this explanation's having come before my mind earlier. So what had my state of mind, as I spoke the words with the double meaning, to do with the words of the explanation? How far can these words correspond to it? Here there is obviously no such thing as the explanation's fitting the phenomenon.
>
> (*Remarks on the Philosophy of Psychology*, Vol. I, § 672, trans. G. E. M. Anscombe, Blackwell, 1980)

The explanation does not 'fit' the phenomenon, in the way in which the explanation of a heart attack fits the heart attack (cf. the notion of 'direction of fit'); rather, what phenomenon it was (e.g. my meaning 'river bank' when I said 'bank') is, at least in part, determined by what explanation is given of what happened ('I meant "river bank"'; 'I was talking about a river'; etc.).

Later on:

> The peculiar experience of meaning is characteristic because we react with an explanation and use the past tense: just as if we were explaining the meaning of a word for practical purposes.
>
> (Ibid., § 688)

Of course, a person may not get the chance to assess what he earlier meant; and people may not in fact consider whether their use of 'year' is a new one, in the future hypothetical case. Indeed, those last-mentioned people might never exist (a significant change in the earth's revolution round the sun might never take place in the course of human history). But a certain criterial 'test' may be all that gives sense to questions about what someone means, or about whether meaning-change occurs or would occur, despite the fact that in many cases that test is inapplicable, unusable. This in itself (it seems to me) is not enough to deprive statements about those cases of a truth-value; 'So-and-so would constitute a change in the meaning of "year"' is true or false, as is 'Caesar meant such-and-such by those words'.

These comments will on their own sound somewhat dogmatic; but the rationale for them, and for a 'criterial' approach generally, is something that will be discussed at much greater length in Part III. The notion of a criterion outlined in Chapter 6 is what is involved in the claim that a community's assessment of whether there has been (*has* been) a change in a word's meaning is the criterion governing the concept 'change in meaning', at least in many cases. And it is the notion to which I am implicitly appealing when I say that 'second' is a pure unit, while 'day' and 'year' are not.

4.4 RIGIDITY

In his *Naming and Necessity*, Saul Kripke introduced the notion of a 'rigid designator'.[4] The notion was defined so as to apply only to terms capable of referring: a term was a rigid designator if it picked out (i.e. referred to) the same thing in every possible world. Indeed, the use of the expression 'designator' showed this. But a wider notion of rigidity, applicable to non-referring terms, seems useful. For example, if one is wary of attributing reference to general terms (common nouns), one may well want to hold that such a wide notion is needed to apply to natural kind terms, for pretty much the sorts of reason that led Kripke to apply his (strictly inapplicable) notion of rigid designation to such terms.

But what, it might be asked, is rigidity, if not rigid designation? To tackle this question, let us look at two typical considerations in favour of regarding a given singular term as a rigid designator.

The first is that one cannot give the sense of the term by means of some paraphrase, such as a definite description. 'Saul Kripke' cannot be understood as in any way short for, or doing the job of, a description along the lines of 'The man who is/did such-and-such'. A description may be used to 'fix the reference' (cf. section 4.2) of a designator, but it cannot do the job of the designator. This is shown by the possibility of using any description that happens to pick out the item in question to fix the designator's reference: no particular description is special.

A proponent of the 'cluster' theory of names, according to which there is associated with a name a cluster of definite descriptions, no one of which is essential, can also deny the paraphrasability of names. But arguments in favour of rigid designation will involve rejection of such 'cluster' theories; and this brings us to the second consideration in favour of a term's rigidly designating, which has to do with certain sorts of modal facts. The argument can be directed both at simple description theories and at cluster theories. If 'Saul Kripke' were somehow short for 'The man who wrote *Naming and Necessity*', then there would appear to be a reading of 'Saul Kripke might not have written *Naming and Necessity*' according to which it is necessarily false; whereas (it is argued) there is only one available reading of the sentence, and that is one according to which it is true. If, on the other hand, 'Saul Kripke' were associated, not with a single description, but with a cluster of such, then we could not substitute a large number (or all) of those descriptions for 'the F' in the sentence, 'Saul Kripke might not have been the F', always getting true sentences; whereas (it is argued) sentences of the form, 'Saul Kripke might not have been the F' are generally true.

Considerations analogous to the above are easily shown to apply to a term like 'gold', without making any use of the idea of reference.

Indeed, there is more than one line concerning the logico-syntactic category of 'gold' that one can take, compatibly with adducing such considerations. Thus, one might hold that the basic expression is the one-place predicate '__ is gold' (applicable to things of gold); or one might hold that it is the (perhaps 'ideal') nought-place predicate, or feature-placing sentence, 'There's gold', or 'It is gold' (cf. 'It is raining'). In the first case, one can argue for rigidity (a) by denying that the sense of '__ is gold' can be given by any complex predicate, such as '__ is metallic, malleable, yellowish'; (b) appeal to such modal facts as that if something is metallic, malleable, and yellowish (or whatever), then nevertheless it need not be gold (or *vice versa*) – and that this applies whether we have in mind a single description or a cluster of such. In the second case, one can argue for rigidity (a) by denying that the sense of the feature-placing sentence 'It is gold' could be given by any complex such sentence, such as 'It is metallish, malleable, yellowy'; (b) by appeal to such modal facts as that if it is metallish, malleable and yellowy somewhere, then nevertheless it need not be gold there (or *vice versa*) – and that this applies whether we have in mind a single complex sentence or a cluster of such.

The issue is complicated by the possibility of adopting essentialism, in which case – to speak for brevity in terms of descriptions – there will be *some* description of gold which cannot fail to be true of gold: namely, the description of it as having whatever essential property gold in fact has. This complication need not detain us here.

With natural kind terms, then, a case can be made for rigidity without invoking reference. If we take some predicate as the basic expression, then we effectively substitute the notion of *being true of* for that of *referring to* in our arguments; while if we take some feature-placing sentence as the basic expression, then we similarly substitute *being true (somewhere)* for *referring to*.

One might think that the notion of rigidity applied to many kinds of expression. But one should not get carried away. Take as an example Prior's celebrated argument from the (putative) logical operator 'tonk'.[5] This operator is introduced by certain introduction and elimination rules, the consequence of which is that simply using the operator will lead to contradiction. It is tempting to construe this argument as tending to show that *bona fide* operations such as conjunction and negation have something rather like rigidity: these operations cannot be captured by giving their truth-tables or their introduction and elimination rules, even if (in fact) the tables and rules that we give for, say, conjunction do apply to '&' and only to '&'. We might think it appropriate to say that the truth-tables merely 'fix the reference' of the logical operators. But perhaps all that Prior's argument from 'tonk' shows – if it is successful – is that the logical operators are *simple*, in the sense of being indefinable, or unsusceptible of elucidation in terms of conceptually prior notions.

The two steps in an argument for rigidity that I mentioned above would do little on their own to establish that an expression, or type of expression, was anything more than simple in this sense. Consider the predicate 'red'. It is surely true that the sense of 'red' cannot be given by means of a complex predicate, and that if something satisfied a given such complex predicate, then it need not in that case be red (or *vice versa*). But all that this shows is that 'red' is in some sense a *simple* predicate, not that it is a *rigid* predicate.

A phrase often employed when arguing for a designator's being rigid is 'the *same* ... in every possible world (in which it exists)'. 'Saul Kripke' is said to pick out the *same man* in every possible world in which it picks out anything – unlike 'The man who wrote *Naming and Necessity*' (in at least one construal of that term). With 'gold', it can be said: 'The term picks out/applies to the *same stuff* in every possible world'. It might be asked: Why cannot one say that 'The man who wrote *Naming and Necessity*' picks out the same man in every possible world in which it picks out anything – namely, the man who wrote *Naming and Necessity* (where this description is intended to have 'narrow scope')?

Part of the reason is that if an expression like 'the man who wrote *Naming and Necessity*' occurs in a 'namely'-rider, then it will call out for a *further* 'namely'-rider. The terminus of any such series of 'namely'-riders must be a name (or perhaps demonstrative): 'Who introduced the notion of rigidity?' – 'The man who wrote *Naming and Necessity*; namely, Saul Kripke'. This is because a definite description is a different sort of expression, logico-syntactically, from a name, in essentially the way that Russell noted in his Theory of Descriptions. And we need to grasp this logico-syntactic difference before we can properly understand the notion of rigid designation. Correlatively, we need to grasp the analogous logical differences at the levels of predicate, adverb, etc., before we can properly understand the notion of rigidity as applied to predicates, adverbs, etc.

But there is more to the distinction between rigidity and nonrigidity than this last-mentioned logico-syntactic one. We have said that a rigid expression picks out/signifies the same φ in every possible world, for some φ. And phrases of the form 'the same such-and-such' suggest criteria of identity. A name like 'Saul Kripke' is associated with its own criterion of identity: that for human beings generally. A description such as 'The person who owns the best-thumbed copy of *Varieties of Reference*' is not in this way associated with any criterion of identity. Where this description switches from being true of John to being true of Elizabeth, we do not say that Elizabeth is the same φ as John, for any φ. (Nor, *pace* Geach, could we introduce a name 'on the back' of such a description, relative to whose governing sortal the name-sharing Elizabeth and John were the same φ.) The term 'person' involved in the description indicates the only criterion of identity that is in the offing; but it is the criterion that is associated with the name(s) or demonstratives which could serve as true 'namely'-riders to the description, rather than a criterion associated with the description itself.

The criterion of identity for 'gold' is expressed by 'same stuff', and has to do, if Kripke is right, with the possession of empirically discoverable essential properties. The criterion of identity for 'metre' is expressed by 'same length', and has to do with measurement with 'true' standards. The criteria of identity for both 'second' and 'year' are expressed by 'same duration', but they amount to something rather different for the two terms, on account of that difference between those terms to which I alluded in the last section. The criterion of identity for 'second', and for 'pure' temporal units like it, has to do with measurement with 'true clocks', and will be the focus of our discussion in the next chapter. The criterion of identity for 'AD 1' is expressed by 'same time'; it likewise will receive attention in the next chapter.

The criterion of identity for 'red', 'blue', and so on, is expressed by 'same colour', and has to do (I think) with indistinguishability by normal observers. Is 'red' a rigid expression? Well, it does seem that it picks out the same colour in every possible world. As with 'year', above, it is true that were the eyes of humans to evolve so that they could no longer distinguish such-and-such wavelengths of light, people would correctly apply the word 'red' to shades which weren't red (i.e. to shades which wouldn't be the shades to which 'red' in fact applies). If you like, you can account for this in part by insisting that the criterion of identity make mention of *actual* normal observers. Whatever you say about the formulation of the criterion of identity for colours, it seems, for all that has been said, that 'red' will be as rigid an expression as 'Saul Kripke', 'gold', 'year' and 'AD 1'. And given the plethora of possible criteria of identity, there seems nothing to stop us going on to say that, for instance, 'cricket' is rigid, so long as we have some criterion of identity for games, expressible, for instance, by '__ shares most of its rules with __ '. If ever creatures were to play a two-sided game with bat and ball, wicket, innings, etc., then they would be playing cricket. (Vague criteria of identity involving 'most' may offend – but they should not, given that perfectly good criteria of identity will often have to be vague or indeterminate for some cases. Consider 'same person' and the 'split-brain' thought-experiments.)

But surely there is *some* important difference between 'gold', 'year', *et al.* and terms like 'red' and 'cricket'? If it is not the difference between rigidity and non-rigidity, or between syntactic simplicity and syntactic complexity, what sort of difference is it?

Kripke famously connects his views on the rigidity of names with a causal theory of reference for names. A causal theory of names says, roughly, that a person's use of a name is correct, and manages to pick out the name's referent, in virtue of the fact that the use itself is causally connected with a chain of such uses going back in time to an original dubbing of the referent (e.g. a baptism). Hence to use a name correctly one need *not* have any particular description of the referent in mind, or cluster of descriptions, even if one does in fact 'fix the reference' of the name by means of some description or descriptions.

Similarly, it might be argued, a person's use of a specific date, for instance 'AD 3', is correct, and succeeds in meaning what it does, in virtue of the fact that the use itself is causally connected with a chain of such uses going back in time to an original fixing of the sense of the date, or more likely of a date or dates within the system in which the date plays its part (e.g. the system of dates AD and BC). To use a date correctly one need not have a particular description in mind, such as 'the year beginning two years after Christ's birth', even if one does in fact 'fix the reference' of the date by means of some such description.

A causal theory of the Kripkean stamp plays at least this role: it helps to explain *how* an expression of a certain type can manage to mean what it does mean, given that the expression is logically simple, and hence not equivalent to any (logically complex) description or description-like expression. One is tempted to think that 'Socrates' must have some equivalent, such as 'the teacher of Plato', or must correspond to a cluster of such descriptions, because this hypothesis *seems* to be needed in order to explain *how* the name 'Socrates' manages to refer to Socrates. The causal theory of reference presents a believable alternative hypothesis, while simultaneously doing justice to the syntactic simplicity of names.

Similar remarks apply to natural kind terms, such as 'gold', and to dates and temporal units. One is tempted to think that such terms *must* have some sort of descriptive equivalents if they are to be used successfully; which view, however, is belied by the syntactic simplicity of the terms.

4.5 SYNTACTIC SIMPLICITY

But are (any) dates and temporal units syntactically simple in the way I have been alleging? 'AD 3' appears to be syntactically complex, being built up out of '3' and 'AD'; and (it may be argued) this appearance is surely not misleading when one considers that 'AD 4 came after AD 3' looks to be a necessary truth, or very close to one. Likewise, the necessary, or near-necessary, status of 'A minute contains sixty seconds' may suggest a certain complexity of deep, if not surface, structure. Such facts as these link up with certain modal facts which seem to undermine the possibility of modal arguments for rigidity along the lines mentioned earlier (pp. 98–9). For instance, if 'one minute' were a rigid expression, wouldn't if be impossible to argue: 'If anything were to last sixty seconds, then it would last a minute'? – whereas, in fact, such a conditional is necessarily true.

There are two possible answers to this objection. The first, placatory, answer is this: it may be admitted that many if not most units, and many if not most dates, get introduced by means of definitional equivalences involving pre-existing units or dates. But not *all* units and dates may be thus introduced; some must be introduced 'empirically', and *these* expressions will be syntactically simple when they are thus introduced, even if they have the surface complexity of other expressions in the system. For example, we may 'start off' with 'AD 1' and define subsequent years in terms of it; or 'start off' with 'one minute' and define other temporal units in terms of it. And if our initial expressions are (not only simple but) rigid, we may at any rate speak of the system which is definitionally based upon them as having some sort of 'rigidity' as a system.

That this answer is not forced upon us is apparent from something which one who adopts it must admit: that even the 'initial expressions' will quite likely share with the other expressions in the system that surface complexity which suggested in the first place that all such expressions were syntactically complex. This is especially the case with dates: given that we define 'AD 2 ', 'AD 3', and so on, by reference to 'AD 1', it will remain the case that 'AD 1' has the same surface complexity as the other dates, consisting of a number preceded by 'AD'. If 'AD 1' is nevertheless to be construed as syntactically simple, then that surface complexity will not in general imply syntactic complexity. This in turn means that we must either admit that *all* the dates in the system are syntactically complex, or allow that the surface complexity of the dates does not force us to the conclusion that all dates but one get defined in terms of that one (even if that is a *possibility*).

Someone who grasps a system of dates, or a system of temporal or other units, must grasp certain recursive rules of the system relating to the construction of dates/units (e.g. the construction of 'AD 1' out of 'AD' and '1'). But this fact does not imply that dates or units are in general syntactically complex. Take the metric system. The sense of 'metre' was, we may take it, fixed by reference to the metre rod in Paris. 'Centimetre', 'kilometre', and so on, were then effectively introduced by means of such propositions as 'A centimetre is one-hundredth of a metre'. Were these propositions *definitions*, properly speaking, in the sense in which, for example, 'system of planets revolving round a sun' is the definition of 'solar system'? I think not. The term 'metre' may have fallen into complete desuetude, leaving 'centimetre' and the rest in use. These terms will have maintained their sense simply because they will still form a system backed up by the practical means of operating with them – namely, metrical rulers and the like. Learners of the language will have no need of the concept of a metre.

The point is that once 'centimetre' *et al.* have been introduced, it is only necessary that enough equivalences remain in force for the system still to have application. No particular unit or units are definitionally central. The system's 'remaining in force' is more a matter of its practical application than a matter of people's dispositions to accept certain propositions as true, or necessarily true. The relation of 'metre' to the metre rod is indeed analogous to that between 'centimetre', etc., and 'metre'. Appeal to the rod helps 'fix the reference' of 'metre'; appeal to 'metre' helps 'fix the reference' of 'centimetre', etc. Both the rod and the word 'metre' could drop out once they had been thus appealed to.

The same sort of arguments will apply to temporal units, and also to dates. Consider, for a change, what I have called 'general dates'; the argument applies equally well to specific ones. The proposition '1 December is the day before 2 December' has, at the moment, a quasi-necessary status in our system of dates. But changes in the orbiting patterns of the earth might lead to alterations in the system, such that every alternate year the month of January had half as many days, and these were numbered: '1 December', '3 December', '5 December', and so on. (It might be thought desirable to keep '25 December' in every year, so that omitting the dates from '16 December' to '31 December' every other year would not be an option.) Such a change would not, it seems to me, amount to a change in the *meanings* of '1 December' and the rest. And this connects with facts about what the utility of a system of dates consists in. Did dates undergo meaning-change when the Julian calendar replaced the Gregorian one? Surely not.

Indeed, as things are, one may wonder how appropriate it is to call the sentence, '1 December is the day before 2 December' a necessary truth. The status of this sentence looks to be much the same as that of the sentence, '1 December is the day after 30 November'. Now, a person's grasp of the expression '1 December' is going to be a matter of how that person can fit the expression into a general system of such expressions – so that the person's inclination to assert the sentence, '1 December is the day after 30 November' will be one of the things contributing to his grasp of the expression, as will his inclination to assert, '2 December is the day after 1 December'. But all this is compatible, both with the possibility of such sentences' coming to be false without a clear case of meaning-change, and with the syntactic simplicity of dates.

That temporal units and dates have a systematic surface complexity is not the only reason why one might think that they must have complex semantic equivalents. Dates and units are non-observational terms, in the sense that one cannot just see that it is 1 January 1990, nor just see that some process took three minutes – though one may be good at estimating such things. (More will be said about what role human observation *does* play in temporal measurement in the next chapter.) Now very many syntactically simple non-nominal expressions are ostensively learnable observational terms, for example predicates such as 'red'. And the syntactic simplicity of these terms seems at least partially explicable in terms of their observationality. Hence one may come to associate syntactic simplicity with observationality, or at least with learnability by ostension; and one may then infer syntactic complexity from non-observationality in the case of dates and temporal units.

Of course the availability of a Kripkean account of the matter vitiates such an inference. Neither 'Socrates' nor 'gold' could be said to be observational terms in the sense in which 'red' is, but we do not need to conclude that 'Socrates' and 'gold' are therefore syntactically complex. The same will go for 'minute' and 'AD 3' if Kripkean causal theories are acceptable.

Would a causal account of the semantics of temporal units and dates mean that lengths of time and particular times had to enter into that account as causes? And would this land us with an interesting species of causally efficacious intangible entity? The answer, of course, is 'No'. All that is needed in a Kripkean causal account is that correct uses of some term have a causal history, via other such uses, going back in time to an initial introduction of the term into the language – by ostension perhaps, or perhaps (as with temporal terms) by giving sentences stipulated as true, such as 'The year beginning with Christ's birth is AD 1', or 'Anything that happened in the year beginning with Christ's birth happened in AD 1'. Once the term, plus others in the system, are in place, these initial 'reference-fixing' sentences lose their crucial status. And nowhere do such things as lengths of time or particular times have such a role as prodding the whole thing into action.

If we are right to draw the sorts of distinction between temporal units and between dates which I have been drawing – especially between rigid and non-rigid, pure and impure, and so on – then it follows that phrases like 'the same length of time' and 'at the same time' will to some extent be equivocal. We might put it by saying that the criteria of identity of 'day' are different in kind from those of 'second'; that the criteria of identity of dates AD are different in kind from those of dates in the possible 'Big Bang' system; and so on. The criteria governing rigid, pure units and dates are, however, of particular interest because of their embodying our notions of 'absolute' duration and 'absolute' (if reference-frame-dependent) simultaneity, respectively. The purposes attaching to the use of these notions are, roughly speaking, those of empirical enquiry.

It is to these notions that we turn in the next chapter.

5

Periods and Instants

5.1 TRUE CLOCKS

In the last chapter, we said that units like 'second' and 'year' signified the *same time* in different possible worlds or situations, distinguishing these units from ones like 'day'. And units like 'second' were said to be incapable of signifying a *different time* without meaning-change, while ones like 'year' and 'day' were said to be capable of this. But in virtue of what do two periods, or two occurrences last the 'same', or a 'different', length of time?

It is important, when tackling questions like this, to distinguish matters constitutive from matters criterial. That is, we should distinguish the questions: 'What constitutes one occurrence's lasting as long as another?' and 'What counts as establishing that one occurrence lasts as long as another?'. There may, of course, be arguments to show, at least in certain cases, that a constitutive question is vacuous, or collapses into a criterial one – in which case, the *Wittgensteinian* notion of the criterial may come into play. But it is as well to bear the distinction in mind, as a *prima facie* possible one, from the outset.

Answers to 'constitutive' questions about identity will generally be of interest in so far as they help elucidate the key concept or concepts. Such answers, on the whole, will be of the form of an analysis of the locution 'is/has the same φ as' (for whatever φ). But a locution may be relatively primitive, in the sense of being unsusceptible of analysis, or elucidation, in terms of better or independently understood terms. Any 'analysis' will, in such a case, be unhelpful, and will have an air of question-begging about it.

Attempts at a 'constitutive' analysis of 'lasts as long as' risk being unhelpful in just this way. Thus, to say that it took as long for me to eat my sandwich as it did for you to drink your tea if and only if my sandwich-eating contained as many instants as your tea-drinking is to use the notion of an instant to elucidate that of a duration – and the notion of an instant is *at least* as ill-understood as that of a duration. (And this is quite apart from the questions, or pseudo-questions, raised by such an analysis, as to whether time is discrete/continuous/dense.) To say that the two occurrences lasted as long as each other if and only if, had one started simultaneously with the other, they would have ended simultaneously, is to use the notion of simultaneity to elucidate that of a duration – and again, it seems that the notion of simultaneity is at least as ill-understood as that of a duration. (And this is quite apart from what to make of the counterfactual conditional involved in such an analysis.)

Of course, it may be useful simply to draw attention to the connections between such concepts as that of simultaneity and equal duration. The problem is that if doubts begin to arise about the sense, say, of statements about equal duration, then we will not be able to allay those doubts by talking about simultaneity if simultaneity is no better understood than equal duration. Simultaneity and equal duration will probably stand or fall together.

Hence, when conventionalism abut the notion of equal duration threatens, it is difficult to tackle the threat by insisting that the constitutive question should be kept distinct from the criterial one, and assuming that objective answers exist to questions as to whether A lasted as long as B, quite independently of what would count as establishing that A lasted as long as B. The conventionalist has a foothold as soon as we admit that the notion of equal duration is at all puzzling: for he can then propose that our puzzlement will only be eased once we allow answers to the criterial question to bear upon the constitutive question – purely constitutive analyses being patently unable to ease our puzzlement.

The general test for A's lasting as long as B is that a true clock would give the same answer to the question how long each had lasted (having been used to time each). The only way to go about establishing, directly, that two non-simultaneous occurrences last as long as one another, is by using a regular process, such as the earth's rotation, as a clock: and it is only when such a clock is reliable or 'true' that using it can qualify as a means of establishing that two processes last as long as each other. (Indirect methods – such as inferring A's duration from the known durations of C and D, whose successive occurrences constitute A's occurrence – rely on, or are beholden to, applications of the direct method.) Our own subjective judgement of time may be taken for the moment as relying on some psychological or biological clock.

So what is a 'true clock'? For the moment, it is enough to say that a clock is a system of repeated events, such as revolutions round the sun, or the falling of water-droplets. A true clock is one whose repeated events are all of the same duration. But in virtue of what are those repeated events of equal duration? By what we said previously, they are of equal duration if and only if a true clock would give the same answer to the question how long each one had lasted. We seem to be saying what equal duration is by using the notion of a true clock, and saying what a true clock is by using the notion of equal duration.

We thus encounter a circularity in our account. On what grounds can we claim that this circularity is benign? The conventionalist will maintain that the reason why the circularity is benign is that a true clock is just one whose repeated events are stipulated to be of equal duration. As Reichenbach puts it:

> a physical process, such as the rotation of the earth, is taken as a measure of uniformity by *definition*. All definitions are equally admissible.
>
> (*The Philosophy of Space and Time*, Dover Publications, 1958, ch. 2, § 17)

While all definitions are, for the conventionalist, 'equally admissible', still there are some constraints on what we do here. Our stipulations must adhere to certain conditions: we cannot, for example, use two clocks as true clocks which yield different answers to questions about relative durations. But within the limits imposed by such conditions, a true clock is a true clock because we have chosen it for a standard. The conventionalist is also at liberty to say, what appears evident, that we choose some clocks as standards, rather than others, for various reasons. Thus in the first instance, we rely on the approximation of a clock's measurements to our own subjective judgements of time, and beyond that, on the fact that the measurements of some clocks allow simpler and neater explanations and predictions, given the rest of our empirical theories and data, than do those of other clocks.

But do we need a theory, such as conventionalism, to account for the non-viciousness of the circularity we mentioned earlier? Why can't we just rest content with an account of equal duration that is in terms of true clocks, and an account of true clocks that is in terms of equal duration?

At any rate, it might well be thought that we have here the sort of circularity that so often seems to crop up when we try to give criteria of identity. There has been much discussion as to whether

Davidson's criterion of event-identity[1] in terms of same causes and effects is viciously circular. Explications of identity over time in terms of spatio-temporal continuity often seem to flirt with circularity, insofar as the only way to draw the right spatio-temporal boundaries for a thing is by tracking the thing itself through time, which seems to presuppose a criterion of identity for that sort of thing. And so on and so forth. What counts as vicious circularity is clearly itself a complex matter.

Nevertheless, the case of identity of duration may well be thought rather different from such cases as those of event-identity and diachronic identity. As often, we should be careful not to play fast and loose with the term 'identity', assimilating all those contexts where it is used. There may be special reasons why the circularity in our account of equal duration should not benefit from any general amnesty for criteria of identity that appear to be circular. What would be instructive would be a case sufficiently similar to that of equal duration, concerning which our intuitions are rather more keen.

Such a case, I think, is that of sameness of colour. Certain things count as establishing conclusively that two surfaces are of the same colour (e.g. red, blue or whatever). If a normal-sighted person, in normal lighting conditions, cannot distinguish between the surfaces – or more simply, if such a person, being linguistically competent, applies the same colour-term to each surface, then that fact is enough to establish that the two surfaces are of the same colour. Empirical data could not show that normal-sighted people are wrong to think that blood is the same colour as ripe tomatoes. Here, what I called the 'constitutive' question may indeed be thought to collapse into the 'criterial' one: somebody who thought that science *could* show us all to have been wrong about colours is probably best described as confused about the concept *colour*.

Now which people count as 'normal-sighted' people? Normal-sighted people (where the question is colour-discrimination) are those people who make pretty much the same colour-discriminations as other normal-sighted people. No doubt it is partly a statistical matter: the prevalent colour-vocabulary will embody the colour-discriminations of the majority. And it is essential that there be enough agreement between people for colour-terms to count as objectively applicable.

It seems, then, that two surfaces are of different colours if and only if a normal-sighted person would be able to distinguish them in normal conditions; and a person is normal-sighted if and only if he can distinguish when two surfaces in normal conditions are of different colours. The circularity in this case surely is one that we can avoid by what might be called conventionalism about colour. That is, it is somewhat in the nature of a stipulation (it is at any rate 'true by definition') that where there are a majority of people in a linguistic community who agree in their colour-discriminations, then a normal-sighted person's inability to distinguish two surfaces just determines that a single one of their colour-predicates is applicable to those two surfaces. And this of course means that it determines that the members of that linguistic community are correct in saying that those two surfaces are of the same colour. The fact that a different linguistic community may make different colour-discriminations does not affect the issue. Two sorts of question can thus be classed as senseless: an example of the first would be: 'But are blood and ripe tomatoes *really* of the same colour?', while an example of the second would be: 'But is it the ancient Greek or the modern Eskimo who makes the *right* colour-discriminations?'.

How far similar, and how far different, are the cases of sameness of colour and sameness of duration? One quite important difference is this: that whereas the ultimate arbiters on matters of colour are normal-sighted people, the ultimate arbiters on matters of duration do not seem to be people at all. Rather, the arbiters on matters of duration are the clocks we have chosen as being the truest. We are quite willing to admit that our subjective estimates of time are rough and ready, and indeed often unreliable. Most of us wear watches. This deference to our instruments might be thought to betoken a certain objectivity, or degree of objectivity, lacking from the colour case.

What would be the situation if we agreed with each other's judgements of duration to the same extent as we in fact agree with each other's judgements of colour? It would then surely be possible for us to have a vocabulary of lengths of time, of the same type of 'objectivity' as is enjoyed by our vocabulary of colours. The ultimate arbiter as to whether I had taken as long to eat my sandwich as you had taken to drink your tea would then be the person with a 'normal sense of time'. (Just as there are colour-blind people, there would no doubt be 'time-blind' people, in the sort of situation we are imagining.) We would simply disallow the measurements of instruments which systematically contradicted our judgements of time.[2]

In connection with this last scenario, the possibility suggests itself that we might all be subject to some general influence that distorted our sense of time – by distorting some biological rhythm, say – in such a uniform way that our agreement was not undermined, but so that we were led to say that there was a general tendency for the processes of nature to 'slow down' together, or 'speed up' together. Of course, an analogous possibility exists for clock-dependent duration-talk: the workings of clocks might, it seems, be subject to some uniform external distorting influence. These cases echo Poincaré's parable of the inhabitants of a disc whose measuring instruments are affected by how far they are from the disc's centre, owing to the decrease in temperature from the centre to the edge. The measurements of the people in Poincaré's fable are systematically affected without their scientific theories' being undermined. Such hypotheses make us consider what exactly is involved in the 'objectivity' of a measuring practice. Let us turn to this question now.

Would people in fact be operating with concepts of *duration* in the case of a uniform distorting influence? It is intrinsic to our measuring concepts that instruments of measurement are taken (by us) to be usable only when not subject to (what we count as) distorting influences. In the imagined case, let us first assume that those involved are capable of coming to detect the external influence on their biological rhythms (or, indeed, on their clocks), and that if they did, they ought to classify it *as* a distorting influence – i.e. one that affected what 'judgements of duration' they made. If they simply discounted this fact, not taking it to undermine their 'judgements' at all, then there is every ground for saying that their practice can not have been one of *measuring*; i.e. that *we* can not use 'measure', 'duration', etc. in our descriptions of what those people's practices were, and of what their judgements were about. We cannot say that they would be (incompetent) practitioners in the business of measuring temporal duration: their practice has some other sort of rationale, if it has a rationale at all. For *us* to call their practice 'measuring', *our* concept of 'measuring' must be applicable; which in effect means that their practice must share certain essential features with our practice of measuring.[3]

If, on the other hand, those detecting the external influence on their judgements emended their judgements, attempting to compensate for the influence, we surely could after all describe them as using concepts of duration. (Though what would count as 'attempts to compensate' would require some spelling out.)

The hard case is that in which *we* should describe things in terms of a distorting influence, but the people involved would simply deny that it was a distorting influence at all. Any tests we might bring to bear in order to demonstrate the effect of the influencing factor would employ our own instruments (especially, clocks); but according to *their* clocks, ours do not keep proper time. We are rather in the same position as we would be if faced with inveterate 'grue'-users – ones who kept invoking concepts ('bleen', 'emerire', etc.) that together ensured that their generalisations, explanations, and so on, were as simple as ours.[4]

Again, however, there appear to be grounds for saying that the other people would simply not be using concepts of duration. (Likewise, the 'grue'-users would not be using colour-concepts.) For can we say that a rule exists in their practice which states that distorting influences undermine measurements? I spoke of their denying that the Influence was indeed a distorting influence; but are they really talking about distorting influences if none of our tests for distorting influences are admitted by them as establishing anything? What allows us to translate some phrase of theirs as 'distorting influence' in the first place? The point, once more, is the familiar one that 'agreement in concepts requires agreement in judgement'. At *some* level we must agree on something (that such-and-such establishes so-and-so); but if we do thus agree, and so get to share some sort of concept, disagreements the next level up will (unless we can never attain the proper conditions for judgement at all) be resoluble.

(All this talk of 'other people' should not mask the fact that the subject being discussed is the objectivity of measurement. What other people might do is also what we might do; and such possibilities throw light on the essential nature of measurement, i.e. on the concept of 'measurement'.)

The matter is complicated, of course. A practice such as that of measuring duration has a number of important features, and another practice may resemble it in some and not other respects. We may, for instance, often observe some member of the tribe counting the events in some artificial cycle, which he sets running when a process he is observing starts up and which he stops when the process ends; the number of events to have gone by he then records. (More could be added to the story.) This on its own lends support to the view that the practice is one of timing processes. And we can know that what these people are doing is 'counting', 'observing', or whatever, because *these* practices are quite general, and (we can assume) are in most other contexts carried out pretty much as we carry out procedures of counting, observing, or whatever. So the fact that it is impossible to get them to admit a distorting influence as such, or indeed to be sure that they have the concept of a 'distorting influence', might not on its own count as conclusive evidence that the people of the tribe lack concepts of duration. Indeed, perhaps 'distorting influence' is itself sufficiently general a notion that we could in fact have proper grounds for attributing it to them – they might measure weights and lengths as we do, and show awareness of distorting influences in these areas.

Despite these complications, there are some things we can usefully say on the subject of the objectivity of measurement. A certain kind of agreement in practice is necessary for that practice to count as objective. A certain kind of response to what are admitted to be external influences on 'measurements' must be forthcoming. The coordination of different systems of measurement within the same sphere (e.g. duration) must be an essential aim; though here, of course, the criteria for there being one 'sphere', and not more, will include the practitioners' attempts at coordination. And so on and so forth.

There is a strong temptation to add that in normal conditions a person will apply a term objectively only when he applies it *because* so-and-so – the 'because' indicating some sort of empirical, causal explanation. But we must ask whether we have here a conceptual truth about objectivity, or a methodological principle for empirical explanation. Linguistic agreement constitutes a form of widespread regularity; and regularities in general lead us to look for other regularities 'underlying' them (especially at the microphysical level). That our quest is often successful is a notable fact; if it weren't, it is likely we should not adhere to the methodological principle. But it is not a necessary truth that we should, in any given case, be successful. And it cannot be a necessary condition on some concept's counting as objective that a quest for a regularity underlying our use of it should ('in the end', or 'in principle') be successful. Corresponding remarks will go for the empirical explanation of individual applications of terms.

Let us return to the question: What counts as a correct statement of duration? We cannot say of the actual expression 'took five minutes' that whether or not it is applicable is ultimately to be decided by subjective judgement in normal conditions. We lack the finetuned biological clock of our imagined 'time-sensitive' people. It seems rather that whether or not 'took five minutes' is applicable in some case is ultimately to be decided – where it *can* be ultimately decided – by the measurements of true clocks. And the notion of a true clock helps to *constitute* the notion of equal duration, in the same way in which the notion of a normal-sighted person helps to constitute the notion of sameness of colour, or in the same way in which the notion of a time-sensitive person *would* help constitute that of equal duration in the 'time-sensitive' language.

We earlier characterised a 'normal-sighted' person as one who agreed on the whole with the colour-discriminations made by other normal-sighted people. Our temporal talk likewise rests upon there being sufficient general agreement between the measurements made by different kinds of clock. Clocks can be tested for accuracy only by comparison with other clocks; people can be tested for colour-sensitivity only by comparison with other people. (A colour-sensitive machine only counts as such if it delivers pretty much the same verdicts as colour-sensitive people.) Within such a context of sufficient general agreement, it is not necessary to use any *particular* person, or any *particular* clock, as a standard. Any person, and any clock, is defeasible as an authority.

That no particular clock (or type of clock) need function as the standard in a system of time-measurement is connected with what was said in the last chapter concerning the rigidity and purity of (many) temporal terms. And it goes against a certain strain in traditional conventionalism about duration. Reichenbach compared the measurement of duration with the measurement of length, and wrote:

> Whether two distant line-segments are equal is not a matter of *knowledge* but of *definition*; and this definition consists ultimately in a reference to a physical object coordinated to the concept of a unit.
>
> (*The Philosophy of Space and Time*, Dover Publications, 1958, ch. 2, § 17)

The putative need for an 'ultimate reference to a physical object' is analogous to the putative need for an 'ultimate reference to colour samples' as the basis of a colour vocabulary. Both needs are putative only. And once the independence of temporal measurements from any standard is recognised, we can see more clearly that the objectivity of those measurements derives rather from a certain systematicity in background agreement – and that 'stipulation' is not really what is at issue at all. To say that what counts as a normal-sighted person or as a true clock is a matter of stipulation is to use a pretty attenuated concept of stipulation. A context of *general* agreement is required at the start, and it is only within this context that people or clocks can achieve honorific status. And although it is as silly to ask: 'Are a true clock's readings *really* right?' as it is to ask: 'Are a normal-sighted person's judgements of colour *really* right?', it is never silly to ask of a *particular* person or clock whether he, she or it is really right, since one can always ask of a particular person or (type of) clock whether he, she or it is normal-sighted or true. If we ask what makes a person normal-sighted, or what makes a clock a true one, we may either want an empirical answer ('her visual system is thus and so'; 'its mechanism is thus and so'); or a philosophical, constitutive one. And the latter sort of answer will allude to such things as the agreement obtainable between people/clocks; it will *not* deliver the true but empty: 'He/she/it gets it right'.

Problems remain. One such concerns whether what has been said about the connection between duration-statements and true clocks provides us with the materials for some sort of *analysis* of duration-concepts. Can we go further than we have so far done, and tackle questions like, 'What is it for five minutes to elapse?', or 'What is a five-minute period of time?', employing in our answers such forms of words as, 'For five minutes to pass is for it to be the case that . . .' – or, 'A five-minute period of time is a . . .'? Can we, in fact, arrive at the sort of *identity-statements*, Socratic and statuesque, after which the metaphysician so characteristically hankers?

These are topics to which I will return later on, in Part III.

5.2 PERIODS VERSUS INSTANTS

We have just been dealing with the question 'In virtue of what do two occurrences last the same time?'. In this section, the analogous question to be considered is, 'In virtue of what do two events take place at the same time?'. Just as the rigidity and purity of units involves us in the first question, so the rigidity and purity of dates involves us in the second. Thus, 'AD 2000' is rigid (roughly) in virtue of its signifying the *same* time in different possible worlds, even ones (like ours) in which Christ's birth took place some years BC.

Two events take place at the same time if and only if they are simultaneous. This belongs to the species of vacuous constitutive truths. By contrast, the criterial answer to, 'In virtue of what do two events take place at the same time?' would outline what counts as establishing that two events are simultaneous.

There seem to be various ways in which one might go about establishing that two events were, or will be, simultaneous. Using two synchronised true clocks, one to record the time at which one event occurred, the other to record the time at which the other event occurred, is a possible technique; it of course relies on a way of establishing the simultaneity of a recorded event and the clock-event which 'records' it (e.g. a second-hand reaching a certain point). Another technique might be to compare the 'traces' left by each event on something presumed to be undergoing a uniform, or at any rate known, rate of change – such as the depositing of geological layers. And of course there is subjective judgement. It is well-known that the advent of relativistic physics has made the whole subject of simultaneity, and the tests for establishing simultaneity, a complicated one; though it is worth pointing out that it is not a consequence of relativistic physics that 'there is no such thing as simultaneity', even if it is a consequence that there is no such thing as *absolute* (reference-frame-independent) simultaneity.

The questions 'What are Fs?' and 'What are the criteria of identity for Fs?' are very often interlocked. It is impossible to give a proper answer to 'What are times?' without discussing simultaneity. Nevertheless, there is a certain ambiguity in the expression 'at the same time', an ambiguity, if you like, to do with the question what *times* are. Sorting out that ambiguity will in fact be making plain some constitutive facts about simultaneity.

At the same time as Myfanwy was writing a letter to her aunt, her aunt was writing a letter to Myfanwy. The two letter-writings were, we may say, simultaneous. This clearly does not mean that the two events began and ended simultaneously; Myfanwy's aunt may have put pen to paper a minute after her niece. The best we can say, from a merely 'topological' point of view, is that there was a period during which both aunt and niece were writing. But this is not a general guarantee of simultaneity. It will hardly do to say that at the same time as Henry VIII was ruling England, Catherine of Aragon was giving birth to a baby girl. Matters such as the relative lengths of time taken by each event are clearly of relevance here.

But it might be thought that it is only in a 'loose and popular' sense of 'simultaneous' that Myfanwy's letter-writing and her aunt's could be said to be simultaneous. *Strictly* simultaneous events are ones which start and end simultaneously, it might be said. What's more, the crucial idea, namely that of two events' starting or finishing at once, is an idea to do with *instants*: we are concerned to know when two things, such as beginnings-to-write, happen at (exactly) the *same instant*. Hence a provisional answer to the question 'What are times?', insofar as times are the entities at issue when it comes to (*strict*) simultaneity, will be: 'Times are durationless instants'.

What of dates? Dates like 'AD 2000' and '1 January AD 2000' pick out periods (a year, a day). Times o'clock, such as '1 p.m., 1 January', may on the other hand be thought to pick out, not periods, but instants, i.e. durationless points in time. In fact this view of times o'clock is not without its problems: for instance, it is hard, without some fancy footwork, to avoid the conclusion that it is impossible ever to give the right time – all our reports of the time of day are only 'roughly true', i.e. literally false, if only because it must take a certain time to say what the time is.

But in any case philosophers who think we are 'committed to' instants do not in general base their arguments on the putative existence in ordinary language of dates that pick out instants. Let me say here that it is not my concern to address those philosophers whose commitment to instants extends to insisting on our 'full-blooded ontological commitment' to instants, where ontological commitment is defined *à la* Quine. Some philosophers draw attention to locutions such as 'For any time t, if p at t, then not-q at t', thinking that such locutions must be construed as cases of first-order ('ontologically committal') quantification, and quantification 'over' instants at that. But it is evident that first-order quantification is not needed so long as the examples are based around the form 'at t', as the quoted example is, and as most such examples are – for quantifying with variables for temporal adverbs (of the form 'at/on t') is then perfectly acceptable. The question whether, in the realist's terms, one is quantifying over instants, rather than periods, *is* of interest to me here; though I do not, by the by, hold with the realist way of putting things. I talk of 'periods' and 'instants' because it is a far less cumbersome way of talking than the alternative – even if a potentially more misleading one.

Thus there is an issue which might be dubbed the issue 'whether we need instants', which is *not* the issue whether we need designators for instants (or variables whose substituends would be such

designators). Nor is it an issue to which we are properly introduced
by the asking of disembodied questions like, 'What is an instant?',
in the hope of answers of the form, 'An instant is a such-and-such'.
It is an issue that arises typically as a result of our adopting, as a
model of time, a given number-series, such as the series of real
numbers.

The thesis that time is infinitely divisible can be expressed in
various ways. One way of expressing it is as the view that, however
short a time something took to happen, it would always be logically possible that something else should have taken an even shorter
time to happen. Now, some philosophers might want to say that
there existed temporal 'atoms' which it was *logically* possible for
events to be shorter than – and even that the existence of these
atoms was a ('metaphysically') necessary affair. However, the notion of a period, shorter than which it is *metaphysically* impossible
for any other period to be, is a very obscure one. As so often, it is
really up to the exponent of 'metaphysical (im)possibility' to make
himself understood here: I myself cannot see what could be meant.

At any rate, the view of time as infinitely divisible – as *not* 'discrete'
– is one that I shall be assuming in what follows. It is frequently
said to come in two distinct forms: the view of time as 'dense', and
the view of time as 'continuous'. Two number-series are associated
respectively with these two views of time: the series of rational
numbers, and the series of real numbers.

Now it is possible to make use, say, of the series of real numbers
in explicating a certain thesis about durations. Consider a toy train
whose speed, we have ample empirical evidence to think, is constant. The train always goes at a yard a minute (it is very slow). We
draw a square on the floor whose sides are each one yard long. We
then build a straight track for the train along the diagonal of the
square, and allow the train to traverse the length of the track. How
long does the train take to complete its journey? The answer would
seem to be: The-square-root-of-two minutes. If the situation envisaged is possible, which it will be so long as *space* is non-discrete,
then it is possible for a duration to be assigned an irrational number,
regardless of the unit-system (we didn't have to choose minutes).
Thus, we need the real number series to be able to assign certain
measurements to lengths of time.

Of course, in this example, the 'measurement' is not one that we
could make directly. A clock, as we said above, will typically work
by generating a series of repeated events, and however short those

events, there will never be any number of them that could give us the reading 'The-square-root-of-two minutes'. On the other hand, we might be using a clock that, for example, had hands that moved through space at a constant speed; but such a clock could only be taken to give the reading 'The-square-root-of-two minutes' on exactly the same basis as that upon which we rest our indirect calculation that the train took that time to complete its journey. The distance moved by the clock-hand is assigned an irrational number, and the time taken for the hand to move that distance is consequently also assigned one, on the assumption that the hand's speed was constant.

Despite the impossibility of 'directly measuring' irrational quantities, there seem good grounds to say that (because of situations of the sort envisaged above) the use of irrational numbers in the measurement of durations could make for the neatest and most powerful overall empirical theory. What this would *not* commit us to is the thesis that, in representing time by means of the real number series, we are thereby assigning durationless points in time to each of the real numbers. Nor would the representation of time by means of the rational number series commit us to assigning durationless points in time to each of the rational numbers. Indeed, the consequences of this way of looking at it, can, I think, be shown to be unacceptable.

Albert is told to synchronise his tea-drinking with Bernadette's sandwich-eating, in the sense that at no time should he be drinking tea and Bernadette not be eating her sandwich, and at no time should she be eating her sandwich and Albert not be drinking his tea. (Assume for the sake of argument that the temporal boundaries to these activities are as precise as any activities' boundaries could be.) What does the expression 'at no time' here mean? Some philosophers will take it to mean 'at no instant', where an instant is a durationless point. It doesn't matter to the example whether we represent time by means of the real or the rational numbers; let us represent it by means of the reals. If to each of the reals on our 'timeline' there corresponds an instant, there ought to be two distinct possibilities concerning Bernadette's finishing her sandwich. There may be a last instant at which she is eating, and no first instant at which she is no longer eating, or there may be a first instant at which she is no longer eating and no last instant at which she is eating. (There cannot, it would seem, be an instant at which she is both eating and not eating.) The same dichotomy applies to

Bernadette's beginning her sandwich; but however we construe 'Bernadette began her sandwich at noon', the fact that she began at noon and took exactly three minutes to eat her sandwich is equally compatible with either possibility concerning her finishing it. Whether there was a last moment of eating, or no last moment, does not affect how long she took to eat her sandwich.

Now it would have been easy enough for Albert to obey our initial instruction if we had meant that during no *period* should he be drinking and Bernadette not be eating, and during no *period* should she be eating and he not be drinking. There could in principle be a clock that could show whether or not he had satisfied that instruction. But what if instants were meant, not just periods? Albert and Bernadette might each start at noon and each take exactly three minutes to finish their repasts – but then might not Bernadette's sandwich-eating have a last moment and Albert's tea-drinking no last moment? And in this case would there not after all be an instant at which Bernadette was eating her sandwich while Albert was not drinking his tea?

One gets a strong flavour of the senselessness of talking in this way when one asks oneself such questions as: 'If Albert had failed to perform the task for the reason given, what could or should he have done to avoid such failure?'. It would, of course, be quite wrong to say that he should have gone on drinking tea just a little longer: if he had in fact managed to drink tea at that extra moment at which Bernadette was still eating her sandwich, this would have made no difference to the time taken for him to finish his tea. He was quite right to make sure that he took no more, and no less, than three minutes, given that this was how long Bernadette took.

There is, in fact, nothing that Albert could have done to improve his performance, and that is because there is no real difference in temporal terms between his and Bernadette's actions. Now this might lead a devotee of durationless instants[5] to adopt a rather easy-going position, whereby, for example, a certain moment can arbitrarily be called *either* 'the last moment of Bernadette's eating', *or* 'the first moment of her not eating'. There are not then two genuinely distinct possibilities regarding Bernadette's performance; but we nevertheless can talk about durationless moments or instants.

What, on such a view, would be an example of a durationless instant? It seems *prima facie* that there are two options here. The first is to say that a durationless instant will be that bit of time non-arbitrarily represented by a real number on some time-line, and which can arbitrarily be called a last moment of φ-ing, or a first moment of not φ-ing, in certain cases. The second is to say that a durationless instant is a thing such as the last moment of Bernadette's eating, which, however, can be arbitrarily *identified* with the first moment of her not eating, or with the last, or first, moment of something else's happening, etc.

The second option, I think, collapses into the first. For if the last moment of Bernadette's eating can be identified with the first of her not eating, then each cannot be associated with a different real numeral. Two real numerals will pick out distinct real numbers; there is no arbitrary identifying of real numbers. So we must be talking of one instant, representable by one real number, which can be with equal justice called 'the last moment when p' and 'the first moment when not-p'.

Can we then say that there is a single moment when Bernadette is eating and when she is not eating? Such a contradiction would surely be no better for being confined to an instant: certainly, if we want to render 'Never' by 'At no instant', we shall nevertheless still want to say 'Contradictions are never true', and the like. If instead of this we say that it is an arbitrary matter which of two descriptions of what happens we adopt, but that we must in any case not contradict ourselves, then it is clear that a question like, 'At time t, was Bernadette eating or not?' will have to count as misguided if it presupposes that the answer will be 'Yes' or 'No'. 'Say what you like' will be the proper answer. Now if someone asks, 'Would a person wearing a fishing-net be clothed or not?', and I reply, 'Say what you like', it remains the case that there are plenty of good sentences around employing 'fishing-net', with fully determinate truth-values. If we adopt the 'easy-going' line on instants, will we analogously be able to pick out a class of sentences employing the form 'At t' with fully determinate truth-values?

The point of operators of the form 'At time t' is above all to modify empirical statements, so that we can say whether or not certain things are happening at certain times. This function will not be performed by that expression, 'At t', about which you can say what you like as to whether it truly modifies 'Bernadette is still eating'; will it be performed by any other expression, 'At t'? Can we at least say that *while* Bernadette is eating, any given instant will be one when either she is eating or not eating, this being no matter of stipulation? Unfortunately, it appears not. For what is there to *prevent* one's saying of some instant during this period that it is an instant when Bernadette is not eating – or indeed (and more threateningly) that it is an instant when you can say what you like concerning her eating? No detectable difference would be implied by opting for one, rather than another, of these descriptions, after all. If it simply *follows* from the fact that Bernadette was eating throughout some period that she was eating at a given instant within that period, then it is dubious whether talk of instants is anything more than 'fluffed-up' talk of periods. The assignment of a definite truth-value to a statement of the form, 'p at t', will amount to nothing more than a flourish added to some true statement of the form, 'p during period P'.

If any sentence, 'At t, so and so', cannot be ascribed a non-arbitrary truth-value, then it is far from clear whether locutions of the form 'At t' have a use at all. Of course, such sentences do have a use – but that is only because they do not deal with durationless instants. To say that Bernadette and Albert both started together and finished together is to say that there was no time *during which* either was engaged in his or her activity while the other was not so engaged (and that they both did in fact engage in those activities). To understand what simultaneity is, we do not need the notion of a durationless point in time, only the notion of a duration. The same applies to instantaneousness. Something changes from being F to being G instantaneously: this means, roughly, that there is a period during which the thing is F, and a later period during which it is G, and there is no period after it began to be F and before it stopped being G during which it is both F and G, and none during which it is neither F nor G.

These comments about simultaneity and instantaneity amount to 'constitutive' ones; and in the present context, their main purpose has been to throw doubt upon the constitutive thesis that simultaneity and instantaneity are to be understood as committing us to durationless instants. In the next section, I shall suggest how the solution to a certain well-known paradox might rely on the rejection of instants which I have been arguing for.

5.3 THE PARADOX OF THE LAMP

A modern-day descendant of Zeno's Paradoxes goes as follows.[6] A lamp has a single on/off switch. A stopwatch is set going when the lamp is off; after thirty seconds, the lamp is switched on; after another fifteen seconds, it is switched off; after another seven-and-a-half seconds, it is switched on; and so on. Each period of being on (off) is half the duration of the preceding period of being off (on). The question is: when a minute has elapsed, is the lamp on or off? We are to ignore the fact that such a process is physically impossible.

One approach to this puzzle is to make out that whether the lamp is on or off after one minute is not something that can be deduced from the set-up as described; but that this yields no paradox unless we *ought* to be able to deduce the lamp's state from the set-up as described; and nothing shows that we in fact ought to be able to. Well, it seems *conceivable* that the lamp should be a deterministic system, in the sense that its state at a given time is determined by (inferable from) its immediately prior state. And we have, in setting up the puzzle, seemingly given a full account of the state of the lamp for the entire minute prior to the moment we are considering. We can simply stipulate such things as: (i) the lamp can only be on if the switch is in *this* position (closing the circuit); (ii) the lamp can only be off if the switch is in *this* position (opening the circuit). In which case, we *ought* to be able to tell what state such a lamp is in after a minute. The only way to block this inference is by showing that deterministic systems are inconceivable – a hard task.

Apart from the approach just mentioned, various answers have been suggested to the puzzle. All the answers fall into two camps: those which allow that the description of the set-up and of the process is logically in order, and those which deny this. The answer I will propose is of the second sort. The crucial notions, I think, are those of *completeness of description*, and *completability of process*.

In the statement of the puzzle, one has to make use of the phrase 'and so on', or of some phrase or word of equivalent function. We are describing a lamp, and what happens to that lamp during a period of one minute. We say it is on for thirty seconds, then off for fifteen, then on for seven-and-a-half, *and so on*. The following conclusion seems unexceptionable:

(1) For any n, one can, from what has been said, determine (i) whether the nth on/off period (period between two consecutive switchings) is one during which the lamp is on or one during which it is off; and (ii) how long the nth on/off period lasts.

But does it follow from (1) that the statement of the puzzle gives a *complete description* of the period of a minute following the setting going of the stopwatch?

The state of an object during a certain period has been completely described, we may say, if and only if:

(2) For any sub-period (period during the main period), one can infer, from the description, a complete description of the object during that sub-period.

We may restrict, or relativise, completeness of description to a particular predicate or predicates, or to a particular (e.g. 'determinable') range of predicates. Thus, an object has been completely described *as to its colour* during a certain period, if we can infer from the description that the object was red for the first half of the period and blue for the latter half of the period. A complete description of the lamp in our puzzle need only tell us whether the lamp is on or off – matters such as the lamp's colour are of course irrelevant. (It should hardly need saying that (2) is not meant as an *analysis* of 'complete description'.)

That the statement of the puzzle satisfies (1) does not entail that the statement provides us with a complete description of the lamp during the minute in question. We can only claim that a complete description has been given if we may count descriptions involving 'and so on' as complete to start with: something we may not do if the question is whether the puzzle-statement provides a complete description. For the description of the lamp during any sub-period which ends with the end of the minute will have to trail off: '. . . and so on'; hence it is questionable whether, for any sub-period, one can infer, from the puzzle-statement, a complete description of the lamp during that sub-period.

So far, we have merely drawn attention to a question that needs answering – namely, Does the puzzle give us a complete, i.e. adequate, description of the set-up? We need to consider the role and meaning of the phrase, 'and so on', in order to answer this. And there are, I think, persuasive accounts of that phrase according to which certain putative *descriptions* (of objects, processes, or whatever) involving it are logically out of order. The characteristic use of 'and so on' in mathematics can plausibly be seen as indicating the infinite extendability of a rule or technique, e.g. the technique of adding to a certain series – rather than as helping to provide a description of an infinite object, e.g. the object resulting from the 'completion' of an uncompletable series. This seems to have been what Wittgenstein was getting at when he wrote:

The concepts of infinite decimals in mathematical propositions are not concepts of series, but of the unlimited technique of expansion of series.

We learn an endless technique: that is to say, something is done for us first, and then we do it; we are told rules and we do exercises in following them; perhaps some expression like 'and so on *ad inf.*' is also used, but what is in question here is not some gigantic extension.

(*Remarks on the Foundations of Mathematics,* trans. G. E. M. Anscombe, 2nd edn, 1967, Part IV, § 19)

If some such account of 'and so on' is on the right lines, then the use of the phrase in the statement of the lamp-puzzle is illicit. It is a purported descriptive use of a phrase which cannot in the context be used descriptively, but whose use in that context appears to be all right in virtue of its surface similarity to a *bona fide* use in another type of context – in which type of context, however, its function is not to contribute to descriptions, but is to contribute to the framing of rules or techniques, or to meta-statements concerning such rules or techniques.

'Emma played the first piece in the book; then the second; then the third; and so on.' This does seem to amount to a perfectly good description of a task undertaken and (presumably) completed. 'And so on' can be replaced by: 'and where there were n pieces in the book, she went on to play all n pieces in order'. (Since one need not know the value of 'n' in order to utter the quoted sentence, it is misleading to take 'and so on' as an *abbreviation* of, say, 'then the fourth; then the fifth; finally the sixth', or of any such expression.) One might stick with the idea that 'and so on' indicates how to go on (i.e. indicates a technique), by pointing out that, if told what the quoted sentence tells one, a person could extend the sentence in a certain way, if apprised of the information as to how many pieces were printed in Emma's book.

'Emma counted one; then two; then three; and so on, without end.' Here, too, we have a description of an (uncompletable) task. It counts as a description because from it we can infer, if apprised of the information when Emma began counting, and at what speed, (a) whether she will still be counting, and (b) if so, what number(s) she will be counting – for any given period after she began. (The answer to (a) will always be 'Yes'.) The phrase 'and so on', once more, indicates to us a technique; not how to produce a complete description of anything, but how to answer any question of the form: 'During such-and-such a time, will Emma be counting, and if so, what number(s) will she be counting?'. (This is a rather attenuated sense of 'going on', perhaps, but this matters not.)

Now consider: 'Emma switched the lamp off after thirty seconds; switched it on after another fifteen; switched it off after another seven-and-a-half; and so on.' In a sense, 'and so on' here does indicate how to go on, for we *can* go on: '. . . switched it on after another 3.75 seconds . . .', etc. But what are we doing in 'going on'? We are not working towards a description of what Emma has done, as in the case two paragraphs back. Perhaps description is not really at issue, then, and we should take the case one paragraph back as a model. Are we enabled to say, of any given period, whether Emma is engaged in her lamp-switching task during that period, and if so, what she is doing?

I think not. For, as was said above, any description of the last n seconds of the minute in question will itself need 'and so on' tacked on at the end. We have something like Ryle's 'namely'-rider problem, as that is alleged to arise from the Liar Paradox.[7] Our initial 'description' of Emma's activity is meant to work *by* indicating how a description can be produced of her activity during any sub-period; but it turns out that for an indefinite number of sub-periods, we can only produce another form of words, whose function is meant to be to show how we can produce descriptions of activity during the sub-sub-periods; and so on. It is only if, at some point, genuine descriptions of Emma's activity are reached, that the descriptionhood of *these* forms of words could be said to endow 'retrospective descriptionhood' on all those forms of words that had concluded, 'and so on'.

The matter would be different, of course, were we to countenance durationless instants, at least in the non-easy-going way (see the last section). If we did so, we could, it seems, require simply that, from the puzzle-statement, plus the information as to when Emma began the task, it be inferable (a) whether she was engaged in the task, and (b) if so, what state the lamp was in – *at any given instant of time*. Nothing would then be wrong with the statement of the Lamp Puzzle, and the puzzle would remain a paradox crying out for solution or dissolution.

The paradox of the lamp is not the only paradox whose statement employs the innocent-sounding '*ad infinitum*': there are a host of such paradoxes, most of which fall into one of two camps, the paradoxes of the infinitely large and the paradoxes of the infinitely small. (The paradox of the lamp is a paradox of the infinitely small.) As Adrian Moore has written, the 'Wittgensteinian critique' can be applied to all of these. Of such paradoxes as that of the lamp, he writes:

> It is certainly possible for me to spend half a minute constructing 0. It is also possible for me to spend three quarters of a minute constructing first 0, then 1. Can this not be continued *ad infinitum*? It can, but only in the sense that there is an endless series of possibilities. There is not one possibility involving an endless series.
>
> > (*The Infinite*, Routledge 1990, p. 215)

The rejection of the 'actual infinite', made alike by Aristotle and Wittgenstein, goes naturally with a rejection of extensionless points and durationless instants – although Aristotle himself didn't make this 'natural' move. So a 'Wittgensteinian critique' of the lamp paradox can certainly be extended to encompass the sort of approach I adopted in the last section.

I am aware that the argument of this section has hardly been a demonstrative proof. It relies somewhat on the not wholly satisfactory bribe: 'If you accept my theory about instants, you can undermine the paradox of the lamp'. (Bribes of this form, but with other expressions in place of 'instants' and 'the lamp', are frequently offered and accepted in philosophy.) But I trust that the effect of these several sections is cumulative, and that in the end, durationless instants will appear at least as pretty shady characters.

5.4   THE SPECIOUS PRESENT

In Part I, we touched on the question how we ought to interpret 'the time of utterance', especially as that phrase occurs in the (schematic) truth-conditions for present-tensed utterances. It was pointed out that, if a sentence like 'That chapel is enormous' is to count as present-tensed, then 'the time of utterance' could hardly signify any durationless instant, nor yet the time taken for the utterance of the sentence to be achieved. What counts as the time of utterance, and hence what counts as simultaneity with the time of utterance, seems to be a pretty elastic affair: we may be dealing with seconds or with centuries. (Of course, we could *insist* that 'the time of utterance' signify 'the time taken to make the utterance', and rephrase our truth-conditions using the idea of an utterance's taking place *during* some salient period, or *vice versa*, jettisoning the locution '*at* the time of utterance'. This does not affect my main point.) But if simultaneity (or overlap, or whatever) with time of utterance (or of thought or judgement, for that matter) is an elastic affair, so surely must *the present* be something of an elastic affair, at any rate if the notion of the present derives from the existence and possibility of present-tensed locutions and constructions.

A philosophical intuitionist will likely deny that our notion of the present derives from the phenomenon of present-tensed expressions (and what those expressions express, if you like). He will say that intuition or introspection or reflection leads us to form the idea of the present. And a philosopher enamoured of the representation of the 'time-line' by the series of real numbers will argue that the only 'once and for all' representation of past, present and future on such a line will assign a single point or real number to 'the present'.

The intuitionist is a notoriously slippery fish, and I will not here attempt to net him. The argument from the 'time-line', however, I shall try to rebut. The first thing to say is that no 'once and for all' representation of past, present and future need be possible at all; and if my allegation of elasticity in the notion of present-tensedness is correct, we have some reason to think that different representations would be needed on different occasions. 'But surely', an objector will say, 'no *period* could ever count as the present; for *during* that period it will always be possible, in principle, to look forward to that part of the period not yet elapsed – in the future – and to look back to that part of the period that has elapsed – in the past'. This was exactly the line of thought that gripped St Augustine when he reflected upon the present.[8]

The possibility mentioned in this last argument will certainly be a possibility concerning any given period. So much is a consequence of the 'non-discreteness' of time, something I have been assuming in this chapter. But the divisibility of any given period is irrelevant to my thesis about the present.

A certain utterance will be present-tensed in virtue of its truth-value's depending (in a certain way) upon what is the case during a period of time justifiably spoken of as 'the time of utterance'. It may be that another actual or possible utterance is or would be present-tensed in virtue of *its* truth-value's depending upon what is the case during a period of time justifiably spoken of as 'the time

of utterance', which period of time is within the first period of time
– i.e. which begins later and ends earlier than the first period of
time. This, obviously, does not detract from the present-tensedness
of the first utterance. Nor, as far as I can see, does the second, actual
or possible, utterance supply us with a 'more truly present' proposition, nor yet with a closer approximation to *the* present.

Somebody might think that at any rate one species of present-
tensed proposition was special: namely, the species of present-tensed
propositions than whose 'times of utterance' no other propositions'
'times of utterance' could be shorter. If there were such a species of
proposition, it would of course be special – it would be special in
virtue of just the feature that picked it out. But (a) that there could
be such a species of proposition is open to grave doubt, since, as we
have seen, the idea of a durationless point is open to grave doubt,
and the alternative for a 'smallest time of utterance' would be an
atom in a discrete time-series; and (b) even if there *were* such a species
of proposition, it is unclear why propositions of *this* species should
be thought of as being about 'the present' in a way that other
propositions could not be. It is the idea that 'the present' calls for
a 'once and for all' representation on the time-line that leads to this
way of thinking. And one may conjecture that it is the phrase's
being a definite description, together with its taking on an air of
absoluteness when plucked from the conditions of normal usage,
that make philosophers want such a 'once and for all' representation of 'the present'. But of course the sense of a definite description
is often, if not usually, context-sensitive. The (length of) time spoken of in 'We do not at the present time know the culprit's where-
abouts' need not be the same (length of) time as that spoken of in
'The present time is a gloomy one for one-parent families'; for similar reasons, the king mentioned in 'The king is dead', need not be
the same as the one mentioned in, 'Long live the king!'.

Part III
Time, Change and
Causation

6

Time and Change

6.1 A MODAL TRILEMMA

The observation that time and change are connected in some intimate and important way is almost as old as philosophy itself. Change
necessarily takes time: roughly speaking, an assertion of change
will amount to, or at any rate entail, 'For some p, p and later not-
p'. Conversely, certain features of time have seemed to many philosophers to be accountable for in terms of (or even to be reducible
to) features of change.

A notable example of this – if we can take causation to involve
change – is the causal account of the 'direction ' or 'asymmetry' of
time. It has been said that the direction of time ('from' past 'to'
future) is nothing more nor less than the direction of causation.
This thought can be cashed out as asserting that what makes A
earlier than B is the possibility of A's affecting B; or it might be
cashed out as asserting that what makes A earlier than B is the fact
that A is simultaneous with some event which could possibly affect
B: something along these lines. According to this sort of reductivist
view, the impossibility of an event's being both (wholly) before and
(wholly) after another is, roughly, the impossibility of an event's
both being able to affect another and being affectable by that other.

Now reductivism of this sort brings us up against a certain form
of problem. If the above causal account of the 'direction' of time is
correct, then we may reason as follows. 'A happened before B' will
amount to something like: 'A took place and B took place, and it
could not have been that something about the way A happened
was due to B's happening'. (I.e. 'p and q, and not possibly: (for
some φ-ly, p φ-ly because q)', with causal 'because'.) What of this
'could not have been'? Are we talking of a logical impossibility?
Surely not; for to say that Luther's birth took place before the aeroplane was invented is not to say that it is not *logically* possible that
the invention of the aeroplane should have affected Luther's birth
in some way. The aeroplane *might* (logically) have been invented
before Luther's birth, and so *might* (logically) have affected it: it might

133

have affected where Luther was born, for instance. No contradiction is involved in such a supposition.

If, on the other hand, the impossibility we have in mind is not logical in character, it looks as if it has to be empirical or nomological in character. But A may happen before B does, even though, because of the set-up, it is just nomologically impossible that A could affect B in any way. Perhaps the system in question is deterministic and the initial conditions responsible for B simply exclude A: if A hadn't happened, B would have happened anyway, and in just the way it did happen. Or perhaps B lies outside A's 'light-cone' (i.e. perhaps the time and place of B's occurrence are such that any signal from A to B would have, *per impossibile*, to travel faster than the speed of light). If the causal analysis of priority in time concerns nomological impossibility, it seems that according to that analysis B happens before A, since B is unaffectable by A. But of course A may be unaffectable by B (and will be *ex hypothesi*); from which the contradiction follows that each of A and B is before the other. Alternatively, we could follow Reichenbach in saying that where neither A nor B can affect the other, they count as simultaneous;[1] which yields the non-transitivity of simultaneity. (A and B might be unable to affect one another; B and C might be unable to affect one another; but A might be able to affect C.) Since this is non-transitivity of simultaneity even *within a single reference-frame*, it is not susceptible of special justification from the Theory of Relativity, but is simply a consequence of a (reductivist) causal account of the direction of time, the modal expressions involved being interpreted in terms of empirical possibility.

What about 'metaphysical' impossibility? Could we usefully talk of its being 'metaphysically impossible' for a prior event to be affected by a posterior event? Substance would have to be given to the idea of 'metaphysical impossibility'; but it is in any case worth noting that at least *one* popular version of this idea will not appear to help much in a causal account of temporal priority. I mean the version according to which events have 'essential properties', which it is metaphysically impossible that they should lack. How could the metaphysical impossibility of an earlier event's being affected by a later one be derived from essential properties of those events? Seemingly, just by those essential properties' including *having such-and-such causes/effects*. And that it is essential to an event that it should have the causes (and effects) that it in fact has/had/will have is a view not without its adherents. Some read it into

Davidson's well-known 'criterion of event-identity'.[2] But *this* species of impossibility will, like nomological impossibility, be too strong for the purposes of our account. For if it is metaphysically impossible for an event to have had other causes than those it actually had, it will be metaphysically impossible for it to have had, as one of its causes, some earlier event that was in fact causally irrelevant. But there clearly is such a thing as a 'causally irrelevant earlier event'. Which shows that 'is earlier than' cannot be taken as equivalent to 'cannot be affected by', with the 'cannot' construed in this metaphysical manner.

Maybe there are further species of metaphysical modality worth investigating. But I will undertake no such investigation here. For I am inclined to reject all the kinds of approach that have been mentioned: all those approaches attempting to analyse 'is earlier than' as amounting to 'cannot be affected by', whether the modality is interpreted as logical, nomological or metaphysical in character. The problem facing causal accounts of the 'direction of time' belongs to a certain genus, it seems to me, and the same sort of treatment should be meted out to each of the various problems of that genus. Let me turn now to another of these problems, the one encapsulated in the question: 'Could there be time without change?'.

6.2 TIME WITHOUT CHANGE

Change necessarily involves time; but does time necessarily involve change? Could there be a period of time during which nothing whatever happened?

If an assertion of change amounts, roughly, to: '($\exists$p) (p and later not-p)', it might look as if the passage of time itself were a kind of change. For imagine a period in which no 'states of the world' undergo change, but before and after which there has been and is going to be worldly change; at some time during that period, at t1 let us say, the proposition 'It will be, n units hence, that p' is true – 'p' being the sentence that will report the first real change (after the frozen period), when that change happens. If we are talking about a *period* of time, there will be a time later than t1, call it t2, at which 'It will be, n units hence, that p', is false. For what will be true at t2 is: 'It will be, m units hence, that p', where m is less than n. So something will be true, and later false, during the period.

We of course need to speak of a period after (or before) which there is 'real change' in order to set up this sort of case for the view that time involves change. A universe without any history at all is another and more mind-boggling matter; we shall be dealing with *such* creatures at a later stage (pp. 181–2). But in any case, it seems that the changes involved in the passage of time itself are not those of primary interest to us. The question of special interest to philosophers – to this one, anyway – is about whether the passage of time must involve *real* change. The distinction between 'real' and 'Cambridge' change[3] has been much discussed. It is a distinction that would seem to be at least *related* to that between relational and non-relational change. However we are to explicate the distinction, I think we can here take it to be a genuine one; consequently, I will rephrase the question with which we began: Could there be a period of time during which no real change occurred?

In the days when verificationist theories of meaning held intellectual sway, the answer given by a philosopher to this last question would very likely be either 'No' or 'The question is senseless'. For it seems that there could be no way of ever establishing that such a changeless period had in fact elapsed: there could be no empirical observation that might support the thesis that such a period had elapsed more than the thesis that it hadn't – since *ex hypothesi*, all observers would themselves be 'frozen' during such a period. For similar reasons, there could be no empirical observation that could support the thesis that a changeless period *hadn't* elapsed more than the thesis that it had. The result, for a verificationist, would seem to be that 'A changeless period has elapsed' must always be meaningless. So must 'A changeless period hasn't elapsed' be. Whether 'It is possible that a changeless period has elapsed' should count as necessarily false or itself meaningless then remains as a question more or less internal to verificationism – but in any case, the sentence will never be true.

Since the demise of verificationism, there has probably been less consensus as to how to answer these questions about changeless time. Sydney Shoemaker[4] has presented an ingenious and powerful type of argument to the effect that there could, in principle, be evidence that would lend *inductive* support to the hypothesis that a changeless period – even a changeless period of a certain duration – had elapsed. Here is one version of that argument. Imagine that there are just two planets in the Universe: A and B. The inhabitants of A observe that every so often, everything freezes on planet B for two hours (by the clocks on planet A); after these freezes, it seems to the inhabitants of B that nothing special has happened, of course. The inhabitants of B are told of these freezes by the inhabitants of A whenever they come out of them, and by keeping records find that their freezes occur every seven years. They, on the other hand, observe that every so often, everything freezes on planet A for two hours (by the clocks on planet B); something, again, which is unobservable by the A-inhabitants, but which they are informed of, and by keeping records find to come around every *eight* years. Together, the inhabitants of both planets conclude that a simultaneous freeze will occur every fifty-six years. And it turns out that every fifty-six years, nothing special appears to happen: no freeze on either planet is observable, either to inhabitants or non-inhabitants. But this of course confirms the hypothesis of a simultaneous freeze; the alternative hypothesis, that every fifty-six years no freezing occurs, fits less well, inductively, with the observed fact that each planet is subject to a freezing cycle.

It should be noted that Shoemaker's argument, if successful, shows that it is logically possible that there be inductive support for a certain hypothesis. But empirically false hypotheses may have inductive support; and it is even arguable that *necessarily* false hypotheses may have inductive support. Consider someone who goes carefully through a somewhat complicated mathematical or logical calculation, but makes an error, and so gets the wrong answer; on this person's authority, which has proved reliable before, another person accepts the result of the calculation. Does the latter not have a species of inductive evidence for the truth or correctness of the (necessarily false) result? The self-contradictoriness of that result is clearly not immediately apparent. And nor need the self-contradictoriness or incoherence of a putative description of a changeless universe be immediately apparent. One who deemed the notion of changeless time to be self-contradictory or incoherent could respond to Shoemaker's argument by saying: 'The hypothesis of a total freeze can only be justified, inductively or otherwise, if it makes *sense*; and whether it makes sense must be decided by other arguments.' (Indeed, if the notion of changeless time were shown to be somehow *incoherent*, we would perhaps then say that Shoemaker's thought-experiment had failed even to demonstrate the logical possibility of an inductive argument: for the conclusion of an argument must be a genuine proposition, and not just a muddle.)

It would appear, then, that whether one considers the question of changeless time to be a contingent or a non-contingent matter,

Shoemaker's argument must fail to rule out the impossibility of changeless time, nor yet to make it any 'less likely'.

Now what exactly would one be committed to who said that a period of changeless time had elapsed, say on the stroke of midday yesterday? Could such a person not take advantage of the connection between time and change to say, roughly, that it was *possible* for there to have been change *while* any given reliable clock stood at (precisely) 12 o'clock, though no such change actually took place? To say that there's room in a given container is to say that an object might be *inside* the container, even if there is in fact nothing at all in the container; likewise, the argument will go, to say that some time has elapsed between two times is to say that change might have occurred between those times, even if in fact nothing at all happened between those two times.

At this point, a version of the difficulty mentioned in the last section presents itself. It is surely innocuously true that (a) no change took place yesterday when all reliable clocks were in fact standing at precisely 12 o'clock, while (b) it was logically possible that such change should have occurred. This alone cannot establish that everything froze at noon yesterday. But if a general freeze at noon *had* taken place, and had done so for reasons to do with the forces of nature, it would not then have been true that the occurrence of change during that period of freeze was *nomologically* possible. This much is ruled out by saying that the forces of nature produced a freeze – i.e. *prevented any change*. The third option, that of calling the putative possibility of change a 'metaphysical' one, is in this context particularly obscure; if it amounts to saying that it is incompatible with the (alleged) essential properties of no (salient?) entity that there should have been change . . . , then 'metaphysical possibility' looks to be as weak a notion as 'logical possibility'. When would a change-while-clocks-stood-still *not* be metaphysically possible? – i.e. when would it be right to say that a general freeze had *not* occurred? And which entity or entities could it be whose essential properties determined the metaphysical modalities here? (Surely not 'Time itself'!)

The question of 'empty time' does not crop up only in connection with 'freezing', of course. If the Universe came into existence with a Big Bang, was there time before the bang? And if the Universe comes to an end with a Big Crash, will there be time after the crash? In either case, one might want to give sense to the supposition that there was/will be time by saying either: 'It was possible for change to occur before the Big Bang', or: 'It will be possible for change to occur after the Big Crash'. But these modal statements present a trilemma: either logical possibility is meant, which is too weak, or nomological possibility, which is too strong, or metaphysical possibility – which is either too weak or too vague.

One might now begin to feel something like the exasperation of the verificationist, and end up deciding to dismiss the question of empty time as, if not senseless, then at any rate hopeless. But such a response is impossible. For our 'modal trilemma' is not confined to empty time, nor to bizarre or extreme cases: it is to be found in connection with our everyday use of temporal units.

6.3 STATEMENTS OF DURATION

One day, Molesworth inscribes the words, 'I was here', on his school desk. It takes him precisely five seconds to do so. Now to what exactly am I committed by remarking that it took Molesworth five seconds to write 'I was here'? I might say: 'Well, some second-hand somewhere traversed five unit-marks in the time it took Molesworth to write his message.' But clearly my remark does not commit me to saying that there were clocks around when Molesworth wrote 'I was here'. Clocks everywhere may have stopped due to mechanical failure, and it would remain true that it took Molesworth five seconds to write 'I was here'. And things took time before clocks of any sort were invented or used.

What I *do* seem able to say is: 'If a true clock had been running while Molesworth was writing "I was here", the clock would have advanced five seconds in the time it took him to do so.' I seem able to say this – but am I? My claim is a counterfactual conditional. Perhaps, then, it is an empirical claim, to the effect that in virtue of the laws of nature and the initial conditions that would have obtained if a true clock had been running at the time, that clock would have advanced, etc. Well, what if the process which takes five seconds is not so prosaic a one as the petty vandalism of the example, but instead is a hugely violent explosion of energy, such that, as a matter of empirical fact, no clock in the same reference-frame as the explosion could have survived intact? In what sense 'would' a true clock have given a reading of five seconds in this case? Or again, perhaps our set-up is so sensitive that the mere presence of a clock would affect how long the process in question took.

Can the counterfactual conditional be construed in a weaker manner? Might it amount to something like: 'It was logically (not empirically) possible that a true clock should have timed Molesworth's performance; and if one had, it would have given a reading of five seconds'? The crucial question is going to be whether grounds can be given for preferring this last statement to one that is exactly similar, but in which 'five seconds' is replaced by any other duration-term. And it seems that no such grounds can in fact be given.

Let us use the heuristic device of possible worlds. There are various logically possible worlds in which Molesworth writes 'I was here' on his desk while being timed by a true clock; many of these worlds will differ as to what reading the clock gives. Our counterfactual conditional, according to the usual wisdom, is equivalent to the statement that in the *nearest* of these logically possible worlds, the reading of the clock is 'five seconds'. What now could determine 'nearness', so as to support such a statement, rather than any other? Clearly, it won't do to say that the nearest possible world is the one in which Molesworth takes the same time, namely five seconds, to write 'I was here': for we cannot include in the description of our possible worlds statements of the durations of occurrences, unless the sense of such duration-statements is given. The sense of duration-statements is not given, however – our present task is exactly to give their sense.

It might be thought that the nearest possible world (to the actual) will at any rate have to be one in which the *relations* between durations of events is preserved: Molesworth's performance will still have to take less long than that rotation of the earth on its axis during which his performance took place. But clearly these 'topological' relations can be preserved in worlds in which the true clock gives other readings than 'five seconds'. In a world in which the clock reads 'seven years', it, or another true clock that happens to be timing the earth's rotation, will give a very much bigger reading than 'one day'. Of course, this won't be allowable if a true clock was *actually* timing the earth's rotation: in that case, the nearest possible world will also contain a clock timing the earth's rotation, likewise giving a reading of 'one day', rather than some other reading. But if a clock was actually timing the rotation of the earth, then that clock would *ipso facto* have been timing Molesworth's performance itself. Our analysis of duration-statements, however, must apply as well in the case of events or processes that weren't in fact timed as in the case of ones that were.

Our resort, once again, may be to the 'metaphysical'. If it is an essential property of Molesworth's writing 'I was here' that it took the time it did, then the nearest metaphysically possible world in which that same writing occurs, timed by a true clock, will be one in which the clock's reading is 'five seconds'. But this sort of talk is obviously utterly unhelpful. Anyone remotely puzzled by the question how 'So-and-so took five seconds' can mean what it does, will not be content to take on board the thesis that an event's duration is simply one of its 'essential properties'.

6.4 CRITERIA

So what sense *can* be made of statements of duration?

The idea to give up, I think, is the idea that 'It took five seconds for so-and-so to happen' can be said to *amount to*, or to *commit one to*, any proposition or propositions about clocks. 'It took five seconds' is the sort of sentence one can only grasp and use intelligently once one knows about clocks and timing; but it is not a sentence *about* clocks and timing. Our vocabulary of colour-words is only possible against a background of shared colour-discriminations, but 'That is green' does not amount to, 'Normal-sighted people would respond to that by calling it "green" '.[5] As the argument of section 5.1 indicated, there is indeed a constitutive connection between statements of temporal duration and the concept of a true clock, but it is not a connection that generates analyses or reductions of those statements.

So what exactly is the nature of this constitutive connection? There may be more than one account of the connection that would avoid the 'modal trilemma' we have encountered: but the account that seems to *me* to be of the right sort is one that relies on something like the Wittgensteinian notion of a 'criterion'. The account I have in mind goes roughly as follows.

A term gets its *sense*, and, we may add, its objectivity, from what we may call its rules of use. A term's rules of use govern its general application; but with many terms, a particular, central application is what crucially informs those rules. This central application will be one made in 'paradigm circumstances' – and *that* the circumstances in question are paradigm is constitutive of the concept attaching to the term. 'Paradigm circumstances' are those that must hold if a use of the term is to count as contributing to a judgement that is indubitably correct (i.e. true or warrantable) – a proviso here being that 'indubitably' does not mean 'infallibly'. These circumstances need not hold in every case where the term is used meaningfully, nor need it be *possible* for them to hold in every such case. It is a constitutive fact about the term that certain simple judgements employing it, if made in certain kinds of circumstances, count as indubitably correct; and the sense which the term has when used in 'non-ideal' circumstances *effectively derives from* there being 'ideal' circumstances, and from the nature of those circumstances.

Take, as a shop-worn example, 'red'. The paradigm conditions for application of 'red' are: where a normal-sighted, linguistically competent observer is looking at something in normal lighting. If the sincere judgement of such an observer, in such circumstances, is that the object observed is red, this is enough for the object to *be* red. It is not merely that such judgements, made in such circumstances, are a reliable guide to the colours of objects, in the way in which smoke is a reliable indicator of fire. Rather, the *sense* of 'red' is derived from such paradigm applications. The sincere judgement of a normal-sighted observer in normal lighting conditions that an object is red is a 'criterion' of that object's being red. But 'red' can be used in (true or false) judgements, including predications, that are *not* made in paradigm conditions. One can even predicate 'red' in circumstances where criterial testing is impossible.

For a temporal expression like 'five seconds', the paradigm circumstances of application are roughly, or at least include: where a true clock is set going at the start of a process, P, and at the end of that process gives a reading of 'five seconds', then 'P took five seconds' is indubitably correct. The notion of a true clock is like that of a normal-sighted observer, as we noted in Chapter 5. Our present concern is with those applications of a duration-term that are made where criterial testing (testing with a true clock) is physically impossible.

It seems to me that the crucial question is: 'When can we say that a use of, say, "five seconds" is a use of the *same* expression as the use of those sounds or inscriptions in criterially ideal conditions?'. I think that in order to answer this last question we should not attend to the possibilities, in each case, of a person's verifying the (truth or warrantability of) judgements he makes with the help of the sound or inscription, so much as to the linguistic and other dispositions of the person. For example, that someone will (or would, if asked) cite the same sorts of indirect (non-criterial) evidence for the truth of different judgements employing a term is evidence, in itself non-conclusive of course, that he is using the term in the same way in those different judgements; so is this behaving in ways that connect intelligibly with his utterances only on the assumption that he does mean the same on the different occasions.

'If asked about his use of the term "F", Bill would have responded . . .'; 'If he'd acted on the basis of such-and-such desire and the belief expressed by his utterance, Bill would have. . . .' – aren't these just further counterfactual conditionals? And won't the 'modal dilemma' apply here too? No. For, again, what is being proposed is not an *analysis* of locutions of the form, 'N means such-and-such by his use of "F"'; but rather that there are certain defeasible criteria for the expression 'means'; or, if you like, schematic criteria for expressions of the form 'means such-and-such by "F"'. An indubitably true or warrantable judgement of the form, 'N means such-and-such by "F"' will be available, for instance, when a person's use of a term *is* 'tested' by his responses to questions, his relevant non-linguistic actions, etc. 'Indubitably' doesn't mean 'indefeasibly' here: further, defeating, evidence is always a possibility. Of course, we could talk about 'normal conditions', as we do in the case of 'ideal' colour-ascriptions, thus excluding pathological insincerity, etc. But 'Conditions are here normal' is itself never indefeasibly true.

The view of meaning-ascriptions here adopted is clearly not a hundred miles from that of the later Wittgenstein. And in this connection it is worth mentioning Kripke's discussion of 'sensation language' in Chapter 3 of his *Wittgenstein on Rules and Private Language*. Kripke writes that a

> liberal interpretation of the private language argument . . . would allow that a speaker might introduce some sensation terms with no 'outward criteria' for the associated sensations beyond his own sincere avowal of them. (Hence these avowals do not 'replace' any 'natural expressions' of the sensation(s), for there are none.) There will be no way anyone else will be in any position to check such a speaker, or to agree or disagree with him . . . . However, the language of the speaker, even his language of sensations, will not have the objectionable form of a 'private language', one in which anything he calls 'right' is right. The speaker can demonstrate, for many sensations that do have 'public criteria', that he has mastered the appropriate terminology for identifying these sensations. If we agree with his responses in enough cases

of various sensations, we say of him that he was mastered 'sensation language'. All this, so far, is subject to external correction. But it is a primitive part of our language game of sensations that, if an individual has satisfied criteria for a mastery of sensation language in general, we then respect his claim to have identified a new type of sensation even if the sensation is correlated with nothing publicly observable. The only 'public criterion' for such an avowal will be the sincere avowal itself.

> (*Wittgenstein on Rules and Private Language*, Blackwell, 1982, p. 103)

Let us compare someone's saying, 'That drug always gives me a strange sensation quite unlike anything else' (the sensation spoken of lacking any 'natural expression') with someone's saying, 'A five-minute period of changeless time elapsed yesterday'. In the first case, it is simply the person's mastery of sensation language in general that counts as guaranteeing that his utterance makes sense and is true or false: there are no criteria governing his avowal, 'There's that strange sensation again!', analogous to the (behavioural) criteria governing his avowal, 'That hurts!'. So no criterial checking of the first avowal is even *possible*. Similarly, no criterial checking of the utterance 'A five-minute period of changeless time elapsed yesterday' is possible; but, I want to argue, it nevertheless counts as making sense, and as having a truth-value, in virtue of the utterer's mastery of duration language in general, which mastery can be criterially checked in other circumstances.

Of course, if a person's mastery of sensation language in general counts as a criterion for the sensefulness of his avowal, 'There's that strange sensation again!', it is also the case that a sincere such avowal counts as a criterion for its own *truth*. Nothing analogously counts as a criterion for the *truth* of 'A five-minute period of changeless time elapsed yesterday', and this raises the question whether we have to regard such an utterance as either true or false. Does sensefulness guarantee having a truth-value? I am inclined to think that in this case it does; but this is a matter to which we shall return.

6.5　HOROLOGICAL CONFUSION

Where do these remarks leave us? They leave us, I think, with somewhat clearer grounds for saying that time without change is at any rate logically or conceptually possible. To say that everything froze at midday yesterday is not to say that change was either logically or nomologically possible (though not actual) while all reliable clocks stood at 12 o'clock yesterday, nor to say anything of the sort. The best we can do in answer to a question like, 'What did so-and-so mean when she said that a period of changeless time had elapsed?', is (a) to give a general answer to the question, 'What makes something a claim that time has elapsed?', in terms of the criteria governing duration-terms, and (b) to say that a claim of the sort described under (a) was made, together with the claim that nothing had happened during the period in question.

The proposition, 'A period of changeless time has elapsed' makes sense, and moreover involves no contradiction. These two facts seem on the face of it to yield the conclusion that 'It is logically possible for there to be time without change' is itself true.

If the approach of the last section is along the right lines, a question arises about another kind of extreme scenario: that in which there is *general horological confusion*. If the criteria governing duration-terms require a background of general agreement between clocks, it might seem that any circumstances in which there was prolonged and inexplicable general disagreement among true clocks (or among what had counted as 'true clocks') would be ones in which, say, 'five minutes has elapsed' would count as neither true nor false – though circumstances in which we would count such events 'inexplicable' must needs be rare. (We should take it also that by 'true clock' is meant any regular process which is usable as a true clock.) Such a situation of confusion, it might be argued, would be one *unspecified* by the rules governing 'five minutes'; somewhat analogously, the rules governing 'game' do not specify whether some novel activity counts as a game if competent speakers are divided 50–50 in their willingness to predicate 'game' of that activity.

But there are difficulties here; ones that can be brought out by comparing once more with the case of colour-ascriptions. If a new substance is produced in the laboratories, and a general disagreement ensues as to whether it is blue, red or yellow, then there is simply no fact of the matter as to whether it *is* blue, red or yellow. But we must presume a background of sustained general agreement: there must still be agreement as to the colours of other substances and things. For this general agreement ensures that we can meet the condition that normal-sighted people should observe the substance in normal lighting; without the agreement, both between people and with past judgements, there would be no reason to regard us as a population with any 'normal-sighted' people in it, using colour-words with the same meaning as of yore.

Now what could count as a 'background of sustained general agreement' in the case where 'true clocks' begin to give disparate readings? Perhaps we can imagine a case in which a particular kind of natural process, P, was such that the results of timing it with different true clocks on any given occasion yielded different results, despite there being agreement between clocks in the timing of all other events and processes; and we might (*might*) in such a case say that there was never any fact of the matter how long a P-process took. But where the timings of *all* events and processes yielded only confusion, could we say that we were ever meeting the criterial condition, of timing a given process with a true clock? In virtue of what would these things be true clocks, and in virtue of what would they be functioning as they had functioned of yore? An alternative, and seemingly equally admissible, description of the state of affairs is available: clocks and measuring processes have all inexplicably broken down, and it is therefore *impossible* to time any event with a true clock, since there are none to hand. And recall now that the rules governing duration-terms are not such that duration-terms are only meaningfully applicable to situations where it is *possible* to time an event. (Consider the five-second-long massive explosion.) *Our* use of duration-terms is backed up by general agreement, and this goes for instances like: 'A five-hour period of horological confusion could/did elapse'. Of course, creatures doomed to live in a world of horological confusion would be in a different case – for they could have no duration-terms. (The special problems that attach to hypothetical *worlds* – as opposed to periods – of confusion, let alone to static or creatureless worlds, are ones that we will be dealing with later on, in the next chapter (section 7.5). The present discussion is restricted to periods or situations of confusion.)

'Well', it might be said, 'perhaps it would be *meaningful* for us to say of a period of general horological confusion that it had lasted seventeen-and-a-half hours, but would such a statement have to be true or false? After all, someone who calls a new activity a game may say something neither true nor false; but we needn't conclude that she has said something meaningless.'

The criterial conditions for 'game' require not much more than this: that if enough linguistically competent people sincerely react to learning about the activity in question by adjudging it 'a game', then it is a game; and if enough linguistically competent people sincerely react to learning about the activity in question by adjudging it 'not a game', then it is not a game. These criteria do not specify whether an activity counts as a game when there is, say, a 50–50 split in people's reactions; so that when there is such a split, we may say that there is no fact of the matter. In the case of such a split, the conditions for applying the criterial test *have been met* – enough people's sincere reactions have been elicited – but the result does not determine an answer. In fact, it determines that there is no answer. In the case of general horological confusion, the criterial conditions *cannot be met*, just as they cannot if there is a massive explosion of energy, or whatever; for nothing can count as a true clock. Indeed, wherever there is *general* confusion (people disagreeing a lot, etc.), criterial conditions will be unmeetable. Hence, the sort of reasons we have for saying 'neither true nor false' when it comes to everyday disagreements about 'game', or 'red', or whatever, would not be applicable in a case of general confusion. And for such cases, the principle is, I think, 'Bivalence as usual': either the confused period lasted seventeen-and-a-half hours or it didn't. But we must assume a longer background period of general agreement.

Similarly, we can say that 'Five minutes of changeless time has elapsed' will always be either true or false; the unavailability of the criterial test for such a statement does not impugn this.

This at any rate is what I want to argue for: but certain well-known objections to my approach have to be considered before the argument can appear secure. In particular, the adherence I have been recommending to the principle of bivalence is objected to, by anti-realists, in virtue of just those sorts of cases that we have been talking about: cases where the criterial tests for a type of judgement cannot be carried out – where a judgement of that type is unverifiable.

6.6 ANTI-REALISM

An anti-realist of the sort delineated, if not personified, by Michael Dummett argues as follows. The meaning of an expression in a given linguistic community is a function of how (enough) people use it, or would use it. Since language must be teachable, and since it is used for communication, the features of an expression's use that matter for its meaning must be publicly detectable. If somebody knows the meaning of an expression, he must therefore be able to manifest his knowledge: anything unmanifestable will be irrelevant to the expression's meaning, since only detectable features of the expression's use matter.

If, then, it is alleged that to grasp the meaning of a sentence, a person needs to grasp, or have a conception of, the *truth-conditions* of that sentence, we must enquire what 'grasp of truth-conditions' amounts to – and, in particular, how such a grasp is manifestable. Where a (clearly meaningful) sentence is unverifiable, a grasp of its truth-conditions will at any rate not be manifestable as *recognition* of the truth or falsity of that sentence – where 'recognising the truth-value of a sentence' means 'establishing by direct means the truth-value of a sentence'. But in that case it is obscure what a grasp of verification-transcendent truth-conditions *could* amount to, if it is meant to amount to something more than the capacity to assert the sentence with good (but indirect) warrant.

This latter capacity, it seems, is all that could be manifest when it comes to someone's grasping the meaning of an unverifiable sentence. So only the conditions for warranted assertion can in the end be relevant to the sense of such a sentence. But if talk of the truth-conditions of such a sentence is inappropriate, then so is an insistence that the sentence must have a determinate truth-*value*. The principle of bivalence is thus inapplicable to verification-transcendent sentences.

There is much truth in the general philosophy of language which motivates anti-realism, I think. But the anti-realist's attitude to unverifiable sentences can be questioned. The crucial issue, for our purposes, is the issue as to what could count as manifesting a grasp of a verification-transcendent sentence. As Crispin Wright asks:

> What . . . in the responses of speakers to the detectable obtaining of conditions warrants the attribution to them of a conception that the *very same* conditions can obtain undetectably? What could distinguish the performance of someone who had grasped that possibility from that of someone who had not but who was prepared to count the statements in question as verified in the appropriate circumstances?
> ('Realism, Truth-Value Links, Other Minds and the Past', in
> *Realism, Meaning and Truth*, Blackwell, 1987, p. 100)

Take changeless time. How, Wright will demand, can someone with a putative conception of the possibility of five minutes elapsing of changeless time be distinguished from someone without that conception, but who could admit that the assertion, 'Five minutes have elapsed' is verified in certain circumstances (i.e. with clocks to hand)?

The simple answer, it seems to me, is: the first person would be inclined to assert: 'It is possible that five minutes should elapse of changeless time'; and would, moreover, be able to cite, or at least recognise, the possibility of evidence (e.g. Shoemakerian evidence) for the warranted assertion of 'Five minutes have elapsed of changeless time'. This is enough for 'having a conception of' the possibility in question. Take a contrasting case: that of the putative conception of something's being different from itself. It is not possible for someone to be able to cite, or recognise, even indirect evidence for claims of the form 'A is different from itself'; any alleged evidence would simply betoken confusion on the part of the person putting it forward. And unless it can be shown that stories such as Shoemaker's are similarly confused, a conception of time's passing without change does not seem to be beyond grasping. It is, as I said earlier, primarily a matter of someone's having (verifiably) displayed a general mastery of duration-terms that counts in favour of the claim that he means the same on some new occasion of use as on previous occasions. Other things being equal, this will apply to a person's statement 'It is possible that five minutes should elapse during which nothing happens'.

Thus we have a *prima facie* answer to the question 'What could manifest having a conception of an unverifiable possibility?'. It was the anti-realist's answering 'Nothing' to this last question that led him to doubt whether talk of the truth-conditions – and so of the determinate truth-value – of unverifiable sentences could be at all appropriate. If 'Nothing' is not after all the right answer, then we would as yet appear to have no grounds for doubting the applicability of the principle of bivalence to sentences of the sort we have been discussing.

We should also ask how the anti-realist will cope with some of the problems we dealt with earlier. Take duration-statements like 'The explosion lasted five seconds'. The event reported by such a statement may, as we have noted, be practically impossible to verify. It looks as if the anti-realist must talk, as he must in other contexts, of 'verifiability in principle'; but to say that it is or was in principle possible to time the explosion and get such-and-such a reading just looks to land us with our modal trilemma once more. By 'possible' do we mean 'logically possible', or 'empirically possible', or perhaps 'metaphysically possible'? Each option faces its own difficulties.

If we eschew 'verifiability in principle', the alternative, for the anti-realist, might well be thought to be the analogue of 'strict finitism': namely, the view that by 'verifiable' must be meant 'empirically possible for us to verify' ('us' being the speakers of the language in which the duration-statements get made). But this, apart from anything else, will deprive of a truth-value many duration-statements which seem to deserve one – many past-tense ones, ones reporting massive explosions, and so on.

6.7 ARE WE IN ERROR? OR CONFUSED?

The challenge of anti-realism is of course too substantial a one to have been adequately dealt with here, nor do I claim to have done much more than sketch a response to it. But I want now to return to the issue of the criteria, if any, that govern duration-terms.

I have claimed that a criterially central application of, say, 'second' may be impossible in certain circumstances, but that for all that, it will be either true or false that five seconds passed in those circumstances. But might not the conditions for paradigm uses of 'second' go something like this? (a) If a true clock, running for the duration of an event, reads 'n seconds' at the end, then 'the event lasted n seconds' is true; (b) if a true clock, running for the duration of an event, does not read 'n seconds' at the end, then 'the event lasted n seconds' is false; (c) if it is not possible for a true clock to be running for the duration of the event, then 'the event lasted n seconds' is false. (We may include 'static events' among events.) If meeting the conditions specified for paradigm uses amounts to satisfying one of the antecedents of the conditionals comprising the set of those conditions, then the paradigm conditions here imagined for 'second' will be met even when it is impossible to time the event in question (by condition (c)). 'There was a period of time lasting n seconds during which no change could occur' implies 'There was a period of time lasting n seconds during which it was impossible for a clock to run', which however implies, by condition (c), its own negation. Hence, the first sentence of these three sentences is necessarily false; in other words, nomologically frozen time will be an impossibility.

However, if the above were indeed the conditions for paradigm uses of 'second', then a sentence like 'The explosion took 300 seconds, though no clock could have timed it' would have to be false; and in general, untimeable occurrences would be an impossibility. Our use of the word 'second', it seems to me, does *not* have this consequence.

But what is my evidence for this last claim? It might look to be no more than the fact that we do not recognize the enforced absence of true clocks as defeating such claims as 'The explosion took 300 seconds'. But could it not be argued that we *ought* to recognize the enforced absence of true clocks as defeating such claims? One could frame this argument in either of two ways: (i) our practice of not recognizing the unavailability of true clocks as itself defeating our duration-claims is not, as I have argued, a consequence of the criteria governing duration-terms – it is simply error or confusion, committed while using such terms; (ii) our practice of not recognizing the unavailability of true clocks as claim-defeaters *is* a consequence of, or is compatible with, the criteria for duration-terms, but those criteria embody corrupt concepts; or, if concepts cannot be corrupt, our practice is a consequence of certain would-be criteria for would-be concepts.

If (i) goes with the view that (a)–(c), three paragraphs back, give the criteria behind our use of duration-terms, then the problem is that (i) posits a straight contradiction between our practice and one of the criterial conditions allegedly governing that practice (condition (c)). Now of course many of us have contradictory beliefs. The rules governing 'All' are such that 'All Fs are G' is incompatible with 'This F is not G'; but not infrequently a person will say, though rarely in one breath, both that all Fs are G and that this particular F is not G. And here we do not conclude that by 'All Fs are G' the person does not after all mean something incompatible with 'This F is G'. So people's practical use of a term can contradict one of the rules governing the use of that term. But there seem to be two aspects of such cases as these that distinguish them from the case of our allegedly erroneous judgements involving 'second', etc.

First, it is not more often than not that people say or think both 'All Fs are G' and 'This F is not a G' – it is less often than not. Second, and more importantly, a person who has said both 'All Fs are G' and 'This F is not a G' will very likely not realise he has done so – when his attention is drawn to the fact that he has done so, he will (unless perverse or deluded . . .) withdraw at least one of the

things he has said. Now a person who has said 'The dinosaur discovered here probably took about 300 seconds to get from that
ravine to this spot' may be got to admit that, given the set-up, no
clock could in fact have timed the dinosaur to yield a reading of, or
equivalent to, '300 seconds', and his attention may be drawn to this
conjunction of his assertions. But this will very rarely induce a
retraction. Only by persuading him of certain philosophical theories could one get him to retract, just as one can quite quickly get
people to say that they don't really know anything. The borderline
between bringing out the consequences of someone's beliefs and
persuading someone of a philosophical theory may be a touch
blurred, but not so blurred as to render the distinction a false one.

Let us turn to the other thesis to be considered: namely, the thesis
that our practice – of *not* thinking that a duration-claim is undermined if it is learnt that the claim could not have been directly
verified – simply shows that our duration-concepts are corrupt,
or are only pseudo-concepts. Certainly, not any old list of rules or
criteria can be taken to embody a *bona fide* concept. Take Prior's
connective 'tonk'.[6] The introduction and elimination rules for this
connective are such that just using the connective results in one's
producing contradictions. Might not the conditions for criterially
central uses which I have said govern 'second' similarly give rise to
undesirable consequences?

Self-contradiction is clearly an undesirable consequence, and the
fact that the use of 'tonk' produces self-contradiction is enough to
show that 'tonk' is unusable. But the conditions of application which
I have alleged hold for 'second' do not seem to produce any contradiction or incoherence. Is it possible to say that they produce, or
somehow go with, straightforward error? It might be thought that
certain concepts *presuppose* contingent hypotheses in such a way
that if those hypotheses are in fact false, the use of the concepts in
question is radically undermined. For instance, if the use of 'tiger'
presupposes that there is an essential property shared by tigers,
and if this is actually false, then it seems that statements using
'tiger' are, not merely false, but senseless, or at least truth-valueless.

The criteria I have alleged of 'second', however, do not appear to
presuppose any contingent hypotheses that one might here question. Perhaps the existence and availability, in certain circumstances,
of true clocks is in a certain sense presupposed by the use of 'second': but if *this* presupposition is false, then it does not merely follow
that my proposed criteria for duration-terms fails, but that there are

no proper duration-terms at all. For that the use of duration-terms requires the notion of a true clock is independently arguable – I argued for it in section 5.1. Moreover, that there are true clocks is not an empirical hypothesis of the same sort as, say, the hypothesis that tigers share an essential property: 'true clock', like 'normal-sighted person', is a concept arising out of actual large-scale agreement. To say that this agreement might be illusory, or might be 'accidental', would be to adopt the position of a philosophical sceptic.

(Do the criteria which I have alleged of 'second' presuppose that a statement can be true or false despite being unverifiable as such (because made in non-ideal circumstances)? – I don't think that one would be using 'presuppose' properly if one did say this. Of course, I am supposing – *contra* anti-realists – that statements can be true or false even when the criterial conditions governing them are not meetable, and when, *ipso facto*, those statements are unverifiable. But this is a different matter.)

6.8   THREE ARGUMENTS AGAINST CHANGELESS TIME

I have left until nearly last consideration of a handful of arguments against the possibility of time without change. One of these arguments in particular deserves attention not only for its bearing on the question of time and change, but also for its bearing on the semantics of dates, and so connects up with our previous discussion of that topic. I will deal with this argument last.

The first argument I will consider, formulated by G. E. L. Owen,[7] is this: in a period of changeless time, there will be nothing to distinguish one moment from any other, since nothing is happening. But if every moment during the period is exactly similar to every other in all respects, then, by Leibniz's principle of the Identity of Indiscernibles, they will not after all be numerically distinct: there will be at most one moment, and this an instantaneous one. Hence there could not be a *period* of changeless time.

The remaining two arguments are similar to one another, at any rate on the surface, and apply particularly to the idea of changeless time before, or after, the beginning, or end, of the universe. The first one crops up in Leibniz's correspondence with Clarke.[8] Leibniz's argument goes something like this: on the assumption that God created the universe, it seems that He would have as much reason to create it at one time as at another, given that there was no first moment of time; but this would mean that God, in creating the universe when he did, did not act with sufficient reason. But God only acts with sufficient reason. So there must have been a first moment of time; God created the universe as soon as He could.

If one is unhappy with the assumption of theism, and of the Principle of Sufficient Reason, nevertheless one need not pass over Leibniz's argument altogether. For one might still be puzzled by the question: 'If there was time before the beginning of the universe, why didn't the universe come into existence sooner – or later, for that matter?'; and one might reason as follows. One who says that there might have been time before the start of the universe must admit that the quoted question has an answer; but in fact the question could not possibly have an answer; so that it is wrong to think that there might have been time before the start of the universe.

The third and final argument I will discuss, a relative of the Leibnizian argument, is this. One who says there might be time before and after the history of the universe must allow that it makes sense to say that the whole history of the universe should have a different position in time: that everything that ever happens should happen two seconds earlier, say. (This is a harmlessly tenseless 'happens', by the way, adopted for convenience of expression.) But this hypothesis, the argument goes, is senseless; so the position that entails its sensefulness is mistaken.

The first argument can, I think, be dealt with fairly swiftly. I will not examine the question whether, by invoking the Identity of Indiscernibles, the argument 'reifies' moments of time; I am inclined to think not, since identity and indiscernibility, and the principles (allegedly) governing these, have suitable analogues in higher-order discourse.[9] We can quite uncontroversially use nouns like 'moment' without fear of 'ontological commitment': let us then ask, 'Would the moments of time during a changeless period be exactly similar?'. The answer to this, I think, is 'No'. For, as was mentioned earlier, during a period before and after which things happened, there would, with the passage of time, be 'Cambridge' changes going on. At one time, the Thaw would be going to take place n units hence, while at a later time, it would be going to take place m units hence, m being less than n. What about a world without any history? Would it not have to be without duration? Perhaps Owens's argument has more bite here, since in such a world there could be no real change to guarantee occurrence of Cambridge change; but, as we shall have occasion to note later on, such thought-experiments about entire 'worlds' must be treated carefully. One cannot assume that one is talking sense when propounding them.

Turning to the second-mentioned of the three arguments, it seems clear that, if the world came into existence with a Big Bang at time t, before which there was empty time, it makes sense to suppose that it might have come into existence earlier, at time t-2, let us say. This is not to suppose that the *whole* of history should be 'shifted back' by a given amount (which is the hypothesis under scrutiny from argument number three). A system of dates need not be definitionally fixed by reference to an initial event – nor, indeed, by reference to any special event. And the semantic rigidity of dates enables us to say, 'The Big Bang might have happened at time t-2', with as much right as, 'Christ's birth might have happened in 4 BC' (= 'Christ might have been born in 4 BC'). These facts about dates are ones which we discussed in Chapter 4. Our question, then – taking the Big Bang as the world's coming into existence – is this: Is the proponent of empty time before the Big Bang committed to saying that there should have been a reason why the Big Bang occurred when it did, *rather than at some other time*?

I confess I can see no grounds for answering this question positively. There are many unanswerable questions of the form, 'Why p, *rather than* q?', and the present example seems to me to be just another. An explanation of why something happened when it did will typically be some sort of causal explanation, and it seems pretty clear that, unless God had a hand, the Big Bang's occurrence is not susceptible of causal explanation. This will be so whether or not empty time preceded it. (Perhaps the thought occurs that with no prior empty time, there *would* be an explanation of why the Big Bang happened when it did: namely, because it couldn't have occurred earlier – there having been no earlier time – and couldn't have occurred later – because if it had, the time of its occurrence would have been inexplicable. But the last bit of reasoning is simply illicit. For again, why shouldn't the time of the Big Bang be inexplicable?)

I turn finally to the last of the three arguments. Could the whole history of the world have occurred two seconds earlier than it did? And is the proponent of time before the Big Bang committed to answering 'Yes' to this first question?

I said, in connection with argument number one, that it did make sense to suppose the Big Bang to have occurred two seconds earlier; and this will surely apply to any other event one cares to cite. But of course it does not follow, from the premise that any event may have happened two seconds earlier, that *every* event may have happened two seconds earlier. We are now imagining, as it were, a world completely distinct from the actual world, sharing no part of its history (in one sense of 'history').

Let us take a parallel puzzle, of a more sceptical-sounding form. How do we know that what we all took for 1990 wasn't *in fact* 1967, that what we all took for 1989 wasn't *in fact* 1966, and so on, systematically? Now this puzzle is patently absurd; and roughly speaking, its absurdity stems from the fact that what enough of us call '1990' is thereby called '1990' with sufficient warrant – and so is in fact 1990. There is no question, beyond our use of dates and the way a system is embodied in this use, as to what year a given year is. And these facts are relevant to the present case, as we shall see.

The hypothesis that the world might have been 'shifted back', say by a year, appears to entail that either people in that world would be systematically mistaken about dates, or their '1990' would mean something different from what our '1990' means, simply in virtue of the fact (included in the world-description) that what they called '1990' would be 1989. But in what could consist the 'fact' that the year that they called '1990' would in reality be 1989? As we have just noted, what makes 'our' 1990 the year that it is (i.e. 1990), is just the role of '1990' in the settled institution of dates – which of course is not to say that 'This year is 1990' amounts to, 'This year is the one generally called "1990"', or any such thing. In our description of a hypothetical world, what justifies our saying that a certain year would in fact be 1989? Can we say that this year's identity would be determined by the role of '1989', either in the language of the inhabitants of that world, or in our own actual language? The first option is ruled out by our saying that 1989 gets called '1988' in the imagined world; what of the second?

A modal statement involving a date – such as, 'There could have been a civil war in 1848' – manages to say something in virtue, at least in part, of its connection with other, non-modal statements, such as, 'There was great unrest on the Continent in 1848'. For to assess a modal dated statement for truth, where its date is relevant to that assessment, requires evidential support of a non-modal nature. The possibility of something's happening at some time, rather than another, amounts to the possibility of its happening at some point in a network of other happenings (for a bare 'time when' cannot help or hinder its occurrence). A date can only be relevant to the truth of a modal statement insofar as it implies such a net-work. And this will be a network of actual occurrences: a date will not imply any network of merely possible occurrences, in eviden-tial relation to which we are to consider the occurrence mentioned in the modal statement.

Returning to the 'shifted back' world, it is clear that our *fiat* that the year called '1990' in that world would in reality be the year 1989 can be no more than a *fiat* – and a *fiat* without content. The modal statement, 'If everything had happened a year earlier, the Russian Revolution would have happened in 1916' is not properly assess-able for truth: the date '1916' in this context can imply no network of actual events. The appearance which the sentence has of being, not only senseful, but actually true, is generated by its surface kin-ship with such a sentence as, 'If the First World War had started a year earlier, the Russian Revolution would have happened in 1916', in which a network of actual events – a bit of actual history – *is* implied by the date.

But what if time had a beginning (prior to the occurrence of the Big Bang)? Wouldn't it then make sense to suppose that the world's history might have occurred a year earlier, simply in virtue of the fact that, whereas the Big Bang took place n years after time began, it *could* have taken place n–1 years after time began?

Let us assume that it makes sense to suppose that time might have had a beginning prior to that of the world. And let us allow that, on this assumption, the length of the period between time's beginning and the Big Bang would be a contingent matter. The essential question is: Why talk of the history of the world's happen-ing a year earlier, rather than the beginning of time's happening a year later?

The dates in the system of dates AD have the meaning they do in virtue (a) of such equivalences as, 'AD 1789 is Year One in the French Revolutionary dating system', and (b) of sufficient 'agree-ment in judgement' as to propositions of the form, 'So-and-so took place in AD n'. We can conceive of the whole system's being 'shifted back' a year, e.g. as a consequence of Christ's birth having taken place a year earlier; in such a case, the *sense* of, say, 'AD 1789', as used in such a 'possible world', would be different. In shifting back, the system would have changed identity. Thus, the Battle of Hastings would have occurred no earlier: it would still have happened in AD 1066. But what people *meant* by 'AD 1066' would have changed so that their 'The Battle of Hastings took place in AD 1067' would be true.

Assume for the sake of argument that the period between time's beginning and the Big Bang was nine-and-a-half years; and moreover that we have a dating system in which the first year of time is 1 Anno Temporis (etc.). The Big Bang happened in AT 10 – it *could* have happened in AT 9. But similarly, time began in –10 BB. – it *could* have begun in –9 BB. Do we have a 'shift back' or a 'shift forward'?

In the case of 'shifting back' the system of dates AD, we could describe the situation thus because the dates in *other* dating systems remained fixed, both relative to yet other dating systems, and relative to historical events. What of dates AT and BB? The sense of dates AT would surely have altered if *all* propositions of the form 'p in n AT' had changed truth-value, and if equivalences between dates AT and dates in other systems had broken down (while the relation between those other systems had remained fixed). Given *only* that the period between time's beginning and the world's beginning were different in length, dates AT would be the odd ones out – just as, given only the relevant differences in our uses of dates AD, they would be the odd ones out, relative to other dating systems.

If this is right, then although people who said, 'The Big Bang occurred in AT 9' would be right, their 'AT 9' would mean what our 'AT 10' actually means. The Big Bang (like the Battle of Hastings) would have occurred no earlier. 'Time began in –9 BB', on the other hand, would both be a true statement in that world, and synonymous with our equiform statement. Time's beginning would have occurred a year later.

If considerations such as these are effective in undermining the idea of world history's having taken place a bit earlier or later, then they are effective whether or not there was time before the history of the world. Consequently, one who espouses the view that there might have been time before the Big Bang can adduce those considerations as well as anyone. Hence the third argument against the possibility of changeless time is rebutted.

CONCLUSION TO CHAPTER 6

It might be said that in this chapter I have tried to answer a 'substantive question' (concerning changeless time) largely by appeal to 'mere linguistic practice'. But this would be quite mistaken. The conclusion arrived at on p. 145 was that changeless time was a logical possibility: in other words, that logical and linguistic tools are on their own *in*capable of determining the truth-value of, 'Time without change either has elapsed, or will elapse'. This leaves open the possibility that the truth-value of this sentence should be determinable by other means, such as scientific ones.

Of course, 'by scientific means' is not synonymous with 'by the sorts of means used by scientists': scientists often employ philosophical arguments, or arguments with philosophical presuppositions, to defend their pronouncements. Thus the view that time began with the Big Bang is sometimes defended by scientists on quite explicitly verificationist grounds. What sort of scientific grounds could be used in settling such questions is a moot question. What might be called 'evidential reasons' would seem, *ex hypothesi*, to be unavailable. But not so reasons that have to do, say, with the simplicity and generality of the overall physical theory of time and space.[10] Proper philosophical modesty precludes further speculation.

7

The Direction of Time

One sort of change is change *brought about*: caused change. In section 6.1, I referred to the causal account of 'the direction of time'. I want now to take a look at this account. *Prima facie*, the account seems to concern the 'earlier/later relation'; and in one form, it attempts to lay down *what it is* for one event to be earlier than another. Thus, one might say that for event A to be earlier than event B is for it to be possible that A causally affect B. But, as we have seen, this kind of reductive or analytic approach lands us on the three horns of a modal trilemma.

Reichenbach got stuck on one of these horns when giving his account of simultaneity. He introduced the notion of a *first-signal*, as the fastest message-carrier between any two points in space, and went on to say that the decisive empirical evidence was that light was the universal first-signal. Embracing as he did a causal account of the 'earlier/later relation', Reichenbach had to face the following question: 'Where two points in space, P1 and P2, are so distant that no first-signal can get from one to the other in less than a certain finite length of time, of n units, can one meaningfully say that something happened at P1 m units later than some occurrence at P2, where m is less than n?'. To this Reichenbach replied 'No'. If causal connection between two events is nomologically impossible, neither can be later than the other, he thought; the two events are 'indeterminate as to their time order'. And further:

> We define: *any two events which are indeterminate as to their time order may be called simultaneous.* . . . The concept *simultaneous* is to be reduced to the concept *indeterminate as to time order*. This result supports our intuitive understanding of the concept *simultaneous*.
>
> (Ibid., ch. 2, § 22)

The last-quoted sentence perhaps shows a certain degree of wishful thinking: that simultaneity should, among other things, be a non-transitive relation is surely counter to our 'intuitive understanding', and not merely at odds with an erroneous Newtonian physics, as Reichenbach goes on to claim.

The counter-intuitive reduction of simultaneity to indeterminacy as to time order is a natural consequence of the attempt to reduce the notions 'earlier than' and 'later than' to the notions 'able to affect' and 'affectable by', with the modalities construed as nomological. And a construal of the modalities as merely logical, or as 'metaphysical', fares no better, as we found earlier (section 6.1). An attempt might be made to find a more complex reduction, of course: for example,

> A happened before B iff ($\exists$t1) ($\exists$t2) (A happened at t1, B happened at t2, and there is some kind of event, E, such that if an event of kind E had happened at t1, it would have affected an event at t2).

What of the modal expression 'would have' here? We cannot intend 'would have, given the conditions that pertained at t1', since the mentioned conditions might have ruled out an event of kind E's occurring then. We might instead say, '. . . would have, given some possible set of initial conditions', where 'possible' simply means, 'by itself consistent with the laws of nature'. Such a reduction would leave unsolved the problem of an event's being earlier than another by less time than it would take for light to connect the two. And it would also raise questions about times. Can we help ourselves to quantification with date-variables in analysing the concept 'before', if such quantification presupposes a system of dates, and a system of dates presupposes a temporal ordering from earlier to later? It would seem not; but of course the nature of the alleged 'presupposition' would need to be examined to settle this question.

Rather than pursue these matters, I want, as with time and change, to suggest that we eschew a reductive or analytic approach to the concepts 'earlier' and 'later'. How might we do this?

Let us once more turn to *criteria*. Perhaps we can lay down the conditions for criterially central uses of 'earlier' in this sort of way: where event A causally affects event B, then 'A is earlier than B' is indubitably correct. From the central and paradigm case of one event's affecting another, it might be argued, the general and extended use of 'earlier' is derived.

I do not think that this will do. The paradigm case of an event's preceding another simply is not the case where an event causally affects another. Remember what we are getting at when we speak in such contexts of 'criteria' and 'paradigm cases'. The description of a paradigm case must allude to *what people do* in certain circumstances: e.g. in normal lighting, people make such-and-such colour-discriminations. This is because it is the (empirical) fact of our agreements in response – in what we do in certain situations – that enables us to institute, and successfully use, a public concept. People's linguistic behaviour (e.g. calling a surface 'red') then becomes a *part* of what they do in those situations. 'What people do' may encompass what people do with the aid of tools or instruments: thus, a true clock's saying 'five minutes' criterially determines a period's lasting five minutes. But we determine what, for the purposes of our discourse about temporal duration, can count as 'true clocks'; for (a) without a subjective sense of duration, we could never come to take any natural cycle as 'regular' (we could not agree on the results of inter-cycle comparison, for instance) – and (b) only if we can *use* a cycle as a clock is it possible for that clock to have any bearing on the concepts of duration which we actually employ. The same goes for light-meters or other such instruments: it is what we do with them that stands at the centre of the given linguistic practice. And in general, criterially central uses of words are made in cases where a certain agreement in prelinguistic response is already in place.

All this having been said, and returning to the notion of temporal precedence, consider whether the case of event A's affecting event B could count as the paradigm case of precedence. In the description of such a case, no mention is made of what (normal, linguistically competent) people do. Now it might seem that this objection can be easily met. Can't we just say something like: if a (normal, linguistically competent) person judges, in normal conditions, that event A causally affects event B, he will then judge, with indubitable correctness, 'A was earlier then B'? And won't this be the right sort of constitutive truth to count as laying down criteria?

The problem with this, I think, is that the predicate 'judges that A causally affects B' is not the sort of predicate we can use here. A judgement that one event causally affects another is not the kind of 'direct response' that distinguishing colours is, or distinguishing lengths of time is. There is nothing in the way of agreement in prelinguistic response on which to build agreement in linguistic response. Here I am perhaps going against what such philosophers as Anscombe[1] have suggested, namely that we can just see that one thing causes another. What we can on occasion see, it seems to me, is in fact just temporal precedence. Indeed, our judgements of temporal precedence often provide us with evidence of causation. But temporal precedence could only ever be a part of causation (and a non-necessary part, at that – as shall be argued later): it is notoriously not enough for one event to cause another that it precede that other, even if the two events concerned are spatially and temporally proximate. Whether A caused B has to do with facts quite distinct from the occurrences of A and B. Roughly speaking, the extra facts concern *types* of event, or *possible* (e.g. counterfactual) events – not just the actual events A and B. And such facts cannot in the required sense be seen just by observing A and B.

It is tempting to put this by saying that the judgement that A caused B is an inherently complex one. But would we call the judgement that some activity is a game a 'complex judgement', given that that judgement has to do with (even if it is not analysable in terms of) people, rules, winning or whatever? The phrase 'complex judgement' does suggest the possibility of analysis; but it may be that criterial grounds can be laid down for 'A caused B' itself, which nevertheless fall short of providing an analysis of 'A caused B'. The point, then, isn't that 'A caused B' is 'complex' in a way that makes it unsuitable as the criterial basis for the seemingly simple 'A was before B'; the point is, rather, that since there *are* cases where we can, just by looking, see that one event preceded another, it seems that it cannot be a criterion for the truth of 'A preceded B' that a normal observer judge that A caused B. For a criterion gives us the basis for a 'best possible opinion' – other bases for an opinion of the relevant sort will be non-paradigm, and so lacking best possible warrant. But we cannot have a better warrant for our opinion that A preceded B where we have just *seen* that A preceded B. Nor is our opinion in this case one that must have implicitly involved the judgement that A caused B.

7.2 PAST AND FUTURE

If we cannot get our teeth into the question of the 'directions' of time and of causation by examining the rules for 'before' and 'after', 'earlier' and 'later', should we perhaps turn our attention to other kinds of expression than these? I think we should; and in what follows I hope to show that our question can be approached *via* the observation that causal circumstances must be alluded to in the laying down of the criteria governing 'It was the case that'. (Note that this is a claim distinct from, and more general than, the claim that it is a constitutive fact that paradigm judgements employing 'It was the case that' – or in the past tense – should themselves rest upon other judgements that assert or entail causal connections.)

The criteria governing 'It was the case that' are importantly different in kind from those governing 'It will be that'. If asked why he thinks a certain object that he is looking at is red, a person will quite justifiably say, 'Because I can see that it is red'. And justification 'runs out' at this level when it comes to colour-ascriptions. (Tests for eyesight are themselves beholden to people's subjective colour-judgements.) If asked why he thinks that today's red tomato was green a while ago, a person may say a number of things: as, that a friend tells him it was, or that he knows that tomatoes start off green. But these are propositions that can only justify the past-tense statement on certain assumptions: that his friend is reliable, that enough tomatoes have been observed, or whatever. And the reliability of his friend, or of past observations of tomatoes, stands or falls, in the end, according to what people (such as the friend) report in the way of their own remembered observations; just as the readings of 'colour-meters' stand or fall according to what unmediated colour-ascriptions people make. If, on the other hand, the person asked about the tomato says, 'Because I remember its being green', we have reached the same sort of level as we reached with 'Because I can see that it is red'. The only 'assumptions' involved here are that the *speaker* is not 'malfunctioning' (e.g. colour-blind, or imagining things), nor insincere, nor linguistically incompetent. . . .

It must be stressed that the 'justification' we are talking about here is not in any straightforward sense epistemic justification. As we have noted, *that* someone is normal-sighted, or reliable in his memory, is itself open to doubt. It is 'constitutive justification' that concerns us (although the possibility of such constitutive justification naturally has epistemological implications). The concept 'red' is such that certain applications of the word count as criterially warranted; and, I submit, the past-tense operator is such that certain uses of *it* likewise count as criterially warranted.

'I saw it was green' is not only a memory-report: it is the report of a remembered observation. It justifies 'The tomato was green' in the same way that 'I heard my friend say the tomato was green' justifies 'My friend said the tomato was green'. 'I heard my friend say the tomato was green' does not, it seems to me, stand to 'The tomato was green' as a constitutively justifying statement – nor does the more simple, 'My friend said the tomato was green'. My position, in fact, is that past-tense statements backed up by remembered observations are the paradigm past-tense statements. They get past-tense discourse 'off the ground', in the same way that colour-observations get colour-talk off the ground, and in the same way that subjective judgements of duration get duration-talk off the ground.

How do observation-statements function? That people see certain things as green helps endow 'green' with its sense; but it is also clear that it is because things are a certain way that people see them as green. This is not to say that people's agreement over greenness must be 'causally explicable' for their use of 'green' to count as objective – our search for causal explanation here is part of a general search for causal explanation, not a seeking for the grounds of 'true objectivity' in colour-talk. But the concept 'see', and perceptual concepts generally, do, I think, involve a causal element. In general, 'I can see that it's green' is true, when it is true, in virtue of something's causing the speaker to respond in the way that he does. The notion of cause is of course a complex one; but we can see what *sort* of a role it plays here by comparison of 'see' with 'know'. A claim to knowledge is a sort of claim to reliability,[2] and reliability is a sort of 'tracking-capacity'. 'If it hadn't been that p, then x wouldn't have thought that p' is a typical and central consideration in favour of attributing knowledge to x. Very analogous remarks go for 'x sees that p'. And the relevance of causation to all this becomes clear when we remember that 'If it hadn't been that p, then it wouldn't have been that q' is a typical and central ground for asserting 'q because p'. It is this counterfactual-involving aspect of causation, rather than any putative 'mechanistic' aspect, that entitles us to adopt causal accounts of 'see', and other perceptual verbs.

Moreover, when we turn to memory, and to 'direct' or 'perceptual' memory in particular, similar considerations apply. The memory-report, 'I saw that it was green', as much as the observation-report, 'I (can) see that it is green', is typically true, when it is true, in virtue of the utterance's having a causal connection with an observed green object. This 'causal connection' may indeed amount to no more than a continuous capacity, on the part of the rememberer, for recounting his original perception. The point is that 'I remember that p' makes a certain sort of claim to ('counter-factual-involving') reliability, like 'I know that p'; and this reliability brings in causal connection.

In sum, then, both memory and perception are in a broad sense causal notions.[3] And both memory and perception lie at the heart of past-tense discourse. Again, a certain agreement in pre-linguistic response enables past-tensed talk to get going. People have the knack of agreeing where to find what they had earlier buried, of agreeing that they have met before, and so on and so forth. On the foundation of this pre-linguistic agreement is built the agreement that constitutes competence with the past tense; and at the centre of this competence is competence with 'I saw/heard/etc. that so and so'.

Many *present*-tensed statements are justifiable on the basis of perceptual memory: thus, 'The roof of this building is red – I saw it as I came in'. And this is naturally connected with the fact that the 'present time of utterance' will be a quite elastic *period* of time, something I have argued elsewhere. 'I can see that it is' may also justify a present-tensed statement. But what shows that 'see' is a perceptual verb, rather than a memory-verb, if both perception and memory are causal notions in the sense here being argued for? To reply that 'see' applies to present states of the world and 'remember' applies to past ones is, I think, to put the cart before the horse; indeed, *that* it is will be an important strand in the argument to follow. The matter requires a fuller treatment than there is space for, given that our main concern is with the difference between past and *future* tenses. But I think one may at any rate say this: the distinction between the past and present tenses lies not only, if it lies at all, in their forms of 'constitutive justification'; rather, it lies in such facts as these: using the present tense ('The roof is red') commits one to the contemporaneousness of reported event and utterance. 'Contemporary', 'simultaneous', and such like, are terms with enough of a life of their own to make this a non-vacuous observation. (These terms connect in particular with the use of clocks and dating systems.)

What of 'It will be that the tomato is green' ('The tomato will be green')? Do remarks analogous to the above ones about past-tense statements apply also to future-tense ones? No. The justifications for future-tense assertions are of a quite different kind from those for past-tense ones. 'I will see that it is green' does not justify saying 'It will be green' as 'I saw that it was green' justifies saying 'It was green'. (Here I think it is worth pointing out that 'I saw it was green' is itself a memory-report, or rather can be; it is not short for, and does not 'rest upon' the more complex, 'I remember seeing that it was green'. 'I saw it was green' can count as a memory-report because of what lies behind it – because of its history – in the same way in which 'It is green' can count as an observation-report because of what lies behind *it* – the context in which it is made.) An alleged clairvoyant may of course say, 'I *foresee* that it will be green', and thereby attempt to justify 'It will be green'; but she will not usually feel it necessary to add, 'I will see that it is green'. Future observation-statements are just irrelevant to predictions, even to ones, like the clairvoyant's, that claim the same authority as pertains to, 'It was green; I saw that it was'.

None of this by itself rules out the possibility of clairvoyance. For all that has been said, a person may know that something will happen just because it *will* happen. It is similarly possible, for all that has been said, that someone may know that something did happen just because it did – without any 'intermediate causation'. We would then have uses of the future- and past-tense operators that were not paradigm; that were not justifiable in the way that the paradigm future- and past-tense statements are justifiable. There are plenty of such non-central uses in any case.

It is an interesting question what statements do count as justifying future-tense ones. With the exception of future-tense statements that are connected with expressions of intention, it would seem that a justification of a future-tense statement can only ever be an evid-ential, epistemic one, if it is put forward contemporaneously with that statement; it will not be constitutively justifying. The sense of a future-tense proposition is in general to be explicated, I think, by appealing to its 'truth-value links' with propositions of other tenses, especially of the present tense. 'The tomato will be green' counts as *having been true* when 'The tomato is green' counts as true (the same tomato is meant here, naturally). It does not follow from this that a future-tense statement must be regarded as truth-valueless at the time of utterance: our observation about retrospective truth was one to do with the criteria governing 'It will be that', not one to do with 'becoming true' or the like.

Statements of intention, such as 'I will cook the dinner', are clearly of great importance when it comes to the justification of future-tense statements. It is a tricky question whether one can make a future-tense prediction, 'I shall cook the dinner', on the basis of having the intention whose (distinct) statement is, 'I will cook the dinner'; but whatever the answer to this question, it is pretty clear that another person can say of me, 'He will cook the dinner', and justify this prediction by reference to my expressed intention, in a way that is not merely evidential but criterial. (It is not that we have found from experience that an independently discernible class of things, 'expressions of intention', are usually or often followed by certain actions; expressions of intention are individuated in the first place by the actions that would – and so normally do – fulfil them. Hence the possibility of prediction is a constitutive fact about the 'language-game' of expressing intentions.)

I am not sure just how central a role expressions of intention play in future-tense discourse generally; whether, for example, a language could have a genuine future tense without having ways of expressing intention. This last question is hard to answer for all sorts of reasons – as that it is in any case not clear that a (natural) language could lack ways of expressing intention. For present purposes, we need only note the crucial differences between the criterial uses of past- and future-tensed sentences. The future tense is what it is because of 'truth-value links', and (perhaps) because of its connection with intention – *rather than* because of any connection with memory reports, as is the case with the past tense.

Past-tense statements also have 'truth-value links' with statements of other tenses (especially present-tense ones). But a justification of a past-tense statement, made at the same time as that statement, can, as I argued above, count as constitutively justifying on account of the 'causal role' of the events it reports: the past perceptions. And it is this that, for our present purposes, distinguishes past-tense assertions from future-tense ones.

7.3   IS A BACKWARDS WORLD LOGICALLY POSSIBLE?

These are knotty issues; but I hope we have, for the moment, got a sufficiently clear overview of them. Let us now return to the question of the direction of time and the direction of causation. It will do no harm to picture to ourselves a 'time-line', with a certain portion of it representing a period, P, during which it is stipulated that 'p' holds. (This last 'p' is tenseless because *schematic* – we are using a picture, after all.) The 'direction of causation' is stipulated to go from left to right on the line: that is, the representation of (the period of) any cause will be to the left of the representation of (the period of) its effect. The purpose of this picture is to test the hypothesis that the direction of causation is independent of the direction of time, from past to future. If from what I have already laid down in the picture it follows that the direction of time must also be represented as going in a certain direction (notably: from left to right), then the hypothesis will have been refuted.

A competent speaker of some language, Noam, says two things, which we will represent thus: (a) 'A: p', (b) 'B: p'. 'A' and 'B' are both sentential operators in Noam's language; 'p' in Noam's language says to hold what we earlier stipulated to hold for that period P. We represent the period it takes Noam to say 'A: p' by a portion of the line to the left of P; and we represent the period of time it takes Noam to say 'B: p' by a portion of the line to the right of P. There are stipulated to be two possibilities: either 'A' is synonymous with our 'It will be that' and 'B' is synonymous with our 'It was the case that' – or the other way around. Noam's utterances are both taken to be as warranted as possible, given the rules governing 'A: p' and 'B: p' in his language. Is either translation-possibility forced upon us by the picture, or can we infer nothing about the tenses of 'A: p' and 'B: p'?

The available translations are these:

(1) 'A: p' = 'It will be that p', and 'B: p' = 'It was the case that p'
(2) 'A: p' = 'It was the case that p', and 'B: p' = 'It will be that p'.

('p' means the same in both Noam's language and ours.) My contention is that (1) is forced upon us, since (2) is impossible.

'A: p' cannot be synonymous with our 'It was the case that p', since it is stipulatedly made with best possible warrant, but 'It was the case that p' could not be uttered with best possible warrant in the same circumstances. For the criteria governing 'It was the case that p' determine that only if the utterer could truly say 'I saw (heard, etc.) that p' is her utterance made with best possible warrant. And 'I saw (heard, etc.) that p' can only be truly said if the speaker's utterance has as one of its salient causes the fact that p. Noam's 'A: p' is to the left of P (during which 'p' holds) on the time-line: that is, the possibility is ruled out that the fact that p should causally affect Noam's utterance of 'A: p' in any way. Noam could not constitutively justify 'A: p' by (his or any translation of) 'I saw that p'. So 'A: p' cannot mean 'It was the case that p'. So (2) is ruled out.

(1), however, is perfectly possible. This should not need much arguing, since we can take Noam to be a speaker of English, and interpret the dummy expressions 'A' and 'B' as 'It will be that' and 'It was the case that'. English, or that fragment of it involving the past and future tenses, is clearly perfectly coherent. If actually p, then possibly p: (1) is possible.

Much more information about how Noam and others of his linguistic community use 'A' and 'B' would be required before (1) became an *unavoidable* 'analytical hypothesis'. This matters not. It is enough, for our purposes, that (1) provide a possible interpretation and (2) fail to do so.

Noam's two utterances were both true – defeating circumstances aside, this follows from their having been made with best possible warrant by a competent speaker. 'Defeating circumstances' would be things like: Noam getting muddled, or hallucinating during P, or forgetting what 'A' or 'B' meant. Such possibilities can be ruled out stipulatively. But if what Noam said was *true* (both times), and if (1) is correct, then Noam's utterance of 'A: p' is earlier than P, and his utterance of 'B: p' is later than P. The 'direction' from past to future must go from left to right on our time-line.

Once causation is taken as going in one direction along a time-line, we can say that *were* there to be a period P during which p, and *were* someone to utter two sentences like Noam's, respectively 'to the left of' and 'to the right of' P, then an interpretation like (2) would be impossible. 'A period P'; 'someone'; 'two utterances'; these expressions all contribute to a piece of universal quantification. We are saying what must follow *whenever* we have laid down just that the direction of causation goes one way along a time-line.

The argument requires that 'A caused B' not itself be analysable in such a way as to involve 'A was before B'; and that any putative 'criteria' for 'caused' not involve temporal priority. Indeed, the reverse is required: that the criteria for 'before' involve causation (in a particular way). But if 'A caused B' *did* require elucidation in terms of 'A was before B', this would also, clearly, yield the conclusion that causes must in general precede their effects. One who wants to assert the conceptual independence of temporal and causal asymmetries must deny both the Humean view that temporal priority is involved in the notion of a cause, and the view I have been propounding, that causation is involved in the notion of temporal priority.

Nevertheless, my feeling is that causal dependency, of the sort that must obtain between paradigm past-tense reports and the occurrences which they report, is *not* itself a matter, even in part, of the temporal priority of occurrences to reports. As I hinted earlier, the connective 'because' signals, roughly speaking, some kind of counterfactual conditionality. It may signal more than this – but I do not think that of itself it signals temporal order (*pace* Hume).

This naturally affects what reply I think should be made when another doubt is expressed concerning the argument from the case of Noam. This doubt concerns whether the stipulation that Noam's two utterances mean either one thing or the other can be made at all. For perhaps, if causal and temporal directions were indeed 'in opposition' (from our point of view) in Noam's world, that world would be too different from ours for us to be able to suppose that Noam shared any of our concepts – or at least any of our temporal or causal concepts.

If what I have said about the criteria for the past and future tenses is correct, this doubt would appear to be groundless. The criteria governing 'It was the case that' are purely causal; those for 'It will be that' have to do either with truth-value links or with intention. Noam's behaviour, described in ultimately causal terms, can be interpreted: and that interpretation yields an interpretation of his two utterances – the interpretation under (1), above. There is no possibility of a 'backwards world' in which Noam goes in for behaviour uninterpretable and chaotic to us. Noam's behaviour will be interpretable, and his world (therefore) not a backwards one.

I conclude in favour of what might be called a non-reductive causal account of the direction of time. This amounts to a number of things.

First: the actual direction of time, 'from' past 'to' future, is determined by the causal aymmetry of our world. In a certain sense, there is nothing more to the flow of time than the flow of causation. (But one must be careful with these 'nothing but' slogans.)

Second: this determination of temporal flow by causal flow is a necessary thing. The cause/effect asymmetry necessarily goes hand in hand with the earlier/later asymmetry – or, if you like, in any causally asymmetrical world the direction of time is from causes (earlier) to effects (later). We can discern two theses here: that a world in which causes generally come after their effects is not possible, and that a causally asymmetrical world cannot *lack* a direction of time. This last 'cannot' is really just a reiteration of the general idea that time is, as it were, an epiphenomenon of causal regularity. But it needs closer examination.

In discussing Noam's case, it was noted that, whereas there was something to prevent our adopting interpretation (2), there was nothing to prevent our adopting interpretation (1). But couldn't certain details be added to a description of a causally regular world which would undermine the very possibility of tensed thought in that world? As, that conditions are inimical to life? To be sure, no *analysis* of statements about temporal flow in terms of ones about possible tensed thoughts was meant to be suggested by the Noam case. But even so, it looks a little unclear how temporal order is to be assigned to creatureless worlds if we *cannot* appeal to possible tensed thoughts, in the way we did above for Noam. This is a matter to which we shall return in section 7.5.

7.4   THE PURPORT OF THE ARGUMENT

The problem of the last section was this. We were to determine whether a certain description of the world entails another, fuller description of it: specifically, whether a description of the world as being 'causally asymmetrical' (having a 'direction of causation') entails a further description of it as being causally and temporally 'co-directional'. And the tactic I employed to tackle this problem was to ask whether the first world-description entailed certain facts about the meanings, and hence truth-values, of possible utterances or thoughts, uttered or thought in the described world – and whether, if so, the (possible) true utterances/thoughts in question entailed the second world-description. The answers to these questions being, it was argued, positive, I concluded that the first world-description did indeed entail the second.

The purpose of this sort of argument can be made clearer by pointing out that our thought-experiment does not just yield conclusions about the utterances of some possible creature, but about what we would say in a certain situation. 'What would be the case in situation S?' – 'Well, imagine yourself in such a situation; how would you describe it?'. To imagine yourself in a causally asymmetrical world (with direction of time unspecified) is just to imagine yourself in the position of Noam. The twist is this: to determine how you would describe such a world, if you were in it, it may be necessary to see whether, and how, facts about that world influenced *the sense of your description*. (Or rather, descriptions. The reports of interest to us are ones like, 'The ball fell', 'It will rain', and so on – any tensed statements, in fact, especially those made in paradigm conditions.)

Now a philosopher dubious of the possibility of thus drawing a metaphysical conclusion from linguistic or semantic considerations might object to the argument from the case of Noam as follows. Whether an utterance which I now make counts as past-tensed does not depend on facts – e.g. concerning present memory – which have to do with its (present) assertability; rather, it has to do with a certain past fact – namely, either the very fact reported by the utterance, if it is true, or the fact inconsistent with the utterance, if it is false. And he may appeal to the truth-conditions for past-tensed sentences (p. 4), which make mention of things' being the case before the time of utterance, not of things' being the case at the time of utterance. So whether Noam's utterance to the left of event E on the time-line counts as past- or future-tensed cannot be settled as I wanted to settle it.

Of course no one would want to maintain that my utterance now of 'I got out of bed this morning' is about certain present facts, e.g. to do with memory; it is, if you like, about past facts, past facts that are in a way alluded to in the truth-conditions for 'I got out of bed this morning'. (Though since it is the sentence, not my particular utterance, that has those truth-conditions, it is rather misleading to talk of the truth-conditions' alluding to the very facts which I reported by my utterance.) But there are lots of facts around for my, or Noam's utterances, to 'be about'. What determines which facts they are about? Why isn't 'I got out of bed this morning' about tomorrow's *levée*, rather than today's? The answer to *this* question must be: because of features of the utterance itself. The utterance *counts* as being about today's earlier event, and not tomorrow's, because of features it now has (for it is occurring now, and wasn't past-tensed before it occurred!). So to determine which facts my utterance, or one of Noam's, is 'about', it is quite legitimate to investigate features of that utterance itself – its context, its grounds, and so forth.

Well (it might be said), perhaps in order to see how an utterance can be 'about past facts' we do after all need to do this sort of thing. Perhaps, in order to elucidate the sense or function of the past tense, we need to talk about what count as its criterially central uses

– and perhaps these uses are indeed 'direct memory reports'. But does this entail that for an expression of some other language to count as meaning the same as 'It was the case', or for some sentence to count as meaning the same as a past-tense sentence in English, that expression, or that sentence, must be governed by the same criteria as the English expression or sentence? To say that an appeal must be made to the criteria governing 'It was the case that' in order to elucidate its meaning is one thing; to say that those criteria are *essential* to its meaning – that they must attach to any expression of the same meaning – is another. The argument from the case of Noam requires that these two things go hand in hand.

What, if any, aspects of a term's use count as definitive is by no means always a determinate matter. There are cases – certain scientific terms, for example – when it is, or has been, indeterminate whether something counts as 'criterion' or as 'symptom', to use Wittgenstein's terminology.[4] Moreover, elucidating a term's meaning satisfactorily may on occasion be no more than listing various key aspects of its use, *none* of them 'essential' ('game', 'number'). And where we *do* feel justified in calling a certain aspect of a term's use 'essential', this may simply be a way of alluding to such facts as that a proper grasp of the term must involve recognising that aspect of use – it may not entail, say, that the term would undergo meaning-change were that aspect of its use to disappear.

To allege that perceptual memory is *criterially* central to past-tense discourse is in a way to make out that the connection between perceptual memory and the past tense *is* 'essential'. This is part of the theoretical baggage attaching to (my use of) 'criterial'. For the picture of meaning being proposed as apt here is just that it is in virtue of there being a class of central uses that other, non-central uses have the meaning that they do. Take away the special role of the central uses and you effectively remove the guarantor of meaning to the non-central uses.

It is this last consideration which inclines me to think that, in giving criteria for the past tense, we do thereby give something like a rule for what shall count as a past-tensed sentence in *any* language. If our own use of tenses were to change so that perceptual memory reports ceased to have the special, 'foundational' role that they have for past-tensed statements, what *other* aspects of the old practice could there be that, by continuing in the new one, we might take as unifying strands in the history of a single concept, or set of concepts? The possibility of a chain of justification ending in direct memory reports is something that has an influence on all sorts of features of our use of the past tense; it is not 'just another aspect'. Explanations of the senses of past-tensed statements, connections between those statements and others, to say nothing of truth-value assignments reasonably made by competent speakers – all these things would be altered. And where such a change in practice would result in such a radically distinct language-game, surely any (actual or possible) practice akin to this latter language-game – in not giving a criterial status to direct memory – would also be radically distinct from our actual language-game of past-tensed utterances? It would not, in fact, be past-tensed discourse.

Thus it seems that the fact that our own past-tense discourse is criterially connected with direct memory reports is part of a more general fact: that for anything to count as past-tense discourse, it must be likewise criterially connected with direct memory reports. Which was the necessary premise in my argument for a causal account of time's direction.

To move on. I have already drawn attention to that aspect of the argument under which it can be seen simply as relying on the traditional-sounding question, 'How would one describe this situation if one were in it?'. It is worth pointing out another 'traditional' direction from which the argument may be approached: that of old-fashioned verificationism. It turns out that a verificationist argument for the causal theory of time needs help, if it is to work, from premises of the sort I outlined in the last section; which premises, however, end up by themselves yielding the desired conclusion, without benefit of verificationism.

In tackling the question whether the direction of time must also be the direction of causation, we typically ask if a world is conceivable in which effects are universally earlier than their causes – as universally, that is, as in this world they are later than their causes. A traditional verificationist denies that this is conceivable: for, he maintains, as far as the empirical observations of creatures in such a hypothetical world were concerned, things would be indistinguishable from how they appear in the actual world. If *everything*, including experiences, is 'back to front', then no observable difference is possible. And if no observable difference is possible, there is no difference.

But how can we talk about the observations of creatures in the causally reversed world at all? What counts as a person's observing that a ball falls (or 'falls backwards')? More precisely, by what right could we describe the behaviour of a person in such a world as constituting 'a report that a ball falls'? For *if* effect precedes cause, this person's 'report' will precede what it reports – his 'prediction' will follow the predicted event – his 'surprise' will precede the surprising event – and so on. Aren't such phenomena so different from what in our world count as 'reporting', 'predicting', 'being surprised', that we cannot construe them as cases of reporting, predicting, being surprised? It is hardly clear that 'observations would be the same', since it is hardly clear that there would be any observing going on in the 'back to front' world.

Unless, that is, the specification of causal relations in such a world is itself sufficient to determine what in that world count as reports, observations, and so on. But the causal relations in question will need to suffice to determine the *meaning* of bits of behaviour (and of mental episodes, if you like); for example, that a bit of behaviour constitutes a report, 'The ball fell', while another bit of behaviour constitutes the prediction, 'The ball will fall'. Causal relations will have to determine, among other things, what tense a statement or thought has. If I am right about the different criteria for past- and future-tense statements, it will have to be the past-tensed statements that paradigmatically get caused by what they're about (so to speak). And the paradigm (criterially central) utterances of past-, as well as future-, tensed statements, made by the inhabitants of our hypothetical world, will have to be for the most part true. From which it follows that that part of the hypothesis that says that effects by and large precede their causes in the world must be dropped. All this is of course a reiteration of the argument of the last section.

7.5 CONFUSED, STATIC AND CREATURELESS WORLDS

The possible – or impossible – world with which we have so far had to do has been a sort of 'back to front' version of the actual world. What about a world in which no generalisation obtained concerning the priority or posteriority of causes to their effects? – a world in which causes preceded their effects about as often as they succeeded them? Or what about a world in which there weren't even any causal regularities? – a world in which there *were* no causes and effects? (Perhaps the first-mentioned kind of world would in fact have to be an example of the second-mentioned kind.) Does my argument from the connection between causation and (hypo-thetical) past-tense utterances lead us to the conclusion that in such worlds there would be no 'past' or 'future', no 'earlier' or 'later', and hence (it would appear) no time at all?

A world of causal confusion is clearly of the same sort of rel-evance to our present concerns as a world of 'horological confu-sion' was to our earlier concerns to do with duration. A horologically confused, or static, or creatureless world poses questions to do with duration analogous to those we have now arrived at to do with past and future; what follows is an attempt at answering both kinds of questions.

When we discussed horological confusion, we did not speak of 'worlds' so much as of 'situations', or 'periods', leaving 'worlds' for a later occasion (this one). The difference between a thought-experiment about a 'world' and one about a 'situation' or 'period' is very great. Let us begin with situations.

I argued that a period in which clocks broke down would not thereby be one in which events had no determinate durations, or determinate relative durations: for (a) during such a period there would be no true clocks to *disagree* with one another; and (b) *our* duration-terms, sustained by the agreement of our clocks, would – before and after the period – be predictively or retrospectively applicable to the events of the period; and moreover, (c) our *actual* duration-terms are applicable to the *possible* period being consid-ered, i.e. we can truly say, 'If clocks were all to break down over some period, nevertheless a given event of that period would either last five minutes or not (say)'. Now (c) gets its plausibility in large part from (b); that is, it is especially because certain statements that *could* be made *would* be true that we conclude that certain counter-factual statements *are* true. But what if there had never been, and never would be, any agreement among clocks? – or what if the conditions that make for that agreement had never, and never would, obtain (if we can talk of such independent 'conditions')? Or again, to consider the sort of point raised at the end of section 7.3, what if there had never been, and never would be, any thinking life? In these cases, (a) would hold, while (b) would not. So what about (c)?

The scenarios we have arrived at, of course, are that of the 'world' of horological confusion, and of the 'world' without thought. Each of these is a radically different world from ours, in the sense that its history does not share those features (periods of regularity, periods of temporal thought/talk) with 'our' world that make comparison possible of the sort that we can go in for between 'our' world and one in which there are simply confused or creatureless *periods*.

When it comes to past and future, a *period* of causal confusion poses no more of a problem than does one of horological confusion. It is not necessary to ask what creatures would do who found themselves in such a period; obviously, they would be incapable of proper memory-reports, and hence (if the period were long enough) could not sustain the institution of a past tense – but the existence of a past tense before and after the period, and indeed of words for 'earlier', 'later', 'before' and 'after', would render the period one of which something like (b) above would be true: events during that period *would* have determinate relations of priority and posteriority.

So what are we to make of confused 'worlds', or of creatureless 'worlds'? I am inclined to answer that we can after all treat them much as we do confused or creatureless periods. (c) does not absolutely require (b). The general motivation for both (b) and (c), and their analogues for other types of confusion than horological, has to do with the extendability of our concepts beyond their criterially central applications. One way of using a concept or concepts in an extended way is in framing a description of some possible state of affairs for the sake of the description itself, as opposed to framing such a description for the purpose of constructing a blueprint, or to jog someone's memory, or whatever. We use concepts in roughly this way when making up stories, and we are using them thus when we imagine radically different possible worlds in the course of philosophising about time. But the purpose of 'contemplating' the description is different for philosophising from how it is for story-telling. In story-telling, it doesn't much matter if we use concepts to frame descriptions that are somehow incoherent or self-contradictory (indeed, this may be a positive advantage, as in the works of Lewis Carroll). In the philosophising case, we are trying to get a better understanding of the concepts in question, and the incoherence or self-contradictoriness of any descriptions we frame with them is a more serious matter. On the other hand, the standard of 'what you can coherently do with a concept' must in general be derived from language-games (forming a blueprint, describing a period long past, reporting your mental states . . .) of pretty definite character and purpose; whereas the game of 'imagining a world' is perhaps of a not wholly definite character and purpose. What counts as the coherent use of a concept when we are engaged in philosophical imaginings must needs be derivative from what generally counts as such, in quite other language-games.

All this having been said, there do seem to be some general maxims of coherence governing our descriptions. In particular, as I argued earlier, there is the maxim of 'Bivalent until proved guilty'. Imagine a world in which there existed only photons and gold (and whatever is involved in the existence of gold), and in which life could not develop or be sustained; surely the gold would still be either transparent or not transparent? To describe it as 'neither' is to court incoherence. (And while we're at it, if the gold were either, then surely it would be not-transparent (opaque), *for that's what gold is like*?) Of course, were one to describe one's world as containing gold that was neither transparent nor not-transparent, this would not be to commit the sort of *faux pas* one would be committing were one to forget about bivalence when writing a medical report; and this is why it is not a straightforward matter to rebut a philosopher who says, 'But who's to say that in such a radically different world from our own, gold might *not* disobey the principle of bivalence?'. The appropriate response to such a line is to point out that the 'principle of bivalence' applies to descriptions, not to things or stuffs, like gold – so that the question concerns whether there are grounds for dropping, or for adhering to, the principle when we are going in for philosophical imagining. The problem is, as I have hinted, that disagreement over the rules governing philosophical imagining is not easily resoluble.

Leaving aside for the moment the idea of a 'completely static world', the following remarks seem true. To think that either permanent horological irregularity or permanent creaturelessness undermines duration is to predict the success of an attempt to describe a world using concepts like 'event', 'happen', and some more particular concepts (e.g. 'explode', 'collide', or whatever), while effectively eschewing a bivalent use of 'take as long as'. It is all right to eschew 'take as long as' when describing two faces, for it is a category-mistake to describe a face as taking as long as another; but one cannot thus eschew it when describing occurrences. To think that permanent causal irregularity or permanent creaturelessness undermines the earlier/later relation is to predict the success of an attempt to describe a world using concepts like 'event', 'happen', etc., while eschewing a bivalent use of 'before'. It is all right to eschew 'before' when describing two faces, for it is a category-mistake to describe a face as being before another; but one cannot thus eschew it when describing occurrences. Dynamic 'worlds' must be ones in which occurrences have relative durations, and in which occurrences are either earlier than, later than, or simultaneous with one another.

This is a different sort of point from the point that, given a certain description of the causal features of a 'world', one must describe certain other features of that 'world' (temporal ones) in a certain way. Nothing specific *follows*, concerning the temporal ordering of its events, from a description of a causally irregular world; we may take the ordering as going 'one way', or take it as going 'the other way'. Likewise, nothing need follow, concerning the relative durations of events, from a description of a world of horological confusion. The point rather is that once one describes a world as having a history at all, one seems committed to saying that either one sort of world, or another, must be at issue; e.g. a world going from past to future *this* way, or one going from past to future *that* way. For to say that things happen in this world is to say that there is change in it; and to say there is change is, as has been noted, to commit oneself to the truth of '(∃p) (p, and later not-p)'. Some proposition, expressible by a sentence of the form, 'p and later not-p', must be true in the world if it is a world of change, and 'later' gives us a temporal ordering.

A (causally or horologically) regular world lacking any thinking life is a special case. As I have indicated, it seems to me that a specification of causal direction *is* enough to entail one of temporal direction – we are not just committed to saying, 'There would in such a world be *some* direction of time or other'. But without the likes of Noam to inhabit a causally regular world, can we speak of 'past' and 'future' in that world?

It seems to me that we can. For we can say: 'Were there to be thinking creatures in such a world, and were they to have two linguistic forms, "A:p" and "B:p" . . . etc.'; we can, in short, talk of hypothetical Noams. And we do not thereby fall foul of the 'modal trilemma', since one of the three species of possibility *is* enough for our purposes – namely, logical (or conceptual) possibility. In section 7.3, interpretation (2) (p. 169) was argued to be a logical (or conceptual) impossibility. Thus when it comes to a hypothetical creatureless world, we need only point out that it is logically possible that there be creatures in that world with expressions 'A:p' and 'B:p'. . . . which expressions would have to mean 'It will be that p' and 'It was the case that p'.

Turning to a 'completely static world', it is clear that such a world would have the most minimal description. Things would not happen at all, so an application of 'take as long as' would not be necessary, nor indeed possible. The same goes for applications of 'before' and 'after'. But what about a whole proposition like 'Time passes'? Must we include either it or its negation in our description of the static world? (Note also that if we do include it and not its negation, we shall apparently face a parallel question about duration; e.g. must we include either 'The world lasts more than five minutes' or its negation in our description?) While a use of event-concepts seems to involve us in a connected use of concepts of temporal order, does the use of whatever concepts are involved in our very minimal world-description itself involve us in temporal concepts? No; but it might be said that we are *already* involved in those concepts – i.e. we have them in our repertoire – so that we must face questions employing them, such as, 'Would time pass or wouldn't it?', just as we must face questions like, 'Would there exist gold or not?'.

A description of a world as one in which time neither passes nor doesn't pass does sound to be incoherent. But the real question, it might be argued, is whether our world-description has to make any mention of time at all. After all, a story in which the hero's age is described as neither being thirty nor not being thirty is an incoherent story; but a story that makes no mention of the hero's age is neither incoherent nor (in this respect) inadequate. Why must a description of a possible world, framed in the course of philosophising, include, or even notionally include, every (let us say 'non-vague') proposition or its negation?

However, the issue is not merely the issue whether a world-description must include every proposition or its negation. Having in mind the analogy of story-telling, we can happily admit that a world-description, like a story, need not be 'complete'; for our philosophical purposes may be satisfied where we have only an 'incomplete' description. A description, or story, may not entail 'p'; but what is at issue now is whether a description – or story, for that matter – must entail 'p or not-p'. There is no age such that Hamlet must have died at *that* age; but the story will entail the general proposition, 'Either Hamlet died at thirty or he didn't'.

In the case of a causally or horologically confused world, our description of such a world itself entails a general proposition ('($\exists$p) (p, and later not-p)'), whose actual truth would depend on that of some specific proposition involving temporal priority. Since neither the world-description nor the entailed general proposition are *actually* true, we need not say that there must be some specific proposition of the form 'p and later not-p' that holds of the imagined world; rather, some such specific proposition *would have to* hold in such a world. With the static world, the very minimal description does not (apparently) entail the general proposition, '(∃p) (p, and later not-p)', which would itself entail, 'Time passes'. But it seems to me that it *does* entail, 'Either time passes or it doesn't'. A static world might be temporal; or it might not. And if there is to be a debate here, it will not be one upon which the 'metaphysician' (or scientist) can shed any light; light will only be shed by a consideration of the law of bivalence – and, moreover, by a consideration of whether our concepts, including our logical ones ('or', 'not'), start idling when we try to use them in very far-fetched or minimal 'world-descriptions'.

But perhaps a little more can be said. What about the description of the static world itself? What would this actually have to be like? If a 'description of a possible world' amounts to a statement of some sort involving modal operators ('Possibly', etc.) – as I am inclined to think – it looks as if our world-description will amount to something like: 'It is possible that nothing should ever have happened, nor be going to happen'. ('It is possible that nothing should ever happen' means the same.) This will at any rate be so if a genuinely tenseless world-description is not available, as the argument of Part I would have us think. For if that argument was cogent, a candidate for a tenseless world-description would itself boil down to a conjunctively-tensed one of the sort just imagined.

But 'It is possible that nothing should ever have happened, nor be going to happen', since of course it uses tenses, brings in time. One surely cannot add, as a further conjunct in the scope of 'It is possible that', the clause, '. . . and that time should not have passed, nor be going to pass'.

7.6   SHADES OF McTAGGART

What I earlier concluded about the direction of time's being the direction of causation can of course be phrased in terms of the 'earlier/later relation'. But we did not make direct appeal to the concepts 'earlier' and 'later' (or 'before' and 'after') in reaching our conclusion. It was suggested, indeed, that appeal to the rules governing those concepts could not on its own bring us to any conclusions linking their use with the direction of causation. It was constitutive facts about *tense* that helped us on our way, facts about past and future. To draw conclusions about the 'earlier/later relation' from what has been argued, we need to show the connection between tensed locutions, on the one hand, and 'before' and 'after' on the other. That the jobs of 'before' and 'after' (in one sense of 'jobs') can indeed be done with the assistance of tense-operators and temporal units has already been indicated (see pp. 86–7).

McTaggart thought that the 'flow' of time was a feature only capturable by talk about the A-series. This was why he rejected the B-series model as a representation of time. In one sense, his thought may seem to have been right. We can talk about the logical asymmetry of 'earlier' and 'later'; but if we want to say what 'deep' asymmetry underlies that logical one, we shall have to invoke the asymmetry of cause and effect. However, if the arguments of the last section embody the rationale for a causal account of the direction of time, then the 'deep' asymmetry can only explain the logical one because of the fact that the flow from past to future must be in the same direction as the general flow from cause to effect, and because of the connection between the past and future tenses and the expressions 'earlier' and 'later'. It might be said that the 'deep' reasons for the directionality of the B-series line have to do with facts representable only on the A-series line. And of course the B-series line wouldn't be the B-series line without its characteristic directionality.

The argument of section 7.3 is not the only one to show why the direction of time is fixed by the direction of causation. There appear to me to be other good arguments in the literature to the same conclusion. It is tempting to suppose that at bottom there must be a single, or at any rate relatively unitary, diagnosis of the matter, which diagnosis is implicitly made use of by the various available arguments. Certainly, those arguments which rely simply on drawing out contradictory implications from the hypothesis of a world in which effect generally precedes cause, while they show *that* the hypothesis is impossible, do not show *why* it is. Nevertheless, we are at a very basic conceptual level when we talk of past and future, earlier and later, cause and effect; and the intimate connections between very fundamental concepts tend to make talk of 'conceptual priority' among them (e.g. a priority of 'It was the case that' over 'before') difficult to justify.

Still – my own view is that McTaggart had a point. A *mere* asymmetry, of the sort that characterises 'the causal facts' as viewed from the perspective of the B-series, could not alone lead us to talk, with *prima facie* justification, of the 'flow of time'. It is the reality of tense – the autonomy of tensed discourse – which leads us to talk in this way; together with what is 'subjective' about our tensed talk: in particular, the central role of *memory*, whose part in determining what a paradigm past-tense report is has already been discussed.

Nevertheless, in a certain sense – though we must be careful not to be misled by this way of speaking – 'the causal facts' determine, or at least help determine, time's reality. For memory is itself to be understood, above all, in causal terms, not as a faculty whose special object is the Past (as sounds are the special objects of perception of our hearing faculty). Our temporal notions, even our notion of the 'flow of time', have their root in the world's causal regularities.

But here we bump against Wittgenstein's 'limits of empiricism'.[5] The empirical conditions for the existence, and identity, of our temporal concepts are not themselves an ingredient of those concepts. Past, present and future are not 'constructs', in any sense, out of causal regularities. And we may go further, and state that past, present and future are features of reality as fundamental as those regularities – for this just means, can only mean: the concepts *past*, *present*, *future*, and the phenomenon of tensed talk, are at least as basic to our language – and to any language that has them – as are the concepts *cause* and *effect*, and the phenomenon of causal talk.

Appendix
The Notion of a Criterion:
Wright's Objections

I have at various points in this book (in particular, in Part III) made use of the roughly Wittgensteinian concept of a 'criterion', or rather of the concept of the criterially central uses of an expression, and the role those uses play in determining the meaning of that expression. The general idea that what is often needed is not an attempt to 'give the sense' of some key expression by truth-conditional reduction or analysis (of sentences containing it), but instead an attempt to elucidate that expression's sense by reference to its having certain criterially central uses, is one worthy of an extended treatment in its own right. This is not the place for such a treatment. Nevertheless, it seems a good idea to consider certain objections that can be put to the very idea of a 'criterial use'; and in this Appendix, I want to look at the objections raised by one philosopher with a sympathetic understanding of that idea, namely Crispin Wright, taking for my object of study his 'Second Thoughts About Criteria'.[1]

Wright gives the following schematic characterisation of the notion of a criterion, as that notion is characterised by 'orthodox' Wittgensteinians:

1 that recognition of criteria for P can confer sceptic-proof knowledge that P;
2 that P's criteria determine *necessarily* good evidence for P, and thereby fix its content;
3 that the criteria for P will typically be multiple;
4 that satisfaction of a criterion for P will always be a 'public' matter;
5 that to know of the satisfaction of criteria for P is always consistent with having, or discovering, further information whose effect is that the claim that P is not justified after all.

('Second Thoughts About Criteria', pp. 267–8)

185

Wright sees two difficulties, both concerning feature 5: firstly, that that feature is incompatible with feature 1, and secondly that it is incompatible with feature 2.

Feature 5, or something pretty like it, certainly is essential to a proper characterisation of criteria. But it seems to me that the notion of a criterion need not involve feature 1 as stated, so that its incompatibility with 5 should not worry us. This is not to say that a consideration of criterial justification, and of justification generally, may not lead us to reject traditional sceptical arguments about knowledge; but I suspect that the motivation for that rejection will come more from what can be said about 'justification', 'know', 'doubt' and the like, than from what can be said about criterial knowledge on its own. Certainly, the sense of 'criterion' which I have been using in my arguments about duration-terms, etc., does not require feature 1.

The alleged incompatibility of features 2 and 5 is more worrying. What is Wright's argument for it? The gist of the argument can be gleaned from this quotation:

> no type of ground, even one conventionally associated with P, can be *necessarily* 'good evidence' for P if it is regarded as a defeasible ground: for if it is defeasible, it may be defeated; and defeated, moreover, so frequently that, bearing in mind the consequential character of any assertion of P, one would rightly become reluctant to assert P on its basis.
>
> (Ibid., p. 279)

That assertion as such has a 'consequential character' amounts to this:

> When someone asserts P, even on grounds which are admitted to be inconclusive, he sets himself against the subsequent defeat of those grounds.
>
> (Ibid., p. 279)

But:

> defeat always *is* a possibility where criteria are concerned. And it will be in the lap of the gods whether it occurs in any particular case, and *how often* it happens that a particular type of criterial ground for P is subsequently overturned.
>
> (Ibid., p. 279)

Wright's concern is that, whereas criteria are taken to be necessarily good evidence for P, whether they could be so must be a contingent matter, since whether or not the criteria hold is admitted to be a logically distinct matter from whether or not P.

At this point, it is a good idea to draw a distinction between two different sorts of case. According to Wright's usage, Jones's behaviour is said to provide criterial grounds for such an assertion as 'Jones believes that it's raining'; and the verification of (sufficiently) many propositions of the forms 'Fa', 'Fb', 'Fc', etc., is said to provide criterial grounds for the unrestricted generalisation, 'For all x, Fx'. For such cases, there is no description of what it would be to have conclusive criterial support for the assertions, owing in the one case (roughly) to the gap between finitely many disposition-manifestations and a disposition-ascription, and in the other to the gap between a list of atomic propositions and a universal proposition.

But there is another sort of case, exemplified by colour-words. That an object is judged to be red by a sincere normal-sighted person in normal lighting conditions *is enough* for that object to be red. It is, of course, the (ineliminable) expression 'normal' that allows our description of criterial conditions to be a 'guaranteeing' one. The expression 'true' has a similar power when it comes to: that a true clock, timing a process, P, in normal conditions, gives a reading of 'five minutes', *is enough* for it to be the case that P took five minutes. And that a person, or set of conditions, is 'normal', or that a clock is 'true', may not only be open to doubt, but may itself be only susceptible of the kind of inconclusive criterial support of which belief-ascriptions and generalisations are susceptible. The distinction between cases nevertheless holds; and it is one worth making, insofar as it helps us see *in what sense* criterial support is 'always inconclusive'. The cases with which we had most to do in Chapter 6 were ones where criteria, among other things, can provide finite characterisations of *what it is* for, say, a process to count as lasting five minutes. The criteria for belief-ascriptions cannot in quite the same way provide a characterisation of what it is to believe something. This is partly because employing 'normal', or 'ideal', is out of place: an appeal to behaviour 'in normal circumstances' would only work if it (illicitly) amounted to an appeal to behaviour 'explicable as usual by the belief that so-and-so'. (The notion of 'normal circumstances' is similarly out of place for universal generalisations.)

The above considerations mean that we should be careful what, exactly, we take feature 5 to amount to. If one knew that one was a normal-sighted observer, looking at an object in normal lighting conditions, that one was not suffering from linguistic amnesia, etc., and one judged the object to be red, then it seems that one would actually have *indefeasible* grounds for one's judgement. This in itself does not, I think, show that 'red' lacks criteria, or such criteria. (I am not sure whether *Wright's* use of 'criteria' would in fact embrace colour-terms; I trust that *my* use of 'criteria' is anyway sufficiently clear.) We may put the point in the following way. The criterial conditions for the application of 'red' are defeasible if described, *a posteriori*, without use of 'normal', as is, in fact, impractible. Where conditions get described in terms, for example, of light levels, light reflectivity, state of observer's rods and cones, and so forth, we can say that a certain large, vague, and possibly infinite class of conditions count as normal for purposes of colour-observation. That any such set of conditions holds on a given occasion is only defeasible grounds for the conclusion that the observed object is the colour which it is judged to be by the observer. For there is a gap between the statement that such-and-such empirical conditions obtain and the statement that the object is red. Now this gap is not the same sort of gap as exists between a finite description of behaviour and a belief-ascription; but nor is it just the gap that exists between any two statements of logically distinct but nomologically connected circumstances. 'The observation-conditions for the object are thus and so' and 'The object is red' of course *are* logically distinct; but one cannot say that they report empirically connected circumstances in the way in which 'The match was struck in such-and-such conditions' and 'The match caught light' report empirically connected circumstances. And the reason is that, *as things are*, the reported observation-conditions belong to the class of conditions (normal ones) which make possible that agreement in colour-discrimination which is the basis of our colour-discourse. That they belong to that class is a contingent matter; and so is the fact that there is such a class of agreement-enabling conditions. But if there weren't such agreement-enabling conditions, 'The object is red' wouldn't express a proposition at all.

Let S be the statement that certain conditions for colour-observation obtain, and that the observer (part of the 'conditions') judges the observed object to be red. The conditions which S describes are in fact normal, though S itself eschews the expression 'normal' (or synonyms). Knowledge that S is true provides *necessarily good evidence* that the object in question is red in the following sense: it is necessarily true that if a normal-sighted person judges, in normal conditions, that an object is red, then that object is red – and it so happens that the conditions reported by S are ('in this world') normal ones. S nevertheless provides only defeasible grounds for the claim that the object in question is red in this sense, that it is an empirical and contingent matter whether the conditions it describes happen to be normal for colour-observation, and whether, indeed, they will go on being such. Empirical discoveries could undermine the belief that the described conditions were normal and agreement-enabling (or ever had been); in that case, such discoveries could, though they need not, defeat colour-ascriptions that were (or ever had been) made in such conditions.

The 'necessary connection' between criterial conditions and proposition really comes to this: that if there were no conditions able to fulfil the role of criterial ones for that proposition, then the proposition would not merely be necessarily false, but would not exist at all. Wittgenstein made the point a number of times, and in a number of contexts; one quotation will suffice:

> Does it make sense to say that people generally agree in their judgments of colour? What would it be like for them not to? – One man would say that a flower was red which another called blue, and so on. – But what right should we have to call these people's 'red' and 'blue' *our* colour-words? – How would they learn to use these words? And is the language-game which they learn still such as we call the use of 'names of colour'?
> (*Philosophical Investigations*, p. 226, trans. G. E. M. Anscombe, Blackwell, 1958.)

In Part III, I discussed cases of widespread disagreement, or lack of agreement (between people, clocks, etc.). And of course it has to be allowed that whether there is the requisite sort of agreement will, as Wright says, be 'in the lap of the gods'. This may leave room for scepticism – perhaps even scepticism about whether we manage to mean anything by some of our words. But the *notion* of a criterion is not undermined. Returning to Wright's 'second thoughts', the conclusion to draw, I think, is that features 2 and 5 are – after all – compatible.

Notes

INTRODUCTION

1. St Augustine, *Confessions*, XI xiv (17).
2. Wittgenstein, *Philosophical Investigations*, trans. G. E. M. Anscombe, Basil Blackwell, 3rd edn, 1967, Part I, § 89.

1 McTAGGART'S ARGUMENT

1. McTaggart, *The Nature of Existence*, vol. 1, Cambridge, 1927, ch. 33.
2. Mellor, *Real Time*, Cambridge University Press, 1981, ch. 6.
3. For example, Prior, 'Changes in Events and Changes in Things', in *Papers on Time and Tense*, Oxford University Press, 1968, especially pp. 10–14.

2 FACTS, KNOWLEDGE AND BELIEF

1. For more on logical form and grammatical form, see Teichmann, *Abstract Entities*, Macmillan, 1992, pp. 20–4.
2. The analogous problem for 'F' and 'the property of being F' is discussed in ch. 3, § 1, of Teichmann, *Abstract Entites*: similar objections to 'facts' can be framed to those which are there made against 'properties', realistically construed.
3. Perry, 'The Problem of the Essential Indexical', in *Nous*, 1979.
4. Castaneda, '"He": A Study in the Logic of Self-Consciousness', in *Ratio*, 1966, pp. 130–57.
5. Wittgenstein is reported to have approved of Lichtenberg's remark that instead of 'I think' we ought to say 'It thinks' (cf. 'It's raining'). See Moore, 'Wittgenstein's Lectures in 1930–33', *Philosophical Papers*, London, 1959, pp. 306–10.
6. Richard, 'Temporalism and Eternalism', in *Philosophical Studies*, January 1981.
7. Altham, 'Indirect Reflexives and Indirect Speech', in *Intention and Intentionality: Essays in Honour of G. E. M. Anscombe*, ed. Diamond and Teichmann, Harvester Press 1979, pp. 31–2.
8. Castaneda, 'Indicators and Quasi-Indicators', in *American Philosophical Quarterly*, 1967, pp. 85–100.

3 TRUTH-CONDITIONS

1. For example, Russell, in *An Enquiry into Meaning and Truth*.
2. Priest, 'Tense and Truth-Conditions', in *Analysis*, 1986, pp. 162–6; and 'Tense, *Tense* and TENSE', in *Analysis*, 1987, pp. 184–7.

3. Wittgenstein, *Tractatus Logico-Philosophicus*, § 4.465.
4. Prior, *Objects of Thought*, ed. Geach and Kenny, Oxford University Press, 1971, p. 59.
5. See, for example, Bostock, *Logic and Arithmetic*, Oxford University Press, 1974.
6. This wheeze was suggested to me by Michael Martin.
7. Quine, *Word and Object*, MIT Press, 1960, pp. 172–3.
8. For the 'wrapping' terminology, see Prior, 'Is the Concept of Referential Opacity Really Necessary?', in *Acta Philosophica Fennica*, 1963.
9. See Teichmann, ' "Actually" ', in *Analysis*, 1990, pp. 16–19.
10. See Dummett, 'Truth', in *Truth and Other Enigmas*, Duckworth, 1978, p. 17.
11. For more on higher-order connectives like 'S', see Teichmann, *Abstract Entities*, Macmillan, 1992, pp. 141 ff.; for formulae analogous to (2″), see pp. 113–17, ibid.

4 DATES AND UNITS

1. For this approach to 'earlier' and 'later', see Prior, *Past, Present and Future*, Oxford University Press, 1967, p. 41.
2. Kripke, *Naming and Necessity*, Blackwell, 1980, pp. 54–60.
3. This point is lucidly discussed in Kripke, *Wittgenstein on Rules and Private Language*, Blackwell, 1982, pp. 22–37.
4. Kripke, *Naming and Necessity*, pp. 48–9.
5. 'Tonk' is the (anti-)hero of Prior, 'The Runabout Inference Ticket', in *Papers on Logic and Ethics*, ed. Geach and Kenny, Duckworth, 1976.

5 PERIODS AND INSTANTS

1. As expounded in Davidson, 'The Individuation of Events', in *Essays on Actions and Events*, Oxford University Press, 1980, especially p. 179.
2. Agreement in *metric* duration-judgements would presuppose measurement with units, which in turn would require clocks. But general agreement in unaided judgements of *relative* duration seems conceivable. For more on this and clocks generally, see Teichmann, 'Clocks and the Passage of Time', in *The Monist* ('Prosthetic Epistemology' issue), 1995.
3. See Wright, *Wittgenstein on the Foundations of Mathematics*, Harvester 1980, ch. IV, §1 & §5.
4. For the definition of 'grue', see Goodman, *Fact, Fiction and Forecast*, Bobbs-Merrill Co. Inc., 3rd edn, 1973, pp. 74–81.
5. Adrian Moore proposed this view of instants to me.
6. See J. Thomson, 'Tasks and Super-Tasks', in *Analysis*, 1954.
7. Ryle, 'Heterologicality', in *Analysis*, 1951.
8. St Augustine, *Confessions*, XI xv(19)–(20).

6 TIME AND CHANGE

1. Reichenbach, *The Philosophy of Space and Time*, Dover Publications, 1958, ch. 2, §22.
2. See n. 1 for ch. 5.
3. 'Cambridge change' is Geach's term; see Geach, *God and the Soul*, Routledge, 1969, p. 71.
4. Shoemaker, 'Time without Change', in *Identity, Cause and Mind*, Cambridge University Press, 1984.
5. See Wittgenstein, *Remarks on the Foundations of Mathematics*, trans. Anscombe, ed. Anscombe, von Wright, Rhees; Blackwell, 2nd edn, 1964, Part II §75.
6. See n. 5 for ch. 4.
7. Owen, 'Plato and Parmenides on the Timeless Present', *Monist* 1966, p. 319.
8. Leibniz, *Letters to Clarke*; see *The Leibniz–Clarke Correspondence*, ed. Alexander, Manchester 1956, pp. 26–7, 37–8, 75–7.
9. See Teichmann, *Abstract Entities*, Macmillan, 1992, pp. 141–5.
10. In *The Structure of Time*, Bill Newton-Smith seems to be saying that the difference between 'There was a changeless period between E1 and E2' and 'Change could have occurred between E1 and E2' – given that the second is compatible with E1's being temporally adjacent to E2 – has to do solely with the possibility of a good empirical theory's justifying asserting the first (e.g. in a Shoemakerian scenario). The first sentence, he thinks, entails the second, the 'could' construed as a physical modality; the second, however, does not entail the first.

    I do not think that an appeal to grounds of this theoretical sort, for the making of statements positing a period of empty time, is one that can help elucidate the sense of such statements. The sense of 'electron' may well derive from the overall theory in which it is embedded; but we surely do not need to have any empirical theory positing changeless time in order to grasp 'A period of changeless time occurred'. Nor, it seems to me, does our grasp of the latter depend on our having a notion of what such an empirical theory *would* amount to, were there such a theory.

    See Newton-Smith, *The Structure of Time*, Routledge & Kegan Paul, 1980, ch. 2, § 10.

7 THE DIRECTION OF TIME

1. Anscombe, 'Causality and Determination', in *Collected Philosophical Papers*, vol. 2, Blackwell, 1981, p. 137.
2. See Goldman, 'Knowledge and Perceptual Discrimination', in *Journal of Philosophy*, 1976.
3. Two *loci classici* for causal accounts of memory and of perception: Martin and Deutscher, 'Remembering', in *The Philosophical Review*, 1966;

Grice, 'The Causal Theory of Perception', in *Proceedings of the Aristotelian Society*, sup. vol., 1961.
4.   Wittgenstein, *The Blue and Brown Books*, Basil Blackwell, 2nd edn, 1969, pp. 24–5.
5.   See Wittgenstein, *Remarks on the Foundations of Mathematics*, e.g. Part II §71.

APPENDIX

1.   Wright, *Realism, Meaning and Truth*, Basil Blackwell, 1987.

Index